Victorian Secrets

Victorian Secrets

What a Corset Taught Me about the Past, the Present, and Myself

By

Sarah A. Chrisman

Foreword By

Sue Lean

Skyhorse Publishing, Inc.

Skyhorse Publishing books may be purchased in bulk at special discounts for sales promotion, corporate gifts, fund-raising, or educational purposes. Special editions can also be created to specifications. For details, contact the Special Sales Department, Skyhorse Publishing, 307 West 36th Street, 11th Floor, New York, NY 10018 or info@skyhorsepublishing.com.

Skyhorse® and Skyhorse Publishing® are registered trademarks of Skyhorse Publishing, Inc.®, a Delaware corporation.

www.skyhorsepublishing.com

10 9 8 7 6 5 4 3 2 1

Library of Congress Cataloging-in-Publication Data is available on file.

ISBN: 978-1-62636-175-1
Printed in the United States of America

For Gabriel

Table of Contents

Foreword

At the State Capital Museum in Olympia in 2009, at a High Tea Reception for the publication of Shanna Stevenson's book *Women's Votes, Women's Voices: The Campaign for Equal Rights in Washington*, I met Sarah Chrisman. Here was this lovely authentically clothed young woman I'd never seen at an historical event before. She had come all the way from Seattle—taking five modes of transportation to be able to attend. The fifth was a ride with my friend, Mary Murphy, who saw her walking up Capitol Way from the bus station downtown. She pulled over and said, "I think we are going to the same place." Sarah in her long skirts gratefully accepted the ride.

Mary showed Sarah around to the museum guests and they all marveled at her beautiful Victorian tan linen dress. You could tell by looking that it was made of natural fibers with fine hand-stitched detailing.

As a member of the Women's History Consortium (an advisory board to the Washington State Historical Society) with a mission to collect women's history and to celebrate the 2010 suffrage centennial in Washington, I zeroed right in on Sarah. I hoped she would be in the Olympia's Lakefair Festival parade as part of the "Suffragettes on Parade" entry. Naturally, I was hoping she would appear at other suffrage celebration events.

I was astonished to learn that she and her husband had an extensive collection of both women's and men's Victorian clothing. Happily, they were interested in sharing it with the public. Sarah and Gabriel invited me to lunch in their tiny studio apartment near the University of Washington in Seattle. I was to see an extraordinary collection of exquisite antique clothing. Especially thrilling was a black hat and dress very much like that worn by Susan B. Anthony in an old photograph.

At once, I became determined to do all I could to advance this outstanding collection into public view. Organizations were being encouraged to celebrate the suffrage centennial by having a Pink Tea. This was the most formal of Victorian color-themed teas and guests sometimes spoke among themselves about winning the vote.

The opportunity came to have a Pink Tea and historical fashion show for the Olympia Unitarian Universalist Congregation. The Chrismans' in-depth knowledge of Victorian clothing was paired with commentary about leading northwest suffragists, both men and women, who would have worn similar clothing. The idea was to honor key leaders such as Susan B. Anthony, Abigail Scott Duniway, and Carrie Chapman Catt in the long struggle in for the right to vote. Washington women won and lost the vote more than once before becoming the fifth state to enfranchise women in 1910, the first new star on the women's suffrage flag in fourteen long years.

As a first offering, there were a few glitches. Once Gabriel was delayed in being able to change outfits, but Sarah carried on, valiantly entertaining the guests. It was a rather grand start and Evie Greenberg was able to take wonderful photographs, extending the outreach for their collection in a significant way. No small amount of organization, work, and travel are involved in putting on an historical fashion show—not to mention the research and presentation planning involved.

Sarah's experience as she transformed herself into a Victorian lady is laced with candid insights and surprises about the underwear of yesteryear. It was a lucky day that we met, and I am still fascinated by the fact that Sarah has worn a corset twenty-four-seven for so many years. She and Gabriel have educated many people about this amazing undergarment, which the reader will find through *Victorian Secrets* is subject to many misconceptions.

It is fortuitous that the Chrismans live in Port Townsend with the state's best Victorian architecture, wonderful heritage, and steampunk festivals. Sarah and Gabriel add a great deal of historical color to these events. The best part, without a doubt, is that this historical color is authentic.

—Sue Lean, Historian
Washington Women's History Consortium

Introduction

"The desire to . . . be beautiful surrounds us on every hand with grace, elegance, and refinement. The little girl that studies her features in the mirror, while she evinces possibly a disposition to be vain, nevertheless in this act shows herself to be possessed of those instincts of grace which, rightly directed, will beautify and embellish all her surroundings through life."

—Thomas E. Hill,
Hill's Manual of Social and Business Forms, 1891

People often ask me about my clothes. Are they religious? No. Are they for a job? No. Are they a costume? Most definitely not. People are always curious when encountering something unusual, but there never seems to be sufficient time to explain the entire tale, no matter how much I enjoy sharing it. The complicated story of how I came to dress as a Victorian lady on a daily basis cannot really be told in the sort of short, electronic headlines currently popular in modern media. The true tale—including all the motivations, reactions, and everything I have learned since starting out on this path—requires a far more Victorian manner of telling: starting at its beginning and with all the details intact.

Throughout the years, I have found that people are curious to learn more about my choices. They ask me to provide insights into simple ideas, such as Victorian garments being, in many ways, more practical than their modern counterparts. They don't mind listening to me speak of discoveries that refute popular myths. (Have you heard the one about the broken ribs? They weren't *human* bones.)

Yet even the most interested of people have buses to catch, friends to meet, work to get back to—and if they don't, I do. Throughout the nearly four years since this historical experiment (which has become my life) began, I've developed a sort of short "elevator speech" that touches on some of the most common questions and gives a truncated explanation of the lifestyle I have chosen.

This, however, is the long version of that story . . .

1

Nature and Artifice

Godey's Lady's Book (September 1889).

Nineteenth-century fashion plate.

"The corset has also much to do with the figure. A good corset can make an unseemly figure look quite pleasant to the eye. . . . All the different shaped corsets, adapted to various figures, are made in a variety of materials."

—*Godey's Lady's Book*, September, 1889

I looked at the contents of the last package with something between disappointment and dubiousness. "It's a corset," I said, trying not to sound too angry or let
down. This was my birthday present, after all. "Thanks . . . "

My husband beamed at me. "Try it on!"

I didn't want to try it on. I had distinctly told him not to buy me a corset.
We had, in fact, had a rather lengthy discussion about it. Corsets, I had told
him, were unhealthy, uncomfortable, and stifling. Women used to break their
ribs to fit into them, and when the poor things died and their bodies were dissected, their dear organs weren't even in the right places anymore.

Sometimes telling a person something and actually getting through to
them can be entirely different matters, however, as evidenced by the object I
was holding. Gabriel was still smiling. I looked down at the item in my hands:
dark blue lace, patterned with roses, overlaid the blue-gray silk body of the
corset.

"Blue roses," I observed aloud. My favorite color, together with my favorite
flower. It is a combination that never happens in nature, although artifice has
arranged it upon occasion.

Gabriel nodded, smiling endearingly. "The silk color matches your eyes!"

I sighed. The gift was not totally without thought, for all that it was
unwanted. He had obviously put consideration into it, even if he had not heard
a word I'd said in our earlier discussion. And it is distinctly hard for me to turn
down blue roses. *Best get this over with*, I thought.

I unwrapped the plastic in which it had been shipped and turned the
corset around and around, trying to determine front from back, top from
bottom. It seemed far more two-dimensional than the versions of corsets I
had seen in movies. It was actually quite flat and had been folded into a neat
little rectangle before I started fussing with it. I was having trouble squar-
ing the perplexing item in my hands with the masochistic, male-enforced,
body-mangling corset I'd read about in women's studies texts. I wasn't even
quite sure how something so flat and stiff could really fit around a three-
dimensional frame.

"This is an underbust model," Gabriel explained. "It goes under your bra."
He looked embarrassed. "The overbust kind is a lot more expensive, and, well,
I was afraid you wouldn't like it."

Well, at least he didn't buy the most expensive version of a thing I'll never wear,
I thought. I held it up against the underwire of my bra, trying to decide which
way it went. I was fairly sure the laces went in the back, but if it was meant to
be laced together, the heavy metal fastenings opposite the laces seemed totally

superfluous. Why did it have fastenings if it had laces—or, contrariwise, why did it have laces if it had fastenings? Wasn't life complicated enough without an undergarment that clasped *and* tied? I frowned.

It had curves at both ends of the metal supports inside the silk, and I wasn't sure whether it made more sense for the deeper curves to be at the top or at the bottom where they'd let my legs move. I fidgeted with it, holding it first one way, then the other.

Meanwhile, Gabriel unfolded the directions sheet. "It says the clasps go on the right."

I shifted the corset, deeper curves up now. The point between the curves fit right between the cups of my bra and the corset rested against the underwire. On the bottom, the shallower lines hinted at the top curves of my thighs, but hovered so far above them that I realized walking wouldn't be a problem.

The clasps were of a style I hadn't dealt with before, but easy enough to comprehend—a very straightforward, slot-and-grommet arrangement, sort of like a big cousin to the hooks and eyes on my bra.

Montgomery Ward & Co. Catalogue, 1895. Skyhorse Publishing reprint (2008).

"It says," Gabriel continued reading off the directions sheet, "that you should never fasten the very top or the very bottom grommet first, because they could get damaged—"

"I guess that makes sense . . . " I reluctantly recalled my high school physics lessons. In an object under physical strain, the ends of the object generally tend to be under more strain than the middle.

"—and never try to undo the clasps without untying the laces first," my husband said, finishing the reading.

And there went my first idea of how to streamline this insanity. As a young child, I used to leave my sneakers loosely tied all the time so that I could slip in and out of them like loafers. My first thought upon seeing the grommets was that they should be sufficient on their own. Apparently not.

With the grommets fastened, I groped behind my back for the laces. I craned my neck around in a fruitless attempt to see what I was doing.

"I'll help you." Gabriel stepped up behind me and gave me a gentle little kiss, just behind my right ear. He took the laces from my flailing hands and carefully pulled them in, fumbling with the bow a bit until I lent him a finger to hold down the crosstie while he shaped the loops. He then tugged the bow secure and gave me two sweet little pats on the hips. He peered over my shoulder at the mirror's image of the two of us.

I stared at my reflection in the glass. The dear mirror was showing me the most flattering lie possible, and my mind struggled to fit the lovely form in the silvered glass into the image of what I truly knew myself to be. This was not me.

And yet, it was.

I had always struggled with being a bit on the heavy side—not obese, but . . . well, substantial. I was cursed with the sort of inconvenient plumpness that might have been cute on a shorter girl, but on a woman who towered ten inches past the five-foot mark, it was embarrassingly intimidating. (Any female who shares the plight will understand: it's bad enough to be taller than most of the boys back in high school, but to be a fat girl taller than most of the boys . . . Let's just say I'd had a lot of lonely Friday nights. By the time my senior prom rolled around, I was so determined to attend at least one dance that I'd shown up in the company of another girl and her Kermit-the-Frog puppet. At least she'd had a date, even if he was green.)

Suddenly, though, that was all gone. The irritating bulges—on which years of exercise, skimping on meals, and skipping desserts had left no effect—had vanished as though by fairy magic. My miraculously lean flanks shone smooth with the silk that covered them. The curves at my waist were not the convex rounds I had hated for years, but the elegant, inward slopes I had seen on models and had resigned myself to never possessing. They were suddenly mine.

I took a breath. Everything I'd ever been taught about corsets had dictated in no uncertain terms that I should be fainting dead away about this time, but I was completely hale. My wind was strong; the only noticeable difference was a slight catch at the base of my diaphragm muscle, which subtly changed the manner of my breathing: as I inhaled, my lungs rose up, instead of down. They drew my breasts with them, and I laughed to see my heaving bosoms in the mirror.

The laughter transformed my face, and the eyes of the creature in the mirror sparkled at me. I lifted my chin to see what it would look like and the mirror flashed poise.

In the mirror, Gabriel smiled at me. "You look beautiful."

I continued to stare, the image I saw before me still struggling to mesh with the image of myself I held firmly in my mind. I ran a hand down the smooth silk of a curve. "Wow."

"Do you like it?" Ah, the hopeful question that always accompanies a gift.

"Well . . . " I wasn't quite ready to give up a lifetime of teachings yet. Everything that had ever been preached to me about this item dictated that I should be shrieking from oppression. "It's . . . interesting."

Worry clouded my husband's face. "I hope you're not mad at me."

It was my twenty-ninth birthday, and this was his gift to me—one of many, actually. A green silk dress, frothy-edged with antique lace, lay amongst the tissue that had encased it. Next to its box was another; its folds of delicate paper serving as a nest to a black velvet bonnet, glinting with jet beads and the iridescent pouf of an ostrich plume tip. There was a black silk jacket with silver stripes in the lining and an antique velvet cape trimmed with monkey fur. I had woken up to breakfast in bed that morning and then been showered with presents. How could I possibly be angry?

"Of course not," I said, giving him a kiss.

"I know you said you didn't want one. . . . " The worry persisted in his voice. "But, you like the Victorian era so much, and it's the only real way to make the clothes fit the way they're supposed to."

"I know." We collect antique clothing, and it had been a long source of frustration that nothing fit me from my favorite era. I kissed him again and he hugged me.

"So, should I help you take it off before I go to class?"

I looked back in the mirror and hesitated. The wonderland image ran a hand down a silk curve and rested it on a shapely hip. I paused. "Let's . . . leave it on. For now, at least."

At this point in our history, the schedules of academia exercised a large influence on the life my husband and I shared. Gabriel was in graduate school earning his master's degree in library science, and I was studying to become a licensed massage practitioner. (I had already earned two university degrees, but there is a very old saying that "Man proposes and God disposes." Thus it was that I had, fresh from high school, worked ceaselessly for four years to earn two bachelor's degrees simultaneously, only to see the job market for those degrees completely collapse just as I was graduating. I received my diplomas in international studies and French in June of 2002: a date that means little to people until I point out that it was exactly nine months after September 11, 2001. It was just enough time for borders to slam shut and the world's economy at large to hit free-fall velocity on its plummet downward. Those were dark days for the entire world, and it would be unfair to those whose lives were affected far more tragically than mine to make too much of my own disappointments. Later, studying for my massage license, I hoped that a job whose purpose was to help people relieve stress would be somewhat less subject to politics than my original ambitions had been.

After Gabriel left for class and I was alone, I spent a few moments posing in front of the mirror on the bathroom door until I embarrassed even myself with my silly vanity. Then I turned to face my dresser, wondering what on earth I was going to wear. I had effectively dropped two dress sizes in as many minutes, and especially as this was my birthday, I felt like showing off a bit. Unfortunately, my wardrobe had not shrunk with corresponding magic.

Most of my clothing dated from my original college years, when Seattle was still groping its way out of the grunge phenomenon. (It's hard for a community to leave behind something that has put it on the world map, no matter how ignominiously.) It tended to be a bit on the loose side, even without the corset. I tried on my various sweaters, former favorites, and rejected them one by one as I saw how unflattering they were. The T-shirts (baggy, unisex, one-size-fits-all things) were even worse, and my jeans wouldn't even stay up on my suddenly reduced waistline.

After virtually emptying the contents of my bureau and developing a sizable pile of rejects, I finally settled on a pair of cycling pants coupled with a spandex shirt. If clothing can ponder its surroundings, that old striped shirt must have been as surprised as I was to see its new presentation. It dated from years before and even when it was brand new, it had never fit me in nearly so flattering a fashion.

Once I'd squirreled away the mounds of rejected clothing into their proper places again, I pulled out yet another birthday present: a new (to me) Japanese manga that was set in Victorian London. A good book, a day off (it was sheer coincidence that I had neither massage class nor work), and the prospect of a late lunch out followed by chocolate cheesecake for dinner. What better way to spend a birthday?

As I attempted to slump into the sofa in my customary rolled-larva-imitation reading position, I found that the lines of sprung steel up my back prevented it. Truth be told, if I had compared my customary at-rest position in those days to the outline on an evolutionary chart, my posture would have been closer to the ape than to *Homo habilis*. The corset, however, was thrusting me right through two million years of evolution, smack into the realm of *Homo sapien*. Welcome to the human race, Sarah Chrisman!

I couldn't slump, no matter how I tried. My back muscles rebelled. *Sit up straight?! You've never asked us to do that before! And on our birthday, too! The indignity!*

However, it was a bit late to change my mind. I had sent Gabriel off to class, and with the laces tied in the middle of my back where I could barely reach them—let alone see them—I was not at all confident in my ability to remove the corset myself. In my mind, claustrophobic visions formed that included trying to untie the bow, but instead accidentally pulling the stays tighter and tighter, strangling myself while muddling the laces into an irrevocable knot . . .

I decided not to try undoing the laces. I gave up the caterpillar posture on the sofa and pulled a wooden kitchen chair up to the window. In my mind's eye, I pulled up all the pictures I had seen of Victorian ladies reading and perched gingerly on the edge. As a girl, I had used to practice their posture, thinking how pretty they were with their hands up and books high before their faces. I copied it now, shoulders back, head up, the two covers of the book perched against the palms of my hands. Over the top of the book, I spotted the Seattle skyline outside my window. It was rather an improvement over the dusty floor and my own ungainly feet, which usually framed the edge of my larval-postured reading. I crossed my ankles and tucked my feet beneath my seat.

When I still had a bit of book left for later, Gabriel came back from classes and spirited me away to lunch. I had decided on the restaurant some weeks previously: The Old Spaghetti Factory, a nineteenth-century warehouse that had been gussied up into a family restaurant known locally for reasonable prices and large portions. The place is a bit of a Seattle classic, and I had fond memories of going there as a child. My mother would urge me to "Eat up!" and get her money's worth. I'd generally stuffed myself on the free bread and soda refills before the entrée even arrived and rarely failed to go home without a stomachache.

I could tell, however, that in my current circumstances, that was not going to be an option. I may have been wearing pants with an elastic waistband, but beneath them the corset was compressing my stomach with a force that wasn't just *like* steel, but *was* steel, at least in part. My birthday pancakes had only just begun to settle.

I dithered and dallied over the menu, finally deciding on the vegetarian lasagna. Since vegetables represent a higher cost to the restaurant than pasta, this was one of the few items with a description that didn't boast words like "enormous" or "giant." I'd never tried it before, but had always had a desire to taste it. While we waited for our entrées, the waiter brought around the complimentary bread.

I could hear the voice from childhood urging me to eat as much as I could hold. "They'll keep bringing more; don't waste it!" it said. But I knew that if I did follow the old advice, I'd be too full to enjoy the lasagna that was coming, and that really would be a waste. I limited myself to two small slices of the loaf and tucked the rest into my purse.

You wouldn't have gone home with more than that anyway, I reasoned. I figured that I wouldn't be wasting anything if I didn't ask for more. The thought was sensible enough, but it took effort to bat away my mother's repetitive voice from the back of my mind.

After lunch we picked up my birthday cake and got ready for the party. When the guests started to arrive several hours later, I noticed many of them do a slight double take as they walked into the room. My Japanese neighbor, Yukiko, took an especially long look up and down my torso, but said nothing. Part of me wanted to explain, but because I was embarrassed, an equal part did *not* want to explain. I didn't even know the Japanese word for "corset."

As for the others, what could I tell my rambunctious, American girlfriends? They were all educated women, all liberated, left-wing, and forging careers for themselves. Could I say, "Hi, thanks for coming. I'm wearing a corset"? At the very least, I needed some sort of context to work the subject into a conversation.

The context came when I was urging everyone to take more cake. (I had my heart absolutely set on a chocolate cheesecake from the Dilettante chocolaterie, and they make their cakes only in a size intended to feed twenty. There were only eight of us at the party, and Gabriel doesn't eat cheesecake.) After a chorus of protestations from all quarters that everyone was full after their second or third pieces, someone piped up, "Why don't you have another piece? You've only had one, and it's your birthday!"

"Well," I took a deep breath. "I have an excuse." It was now or never and gods alone knew what my friends would make of my confession. "I'm wearing a corset."

To my surprise, there was no chorus of hisses, and my friends, bless them, did not descend to strip me of bondage and burn the symbol of oppression. Instead, there were simply a few curious *ahhhs*, tinged, incredibly, with approval.

"I thought you were!" said one friend, a woman likewise named Sarah. She grinned, and I was rather encouragingly shocked to see a roomful of smiles.

Now that the subject had been broached, everyone wanted to talk about it. "I've been thinking about getting one of those," someone said to my astonishment. *Other women want to do this? I'm not a backward, masochistic freak?* "What does it feel like?"

I considered the question, shifting a bit. How does it feel?

"A lot more comfortable than I would have thought," I answered truthfully. Sure, I was feeling full after one—admittedly large—slice of cheesecake, but I'd suffered none of the cataclysmic maladies prophesied by numerous sources. I could breathe and I hadn't fainted. My shoulders were looking forward to a darn good slouch when the corset came off for bed, but deep down I knew that an upright posture was better for my back. "I've actually been surprised at how comfortable it is."

And surprised by the genuine interest—and even envy—shown by my modern, liberated female friends. The only one who didn't lean forward with approving intensity was Yukiko, but I wasn't sure whether this was a cultural difficulty, a linguistic one, or simply a preoccupation with the exceptionally large piece of cheesecake I had forced on her. (By Japanese standards, it probably would have fed an entire family.)

After everyone had gone home, I examined my own form in the mirror once more. "Everyone seemed to like it," Gabriel commented.

"Yeah . . . " I ran a hand down my side, marveling at how firm it was. "I was surprised."

Gabriel laughed at that. "They're nice people."

"True. True . . . " My hand came to rest on my hip. *But what happens when I meet people who aren't so nice?*

"Do you want me to help you off with the corset?"

I nodded. "Yes, please." My back was aching from being straight for so long, and there was an especially irritated spot right at the base of my spine. Sore curves pained me under my breasts where the underbust corset had been pressing the underwire of my bra into soft flesh. I could breathe more easily than I had expected, but not sigh deeply. I hadn't died, but I was ready to be comfortable again.

"It wasn't as bad as you thought it would be, was it?" Gabriel asked as he untied the corset, loosening the laces at my back.

I fidgeted with the line of clasps, experiencing brief claustrophobia before I got the sliding motion correct and the grommets parted from the hooks.

"No, I guess not."

I felt an immense relief with release, as the two halves of the corset parted and the stiffened silk fell away. I looked down at my skin, at the red pressure lines the steel boning had left on my stomach and sides. I turned around and saw angry red x's on my back from the laces.

"But it's not something I'd want to do every day."

Sears, Roebuck & Co. Catalogue, 1897. Skyhorse Publishing reprint (2007).

2

Ribbed Rumors and Stayed Truths

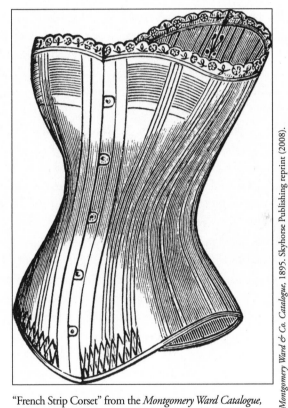

"French Strip Corset" from the *Montgomery Ward Catalogue,*
1895. This model sold for 50 cents each, or $5.50/dozen.

Montgomery Ward & Co. Catalogue, 1895. Skyhorse Publishing reprint (2008).

My first taste of corsetry had intrigued me, but I was frightened by what it might do to my body. For years, I had been hearing how bad corsets were—that corsets deformed women's bodies, broke their bones, tortured them, even killed them. When I had sighed over the bygone Victorian era as a child, my mother had threatened me with the admonition: "If you had lived back then, you would have had to wear a corset!" (This was said in the exact same tone she might have used to say, "If you had been born in Salem, you would have been burned as a witch!") In high school, my German teacher had told us how women used to break their two smallest ribs to fit into corsets because that was the only way to make their figures small.

The Saturday before that fateful birthday, I had attended a cadaver lab at Bastyr University (an accompaniment to a host of anatomy and kinesiology classes I was studying at a different school for my massage practitioner certification). I had seen dissected corpses flayed open, the marks of the vices they had chosen in life etched far beyond skin-deep in their most intimate parts. I had seen the blackened lungs of smokers and held the liver of a woman who'd died of alcoholism; the latter still reeked of alcohol, long after her death.

The scent of mortality had seemed to come away on me with the cloying formaldehyde fumes and lingered in my mind long after shower and soap had taken the smell of death from my skin. It scared me. Yet, the damages that had turned those living beings into corpses were things in which millions of people—modern people, enlightened people—indulged every day. How would a body be affected by something so archaic it had been abandoned nearly a century before, when radiation was considered healthful and cocaine had only recently ceased to be sold over the counter in drug stores?

It was clear to me that I needed to do a bit more research. Luckily, I was married to a graduate student of information science (i.e., library school.) Gabriel found me a selection of books on corsets from the University of Washington's extensive libraries, and he tracked down several websites devoted to modern corsetry. (Sometimes, it seems like a person can find practically anything on the Internet.)

Since I was starting from a position of complete ignorance, the first things I learned about corsets were highly basic terminology and history. I had only recently learned the difference between an underbust corset (one that fits under the breasts, such as Gabriel had given me) and an overbust one (which supports the breasts, and therefore does not require a separate brassiere). Launching myself into research, I began to develop a core knowledge of corset facts.

The metal strips attached to the clasps and running down both sides of the front are, together, called a busk. Originally, the busk was a single piece of wood, metal, whalebone (i.e., baleen—but more on this later), or other stiff material; its function was to support the corset. Being highly intimate and close to the heart, early one-piece corset busks were sometimes carved with romantic sentiments and given as gifts to lovers.

Back in the days when a corset's busk was a single, solid piece, a woman would have to unlace the corset completely to remove it—or else loosen it significantly and pull it over her head like a sweater. (Later, I had the opportunity to watch a historical costumer putting on a Renaissance-style corset in this manner. It took her a full five minutes to drag out the laces as far as humanly possible, then subsequently wriggle and squeeze her way headfirst into the stretched-out corset. She resembled nothing so much as a bloated boa constrictor trying to force its way down a shrew hole.)

In the nineteenth century, someone had the clever idea of splitting the busk and putting clasps on it. This did away with the quaint custom of lovers' engravings upon the busk (since it was split and covered with clasps), but meant the laces could mostly stay in place. They needed to be loosened only a few inches to slacken pressure on the clasps for the corset's removal, no wriggling required. The clasps (which I had seen as a needless complication) were, therefore, actually in place down the front to make it easier—not harder—to put on and take off the corset. I read with interest of the spoon busk, a late Victorian innovation that was said to make corsets dramatically more comfortable, but could find no specific pictures of it and so I filed the knowledge away for future examination.

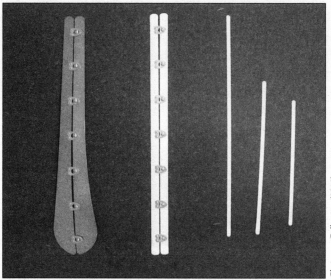

Chrisman Collection (2013).

Left to right: Spoon busk (the curved shape at the bottom is to cup the wearer's belly), straight busk, corset bones.

The corset itself can be called a "figure," "form," "body," "set of stays," "pair of stays," or simply, "stays." The lines of stiff material supporting the corset are "stays," "ribs," or "bones." The first of these terms for the little metal supports is self-explanatory; the second comes from their placement on the body: they're stiff things on the torso, though one would not expect them to be called "knuckles." The term "bones" comes from the most popular material for them in the nineteenth century, which was whalebone. More properly called baleen, it hangs from the upper jaws of certain whales and is actually made of keratin, like human fingernails. However, early whalers were not exactly known for their scientific sophistication (the sperm whale got its name from their odd belief that it stored extra semen in its head) and their misnomer stuck.

Some might call this attention to etymology pedantic, but it is vitally important. The worst slanders that the twentieth century heaped on the corset hinged upon that one word—bones—and the critics got it wrong.

I was absolutely fascinated to learn most nineteenth century writings that reference "broken bones" refer not to women's ribs, and not to human bones at all, but to the whalebone ribs of corsets.

Any garment that is worn regularly will begin to show wear over time, especially if it is worn under tension. Moreover, it must be remembered that the substance in question is a protein analogous to fingernails: It is thicker and tougher, but it was supposed to hang in large plates constantly exposed to sea water. It was not meant to be chopped up into fussy pieces and put under strain on dry land. Baleen gets brittle over time. Understandably, it breaks, just as fingernails break. The notorious "broken bones" and "broken ribs" were actually a millinery, not a medical, emergency.

Learning this opened up an entirely new realm of fascination for me. How many other lies had I been forced into believing over the years, and what truths were they deforming? I devoured research books while nibbling my meals and lurked through web pages to expose the facts.

Another misconception I was fascinated to see debunked was the idea that stays were worn only by privileged, upper-class women. Modern, glossy-paged popular books about beauty and body image are quick to perpetuate this myth,[1] but upon examination, they never offer any actual evidence to support these claims—or at least, none that hold up to analysis. The actual truth of the matter is that corsets were worn by all classes of Victorian women, not just the idle rich. Isaac Singer's invention of the sewing machine in the mid-nineteenth century revolutionized the millinery industry, and corsets were one of many garments that became widely and cheaply available after its universal adoption.

---

[1] Shari Graydon, *In Your Face: The Culture of Beauty and You* (Vancouver: Annick Press., 2004), 49. This is just one example—many others are easily found.

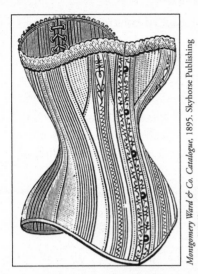

Sateen corset from the *Montgomery Ward catalogue*, 1895. Montgomery Ward sold this model at a price of 50 cents each, or $5/dozen.

What did that represent in terms of buying power? Not very much, really: the *catalogue's* own brand of complexion soap cost 10 cents per bar (3 for 25 cents or 95 cents/dozen).

Businesses such as Britain's R. & W. H. Symington & Company manufactured bodies on a vast scale. According to Christopher Page's *Foundations of Fashion*, their collection of antique corsets—preserved in the Leicestershire Museum—includes an 1895 corset that retailed for only ten pence![2] "[T]he factory-made corset . . . brought fashion within the reach of the whole female population, not only of Britain, but of many other parts of the world as well."[3] By 1880, the Symington company alone (one of the many hundreds of different manufacturers producing corsets) employed more than 1,600 workers using 500 sewing machines.[4] A number of corsets—many of them patented designs—were specifically marketed toward working women and featured corded supports and extra reinforcements in strategic areas to help them stand up to the strains of bending and stooping to which housemaids and cleaning women would subject their garments. The garments were actually designed to help support their wearers' backs during these tasks. The corset's utility for working women could even be seen in the names of certain models, such as the Pretty Housemaid, a popular mass-manufactured body marketed toward working women.[5]

---

[2] Christopher Page, *Foundations of Fashion: The Symington Collection; Corsetry from 1856 to the Present Day, Leicestershire Museums Publication no. 25* (Leicestershire, UK: De Voyle Litho, 1981), 18.

[3] Ibid., iv.

[4] Ibid., 4.

[5] Valerie Steele, *The Corset: A Cultural History* (Singapore: Yale University Press, 2000), 48.

Unlike the stereotyped image of modern, exploited laboring workers (e.g., the popular image of ragged-clothed diamond miners who could never afford to own a diamond), the nineteenth-century factory girls who sewed corsets benefitted directly from their industry. An early photograph of workers at the Symington factory shows rows of girls and young women with corseted figures beneath their working dresses.[6] Actually, once one has become accustomed to noticing the appearance of a corseted woman, it is difficult to locate any nineteenth-century pictures where the women are not wearing stays, regardless of social class. They were completely ubiquitous.

Chrisman Collection (1887).

My own great-grandparents: Helen and Harry Boothby, pioneer farmers in Alberta, Canada (prairie country). I had seen this photo every day of my life until I went off to university, but it wasn't until I started wearing a corset myself that I noticed the spoon busk of Great-Grandma Helen's corset is visible through her dress, underneath the bow at her waist.

---

[6] Page, *Foundations of Fashion,* 5.

As I continued to read and research, more of my long-held beliefs fell apart, like rotten stitching holding together a patchwork of mythology. Broken bones had been a fashion annoyance; the perceived symbol of upper-class authority had, in fact, been available to all; and it was actually seen as a healthful helpmate. My curiosity and interest became bound in this intriguing garment just as tightly as my waist had been laced on that very first day of my wearing it—and the adventures were just beginning to draw me in.

3

A Step Backward in Time . . .
and a Knotty Problem

Harper's New Monthly Magazine, No. CCXLIV, Vol. XLI (September 1870).

Port Townsend, WA.

As the setting for the romantic movie *An Officer and a Gentleman* (starring Richard Gere), Port Townsend is familiar to most Americans who were alive and cognizant in 1982. To locals, however, it is slightly better known as a sweet little Victorian-era town, which has retained its original main street and a number of beautiful buildings from the days when it was the second busiest port in America (New York being the first). Every year, city officials organize the

Port Townsend Victorian Festival, a weekend-long event featuring a grand ball, tea parties, and numerous participants wandering about the town in period attire. I had wanted to attend for ages, but something had always come up to prevent it. The first time I learned of the occasion, I had just missed that year's event. The next year I couldn't get the weekend off work and the year after that I was teaching English in Japan. Then Gabriel was preoccupied, but my mother promised to go to the festival with me—only to cancel on the very morning we had planned on beginning our travels.

This year, the festival was scheduled for the third weekend in March—a scant week and a half after my birthday—and I was determined to go. I had specifically requested it as part of my birthday wishes, and Gabriel had made reservations months ahead of time. As the date grew near, I became increasingly excited. I was particularly looking forward to the highlight of the weekend: a Victorian Grand Ball.

We arrived in town in high spirits with almost our entire collection of antique clothing crammed as gently as possible into the back of a borrowed car. (Our own car, a DeLorean upon which Gabriel doted, lacked sufficient trunk space to hold so much luggage, even if Gabriel had been willing to drive his precious automotive baby on an overnight trip in the temperamental month of March—which he wasn't.)

We were to stay at The Swan, one of the most beautiful hotels in Port Townsend. A century seemed to melt away beneath our feet as we stepped onto the sunlit wooden porch. As we hauled our many bags, we joked that we now understood the Victorian affinity for steamer trunks and porters. My first action when we entered our room was to plunk down, spread eagle, onto the king-size feather bed. "Ah!"

Gabriel laughed, watching me sinking into the billowy depths. "Nice?"

"Nice!" I affirmed. I rolled over, smiling up at him. "And look!" I pointed at a distinctive bull's-eye-within-a-square design carved into strategic places on the walls.

"Yep," Gabriel nodded. "Port Blakely Mill."

We had previously lived a few miles from the old location of the Port Blakely Mill. It was once the biggest sawmill in the world, back in the days when forest giants had slid along the muddy paths of Skid Road in Seattle, when the Evergreen State had breathed in money and breathed out timber. The Swan was built in Port Blakely's heyday and still proudly bears its signature corner pieces. It was a small detail, but life—and by extension, history—is in the small details, and these little touches intensified the feeling of being in the past.

Illustration from an article describing the bounty of the Pacific Northwest.

There were, however, two rather noticeable elements within the room that were unquestionably modern: ourselves. As soon as we'd finished carrying in the bags, we helped each other get changed. Gabriel helped me with my corset, and I helped him with all the incredibly fussy little elements of a Victorian gentleman's outfit: cuff links, shirt studs, removable collar, collar buttons, collar tab, waistcoat, frock coat. . . . I tried to help with the tie, but in the end I proved somewhat hopeless at that item and he had to finish the job himself.

The element of my clothing that worried me the most was not the corset, which I had established on my birthday would not actually kill me, but the shoes. For years, I had pined after kitten-heel boots. A quintessential Victorian element of footwear for ladies, the kitten heel arches ever so slightly forward, balancing its wearer's weight under the instep. It is sometimes called a French heel; in fact, it was in France where I first saw them, displayed elegantly in the front window of a shoe shop, as sweet and as tempting as the bonbons laid out behind the glass of the candy shop next door. Their heels arched downward like the necks of twin black swans, and their leather was glossy as swans' wet feathers.

I had never learned to walk in any sort of high heel (the only pair I had ever owned was secondhand with broken straps, for playing dress-up, when I was five), but from the moment I saw those boots, I wanted them as I had wanted no other footwear in my life. Much to my chagrin, I could not afford those lovelies in the Angers shop, but the yearning had persisted, and now, years later, I finally had a pair.

Montgomery Ward & Co. Catalogue, 1895. Skyhorse Publishing reprint (2008).

An example of a French heel can be seen on *Montgomery Ward*'s "Sunbeam" shoe. Price: $2.25.

Unfortunately, I also had a broken toe. A few days before my birthday, I had been taken down in judo practice by a quick side-sweep that had snagged my left pinky toe so far out of line from the foot that its longest phalanx bone had snapped. It was the second time that same toe had been broken in exactly the same way, by exactly the same sparring partner—a scrappy little guy with a heart of gold who once, while choking me with my own arm, pointed out in a voice as calm as it was cheerful, "Now, this is suboptimal!"

Since then, I had been walking around with medical tape splinting the broken toe to its neighbors. I kept my sneakers fastened loosely and favored my left side as much as I could. Careful scrutiny revealed a slight limp in my gait as I leaned my weight onto the inside of my left foot to relieve the pressure on the broken toe.

My coveted kitten-heel boots weren't towering, nor were they particularly needle-toed, but even so, I didn't relish the idea of cramming my swollen, sore foot into pointed boots that I knew would specifically throw my weight forward and onto my toes. Still . . . the beautiful boots beckoned. I lifted one out of its box, stroking the soft leather and inspecting the tool-work.

Here goes nothin'.

I lifted my ugly-duckling foot to my curvaceous, swanlike shoe. I pulled out the laces as far as they would go and gently worked in my foot, wincing and shoving.

I sucked in air as the broken toe sent out little hot waves of pain in complaint, but the foot was in. I relaced the boot; it felt about twice as tight as its counterpart, but this seemed a minor point of discomfort. The real issue on my mind was what it would feel like when I stood on it.

Gingerly, I raised myself from the edge of the bed, keeping nearly my full weight on my good right foot. Gabriel watched anxiously. "Are you going to be okay?"

With caution, I set my left heel against the floor and leaned forward, testing.

"It hurts," I said, assessing. "But I think it'll be okay."

In judo practice, I had endured worse pain and gone on sparring, being thrown head over heels by men twice my size. What Gabriel and I had planned for the afternoon was a leisurely stroll around downtown. The literal walk in the park would wait for the next day.

Had I been paying less attention, there would have been a limp in my step, but I kept it carefully under control. I asked Gabriel to walk slowly and, with a conscious deliberation of gait, kept pace beside him, grateful for the level ground of Port Townsend's main street, which sat at sea level. The broken toe certainly overwhelmed any discomfort from my corset. Not that the toe was unbearable, just . . . inconveniently noticeable. By the time we returned to the hotel room, I was honestly happier to be removing my shoes than to be getting out of my stays.

The next morning we were up with the sun, eager to get the most out of our mini vacation. We helped each other into our antique outfits, just as we had the previous night. Getting into the corset was growing easier with practice, but Gabriel was still having significant difficulty with the smaller bits of his outfits. As he tied my laces and I helped with his shirt studs, we speculated about the importance of help with clothing as a constant way of cementing relationships in Victorian society. It was rare for people to live alone in that era, and nearly everyone had someone to help them dress: Those who could afford it had servants to dress them, but the servants would help each other for free. Husbands helped wives to dress (and vice versa), unmarried sisters helped each other, daughters helped mothers . . .

Comparatively, modern people are astonishingly alienated from each other. Frequently, individuals feel the need for electronic mediation for communication with someone right in front of them. I know a young lady who has actually become a fan of the Facebook page titled something similar to "Texting a person in the same room as me." How many more levels of separation could be possible? In this instance, first there is the refusal to interact directly in the first place, and then there is the further step backward of joining a virtual club to, at a remove, encourage others to do the same. That a virtual social group could not only replace true contact but actually encourage isolation is a rather sad commentary on the loneliness of twenty-first century life.

What a different culture it must have been when people's entire lifestyles forced interactions. They not just had to talk, but actually touch each other to get dressed in the morning. They were close enough to smell soap, feel warmth, taste the tang in the air of esters given off by their bodies' chemical reactions. *How would society, and relationships, be different in a world with such closeness? How would one's thoughts of someone change if every morning they were close enough to smell the sweat of each others' dreams?* we wondered.

Pondering all this, we got hungry and turned our feet in the direction of our favorite restaurant in Port Townsend. A sweet little place of tight corners and generous portions, what the Salal Café lacks in elbow room, it makes up for in copious quantities of food so delicious it is hard to leave any of it behind. I knew this, and I knew that I'd generally leave the place with a stomachache even when my abdomen hadn't been actively compressed, but I still wanted to go there. Breakfast is their specialty, and this experience was all part and parcel of the special weekend.

When the friendly waitress delivered my sizeable omelet and mountain of fried potatoes, I dug in with vigor. I specifically didn't drink any water because I didn't want it to take up space in my stomach. I knew that this was somewhat of a bad idea (I'm prone to nausea-inducing migraines when I get dehydrated), but I ignored my better judgment as I managed to cram in most—not all, but most—of that delicious breakfast. *I can always drink some water later, after things have settled a bit*, I reasoned. I forgot to take into account exactly how long starchy fried potatoes and cheesy eggs take to digest (compared to, say, lettuce—something a person can eat in large quantities and still feel empty five minutes later). Potatoes and eggs had certainly been common foods in the Victorian era, but then as well as now, it was not a particularly well-advised move for someone of my stature to devour them quite so ravenously as I did that morning.

I was still acclimating myself to the habit of eating smaller, more manageable portions, and subsequent events would have gone better for me if I had followed a piece of advice from 1891: "It is of the utmost importance, if the individual would enjoy health . . . that all the personal habits be perfectly regular. . . . Do not let visiting, traveling, or business interfere with them. You must be regular in sleep, in evacuation of the bowels, in bathing, and in eating. Nature will not be cheated. She requires perfect attention to certain duties. If you attempt to violate her requirements you will certainly be punished."[7]

Sears, Roebuck & Co. Catalogue, 1897 Skyhorse Publishing reprint (2007).

The subject of nineteenth-century food is one that could very easily fill an entire volume on its own, and it deserves a separate book to do it justice. As a passing note of interest, however, I might say that the expansion of portion sizes is a subject that comes under discussion whenever Gabriel and I look at plates, bowls, or other dishes. Holding up antique china to equivalent modern pieces often feels like comparing household goods between Gulliver's Lilliputians and Brobdingnagians.[8] In a great many nineteenth-century dish sets I have seen, the only plate big enough to hold my breakfast that morning would have been the serving platter. I've actually met people who collect or have inherited antique china and specifically use the serving platters as their everyday plates, claiming, "The other pieces just aren't big enough!"

---

[7] Thomas E. Hill, *Hill's Manual of Social and Business Forms: A Guide to Correct Writing* (Chicago: Hill Standard Book Company, 1891), 179.

[8] Fairies and giants

Genuine English Semi-porcelain ware. A delicate anemone flower spray decoration in a steel gray color put on under the glaze; warranted not to wear off or to crack. The shapes are new and gracefully moulded For a low priced pattern it is unexcelled, as to finish, decoration and durability, and is a decided change from the ordinary brown prints.

Order No. 54010.

Per doz.		Each			Each
1 Tea Cups and Saucers, handled $1.40	13 Platters, 8-inch..	$0.14	30 Soup Tureen(with ladle and stand)...$3.50		
2 Coffee Cups and Saucers, handled.. 1.64	14 Platters, 10-inch..	.27	31 Sauce Tureen (with ladle and stand)		.88
3 Pie Plates, 5-inch. .78	15 Platters, 12-inch..	.43			
	16 Platters, 14-inch..	.61			
	17 Platters, 16-inch..	.96	32 Sauce Boat		.24
4 Plates, 6-inch..... .96	18 Bakers, 7-inch..	.18	33 Pickle Dish		.18
5 Plates, 7-inch..... 1.13	19 Bakers, 8-inch..	.27	34 Covered Butter Dish		.53
6 Plates, 8-inch... . 1.31	21 Scalloped Nappies, 7-inch...............	.18			
7 Soup Plates, 7-inch. 1.13					
8 Fruit Saucers ...... .53	22 Scalloped Nappies, 8-inch	.27	35 Covered Vegetable Dish.............		.70
9 Individual Butters. .35					
10 Bakers, 3-inch (for side dishes).......... 1.23	25 Pitchers, ½ pt....	.14	36 Casserole (square covered dish)......		.78
	26 Pitchers, 1 pt.......	.18			
10½ Bone dishes..... 1.23	27 Pitchers, 1 qt.....	.21	37 Teapot		.41
11 1 pt. Bowls......... 1.40	28 Pitchers, 2 qt......	.35	38 Sugar Bowl......		.39
12 1 pt. Oyster Bowls.. 1.40	29 Pitchers, 3 qt......	.54	39 Cream Pitcher ...		.18
Oat Meal Bowls,5-inch 1.40			40 Cake Plate.......		.24

"Oregon Pattern" dish set: *Montgomery Ward*, 1895.

Montgomery Ward & Co. Catalogue, 1895. Skyhorse Publishing reprint (2008).

After breakfast, we went for a promenade along the main street of the town. Water Street is a name that fits the thoroughfare quite literally; it is laid out right at sea level, at the base of a bluff that separates Port Townsend's commercial Downtown from its residential Uptown (whose name is, again, quite literal: Uptown, the old heart and hearth of the city where permanent residents lived in its heyday, is up at the top of the bluff). (Incidentally, Downtown and Uptown are actually named districts in Port Townsend, like Queen Anne Hill in Seattle, or Manhattan in New York.) It was a beautiful day, but tremendously windy, with strong, salty gusts blowing in from Puget Sound. I worried about the plumes on my antique hat in the vicious blasts, so we ducked into shops as often as we could, as much to spare our irreplaceable antique clothes as to see everything possible, and to enjoy the day to its fullest experience.

Even in Port Townsend, where dress-up events are fairly common, people were fascinated to see our authentic Victorian clothing. We had seen replicas—cheaply made clothes of gaudy synthetic fibers—all over town while we walked. The residents of the town were used to seeing those, but in our outfits they saw something else entirely, and they were intrigued. The silk and the wool, the pleats and ruffles and tucks, set the real garments apart from the imitations, and people kept stopping us to ask questions about these details.

Gabriel and I love antique clothing for its beauty and its history, but most of all we love what it teaches us about the past. We acquire discarded items in need of repairs, and mending them not only gives us the joy of saving endangered pieces of history, but also tells us the stories of the ghosts lingering within them. One of Gabriel's suits from the 1880s is constructed of good-quality fabric everywhere except the trouser pockets, which are rough sailcloth. We could tell from that detail alone that its former owner had a tendency to wear through his pockets.

Wearing the clothes on special days taught us more still: about the posture held by the cut of the garments, about the intricacies of fastenings that have become obscure, about the differences in antique and modern materials. We loved learning all these things and sharing our discoveries with those who were interested.

When people made inquiries of us that weekend, we told them about how clothing was a mark of status in Victorian society; about how all the little embellishments and added touches—beads and trim, fancywork, and fine stitching—showed off the wearer's wealth and displayed that they had the time and money to pay attention to the little things in life. We talked about how Victorians would do their best to dress as highly as they could and about the pride of presentation they took in themselves. The townspeople with whom we spoke were extremely friendly and positive, and we were having a grand time of things. With anything, however, there are always exceptions.

By the time we got to a cramped little antique bookstore, my broken toe was causing me considerable annoyance within its boot. To give it some respite, I settled down in a well-used chair near the cash register while Gabriel explored the shelves. The shop's owner made a polite remark to Gabriel about his suit, and he started to tell her about the differences between Victorian suits and postures and modern ones. The Victorian suit he was wearing (an itinerant Irish preacher's outfit from the 1870s) had always looked like a costume on him, despite its authenticity. Then one day, following an anatomy lecture on the effect of modern activities (driving, computer use, etc.) on muscular structure, I had suggested to Gabriel that he try adopting a more nineteenth-century posture: shoulders back, chest out, chin up. By those simple changes, he had instantly gone from a modern man dressing up in a costume to looking like he'd just stepped through a door to the past. Since then, he'd been exercising daily on the rowing machines at the gym near our apartment to strengthen the rhomboid muscles in his shoulders, so that he could hold the posture to which Victorian boys were trained from childhood. He told the shopkeeper all this and I smiled to myself, thinking of all the hours of massage I had given those sore rhomboids.

"Well, it's easy for you!" An over-the-hill customer (clearly a tourist) sneered, looking down her nose at my husband. "Men have always had it easy! It's not like you had to wear corsets!"

At that, I stopped holding my tongue and looked the rotund baby boomer in the eye. "I'm wearing a corset!"

She looked at me as though I'd just declared that I gave birth to live snakes and ate them for lunch on a daily basis. "You are?!"

I nodded coolly. "Yes."

Her expression did not alter except to drop her jaw and leave it gaping open like one of the stupider breeds of dog. She didn't say anything, just stared with an intensity of rudeness most people are required to leave behind with their diapers as a prerequisite of kindergarten.

As we left the store I held my head high, making a concerted effort not to limp on my broken toe.

That was the first of the negative reactions I was to encounter, but by no means the last. As surprising as my own corseted figure seemed to me, I was still within the realm of what might be attributed to lucky genes or exhaustive exercise. Later, as my corset-wearing became more dedicated and my form increasingly dramatic, I was to encounter entirely new levels of venom. But, I'm getting ahead of myself . . .

We had a considerably better reception from a group of costumed women slathered in pasteboard brooches. Having stopped us outside an antiques store, their apparent leader embraced us heartily and cooed over our nineteenth-century clothing, towering over us and proclaiming in a booming, cheerful voice how wonderful it was, whilst her diminutive companion (also dripping plastic gems) grumbled that we shouldn't be wearing real antiques. Ellen (the taller woman) gave us her card, explaining that they were from a group of costumers visiting for the festival. She made us promise to come to the fashion show that afternoon, go to the ball that night, join the club, come to tea . . . I don't recall her asking us to sign over rights to a hypothetical firstborn child, but then again, her list of insistences was lengthy, and I may have forgotten a few of them. By the time she and her entourage swept away in an effusion of well wishes and flurries of polyester petticoats, I was feeling slightly dizzy from the overabundance of good cheer.

I raised an eyebrow at Gabriel, who chuckled.

"Enthusiastic, isn't she?" I asked, catching my breath.

"Uh huh." Gabriel smirked, putting away the card. "She seemed nice, though."

"Oh yes," I agreed. "Very nice." I thought about the group's ensembles: loose rayon blouses, skirts dragging in the dirt, and plastic flowers glued to huge, floppy Target-bought straw hats. They weren't exactly artifacts from which to extrapolate historical data. "But, they don't really seem . . . like our sort of people . . ."

Gabriel laughed again. "Yeah . . . not really."

"Very nice, though!" I added hastily.

"Oh, very nice," he agreed. "You wanted to go to the fashion show anyway, didn't you?"

"Oh yeah!" The ostrich plume on my hat bobbed as I nodded emphatically. "Absolutely!"

"Me too." He looked down. "How are you doing, by the way?"

"Well . . ." I grimaced slightly. "My foot hurts, and . . ." I squirmed. "My back is really hurting, too."

"Oh, I'm sorry!" His eyes grew soft with concern. "Is the corset bothering you?"

"Yeah . . ." I nodded reluctantly. "My lower back has just been getting sorer and sorer." My right hand crept to the ache, almost of its own volition.

"Do you want to go back to the hotel room and see if we can do something about it?"

I frowned, sighing. "I can't really think of anything we could do. I don't really want to change clothes." I was having fun adding delight to everyone's day. "But . . ." My hand rubbed against unyielding steel, under which my back was throbbing.

"Here, let's go back to the room," Gabriel insisted. "There must be something we can do."

Back in the privacy of the hotel, it was a tremendous relief when Gabriel untied my laces and the two halves of the corset fell away after I'd slid the grommets free. I bent my stiff torso backward and forward and reached around to massage my aching lower back. Under my hands, I felt the grooves left by the corset laces against my flesh. Resembling very long shoelaces, the tight nylon cords had imprinted vicious red lines on my delicate skin. Further down, my massaging fingers found a divot.

It was fantastically sore, so I used great caution as I palpated it. Offset only slightly from being directly over the base of my spine, the hole in my tissue was slightly bigger around than the nail of my pinky finger, and about half as deep. If I craned my neck around far enough, I could see the spot in the mirror: it was angry-red, like the lines from the laces, and it seemed to be of a strangely familiar design.

"Hey, hang on a minute." I pulled my hands away from the sorest spot on my aching back and turned an analytical eye toward the corset. I held it up, parallel to its position when I was wearing it. Near the bottom of the left side in the back, I found what I'd expected. "Aha!"

Corset laces, like shoelaces, are nearly always referred to in the plural. From a casual glance at a corset, it looks like there are two of them, since there are two separate ends coming out to tie in the middle. Realistically, it is just one extremely long cord (about five yards in length) tied end to end in an extended loop. In this case, the knot from this loop had gotten underneath the corset body and been compressed into the nerves at the base of my spine all morning. Imagine dropping a marble into one's shoe, lacing it up, then walking around like that all day. Under the circumstances, it shouldn't have been a surprise that my back hurt.

At first I wondered why I had not just recognized the problem from the start. I hadn't felt the pain localized as a simple knot; it had spread across a significant portion of my lower back. Then I remembered an experiment from my biology class back in college. In the lab, we had taken turns blindfolding and poking each other with blunt pins. Starting at the fingertips and moving up the forearm, each student would choose at random whether to poke their partner with one or both ends of the bent pin, and their blindfolded partner would have to say whether he or she felt one or two points. On the fingertips, where there are many, many touch sensors, there were very few errors in judgment. Nearly everyone could tell exactly how many points were poking them and how far apart the ends of the pin were placed. Farther up the arm, as the nerve endings grew widely spaced, it got increasingly more difficult to tell whether we were feeling two pinpricks or just one. The point of the experiment was to demon-strate difference in sensitivity between different areas of the body.

The back is even less discerning than the forearm. The nerve endings are too widely spaced to pinpoint the single knot that was causing me pain, so instead my body had read it as a radiating soreness across an area as wide as my outstretched hand. The nerves back there are slower to react to stimuli as well: unlike removing a stone from a shoe, the relief was not instant when the corset came off. My back still ached, although I could sense a definite improvement.

Once I'd explained the matter to Gabriel, he, problem-solver that he is, instantly went about shifting the knot in the laces to a position on the exterior of the corset. I, meanwhile, propped my broken-toed foot up on a pillow, lay down on the feather-soft bed, and read a graphic novel.

"You know," I remarked cynically, "I bet part of the reason naps figure so prominently in nineteenth-century Southern stories is that they were an excuse for the women to loosen their corsets!"

"Maybe." Gabriel fussed with the knot in the cord. "But I think it had more to do with the fact it was too hot to do anything in the South in the middle of the day. Besides," he grinned over at me, "people like to picture pretty girls in bed." He lifted up the adjusted corset. "Okay, I think I've got it. You want me to help you put it back on?"

I looked over at him reluctantly. My back was aching, my foot was aching, and the feather bed was very comfortable. I looked pointedly at my taped-up broken toe and rubbed my sore back. Then I sighed. I had been looking forward to this trip for years; it would be a shame to waste our time in my favorite town hiding in bed.

Once Gabriel had helped me with my clothes again, we ventured out to learn more details about the vintage fashion show. It required quite a bit of wandering hither and thither and a long walk up the fennel-covered hill that separates the two halves of town. By the time we reached Uptown, my fractured phalanx was in sore want of respite, so Gabriel left me on a bench outside a bak-ery to rest my feet while he scouted ahead to work out the location and schedule of the event. When he returned, he had exciting news.

"They want us to be in the fashion show!" he told me.

"Really?" I cocked my head. I hadn't been expecting that.

"Yeah!" He sat down next to me. "I found the lady in charge; she asked me about my clothes, and I told her about how they're real antiques and that you're wearing real antiques, too, and they want us to be in the fashion show!"

An hour or so later, we were in the back room of a church with a group of people in a hodgepodge of fancy dress. There were some interesting elements: a sweet, elderly woman wearing a shattered-silk cape; another woman of similar age dressed in an antique girl's exercise outfit, which had been fashioned out of an old nun's habit; and a man wearing a replica of an artillery officer's uniform from the early 1900s. Many of the fashions displayed were strangely loose interpretations of yesteryear: a woman wearing a rayon-velvet bodice and long paisley skirt paired with ostrich plumes on her hat and modern pumps on her feet; several women dressed entirely in purple; and a number of teenage girls in modern evening dresses. In the corner lurked a parasol, which someone had apparently fashioned by gluing a massive swath of polyester lace to a plastic child's umbrella.

Being part of the presentation, we didn't get to see the entire formal production, and since we had been invited at the last minute, we didn't have a terribly clear idea of the exact procedure. However, as the line progressed and we moved close enough to hear the commentary accompanying the show, a pattern emerged. The announcer would introduce each person using a microphone as they walked to one corner of, and then across, the stage. Then the person modeling the outfit on display would tell the audience about it—mostly explaining at which thrift shops they had bought various components and calling attention to where they had cut bits off or tacked bits on to make things look vintage.

The lady with the cape had an incredibly sweet story to tell. The garment had been her grandmother's and was stored in a trunk in a dusty attic when she was a child. As a young girl, she used to sneak up to the attic and steal the cape out of the trunk to play dress up. She would fasten it around her waist like a skirt and twirl around and around.

When it was my turn to mount the stage, I told the story behind the item that, of all I was wearing, held the most pride for me: my grandmother's watch. I lifted it from its place suspended by a silk ribbon around my neck and pressed the small button at the top to spring the case open. I concentrated on the heavy feel of the gold in my gloved fingers to steady my hands in front of the crowded audience.

"This watch," I explained, focusing on the carved initials on the case, the intricate design of flowers and leaves in three colors of gold alloy, "belonged to my grandmother, and to her grandmother before her. It gets passed down to all the Almas in the family. I'm Sarah Alma, and my grandma was Alma Sarah. One of my earliest memories," I leaned forward, holding the watch, trying to make the audience see, "was standing in the bank vault with my grandmother, and her taking this watch out of her safety-deposit box and telling me, 'One day, this will be yours!'" I shook my finger in benevolent imitation of my grandmother and the audience laughed.

After I had exited the stage, I took a seat in the pews amongst the audience, my broken toe aching and another dreadfully familiar discomfort beginning that I tried vehemently to deny. Gabriel soon joined me, and after a few minutes, he turned to me with concern in his eyes. "Are you okay?"

I had been regretting my earlier decision not to have any water with breakfast, compounded by further lack of liquid throughout the rest of the morning. A well-known throbbing had started at the base of my skull, blooming out to nailed fingers of pain that tore at the brain behind my eyes.

Not now, I thought, angry at my own weakness. *Not today. Why does this always happen on special days when I least want it?*

"Just a bit of a headache," I answered wanly.

"Uh oh."

My husband was well acquainted with my migraines. They seem to be caused by electrolyte imbalance and always occur when I've either been eating too little salt or drinking too little water. Once they appear, they always follow a schedule of nearly train-like regularity, progressing from my initial denial stages of "a bit of a headache" to a climax several hours later when I wrap myself around the toilet to puke my guts out before dry heaving for a while and crawling into bed to sleep off the aftereffects.

"Let's get you back to the hotel."

I nodded meekly, willing my head not to fall off my shoulders, and allowed Gabriel to lead me back to The Swan. Once there, I tried drinking as much water as I could, but between the tiny little hotel-style plastic cup and the extremely reduced capacity of my stomach (owing to the corset), what I could drink was very little. Even if I had been able to chug gallons of water, past experience had taught me that by the time the screeching ache in my skull had progressed to this point, there was little that could be done but resign myself to vomiting and let it run its course.

I made Gabriel help me off with the corset and lay with a pillow over my face to block out the tiny bits of light glimmering from beneath the window's curtains. The throbbing only grew worse, with a speed that shocked me. As I've said, the pattern of these migraines is unvarying and I know their pace with dreadful clarity, but this one was happening much faster than usual. It should have been several hours between the first warning aches and the point at which all light and sound was magnified to the point of intense pain, but this time it had taken little more than thirty minutes. I wondered if I was destined to just keep getting worse and worse migraines and wanted to moan in frustration, but I knew the noise would feel like a drill to my brain.

Hours passed. I looked over at the clock. I was feeling no better, but if I didn't get dressed soon, we wouldn't be ready for the ball in time to attend it. I pulled myself up from my prostrate position, weaving slightly as the room tilted.

"Feeling better?" Gabriel asked hopefully.

"Not really. I—" I paused, my hand going involuntarily to my mouth as my jaw flooded with thin water, the immediate precursor to vomit. I rushed to the bathroom and hunched over the toilet.

I thought that I was certainly going to throw up. I leaned over the toilet bowl, my knees against the cold tile floor, expecting the vomit to come, but it didn't, and after a while I stood up and staggered back into the main room.

"Would you help me get dressed for the ball?"

Gabriel looked incredulously at me. "I don't think we should go if you're feeling this bad."

"But the tickets are nonrefundable, aren't they?"

"Yeah, but—" He stopped as I rushed back into the bathroom, my head and stomach rocking at cross-angles to each other. When I came out again, he had his eyebrows raised. "I don't think you would have much fun if you're this sick."

I held one hand on my aching head, the other on my lurching stomach. "But I want to go," I insisted. I felt like a seasick hangover victim, but the Grand Ball was the part of the weekend I had been anticipating with the dearest hopes. Not only was it a wonderful opportunity to show off my beautiful birthday clothes, but it was also a dance.

I love to dance, but my husband detests it. It had taken the combined power of both our extended families to force him to grant me a single waltz at our own wedding. Since then, he had danced with me once—again at a wedding, again under extreme duress, and he had complained about it afterward. For him to buy tickets to a ball was an absolute coup, but he had done it for me, to pamper me because it was my birthday treat and he loved me.

I didn't care if I felt like I'd been clubbed over the head and force-fed rancid dog meat; I was going to that dance. I drank some more water, hoping it would do some good. My ball gown wouldn't fit without the corset, so I made Gabriel lace me up as slowly as possible, with my stomach rebelling on several levels. (Not only was it already queasy, but now it was also full of water.)

There were some uneasy moments, such as when my throbbing head belly-kicked my gag reflex again and I rushed to the toilet, yards of pale green silk collapsing around me as I crouched over the bowl, but eventually we finished dressing. Gabriel looked quite dapper in his antique tuxedo and, sick as I was, I couldn't help feeling pride beneath the nausea. My own outfit was another birthday present: a beautiful silk ball gown of palest green. It was a replica of a Victorian pattern (rather than an authentic piece), but a faithful one, with genuine antique lace. Since hats weren't worn while dancing, in my hair I wore an antique celluloid tango comb from 1919 that my mother-in-law had given me (another birthday present).

I was starting to feel slightly better by the time we got to the ball, but then immediately had a sudden setback as the loud music slammed against my skull. I swayed on my sore feet, and Gabriel looked over to where I stood, slightly paler and slightly greener than my dress.

"Are you sure you want to do this?" he asked.

I nodded, and we walked inside the dance room.

It was a classic small-town hall, with a stage up front and a large wooden floor that could be used for anything from county fairs to light sports. Christmas lights had been hung as fairy arcs expanding outward from the center of the ceiling, and doves cut from white paper hung above the dancers. It was beautiful.

I staggered my way uncertainly to a seat, hoping that my head would slow down its throbbing again. "Can I do anything for you?" Gabriel asked.

"Well," I looked uncertainly over at the table of refreshments. "Could you bring me a cup of water?"

"Of course." He pounced at the opportunity to be useful and rushed off to the drinks. I took a full breath—a high breath, rather than a deep one. The corset meant that a large inhalation lifted my ribs instead of pushing out my belly. Closing my eyes, I willed my skull to stop cracking.

Gabriel returned, water in hand. "They have chocolate-covered strawberries," he told me. He knew they were particular favorites of mine. "Do you want me to bring you one?"

I looked down at the water, sipping doubtfully. I still wasn't entirely sure that I wouldn't double over spewing bile at any moment. Still, chocolate strawberries . . .

Gabriel seemed to read my thoughts. "It might settle your stomach a bit if you eat something," he nudged.

"Okay." I was nervous, but I really didn't need much urging. I *love* chocolate-covered strawberries.

When he brought one back for me, I nibbled at it slowly between delicate sips of water. Nibble—stay, stomach, stay! Chew . . . swallow . . . sip. Sip . . . no! Okay . . . stomach—is—Ah! No, okay. Sip. Sip. Nibble.

I feel fairly confident in stating that chocolate strawberries were not carried in the standard doctors' bags of the nineteenth century.[9] Those iconic leather bags were far more likely to contain some variant of aspirin: the active painkilling constituent of the willow plant was identified in 1823, and by 1897 the Bayer company had developed and patented a way to artificially synthesize the drug.[10] There were other remedies of varying efficacies (generally available from drugstores without the bother of seeing a doctor), and of course there has always been the time-honored headache treatment in which I had been engaged earlier: lying quietly in a darkened room.

By the time I had finished the strawberry, I was feeling improved enough to look over to where Gabriel had started a conversation with our neighbors at the adjoining table. They were from the same costume group we had encountered earlier, although the precise assortment had changed somewhat. The short woman who tended to grumble was there, dressed now in an electric blue polyester gown that fitted her like a sack. Ellen had been replaced by a more sedate and soft-spoken woman named Tilly who wore an outfit that was rather more tasteful than others we had seen. Her broad, hoopskirted gown was fashioned of a material that shifted color as the light changed; I couldn't tell if it was real shot silk, but the fact that I could have that uncertainty spoke for its quality. I envied her thick waves of lustrous brown hair, tucked into a lace net at the back of her neck. Feeling the crush of pain in my head receding ever so slightly, I tried to concentrate on the conversation.

Tilly ignored snarky interjections from her companion and continued to tell Gabriel more about their club, as well as about the other groups with which she was involved. She went into special detail about an upcoming tea she was organizing as a fund-raiser for a senior center. She told us about how it had become a regular event; every year on the Saturday before Mother's Day she helped this center organize a Princess Tea. Volunteers served in formal dress, and there would be an antique fashion show as entertainment. She urged us to come help, and we said we'd think about it.

---

[9] There were sickroom recipes for sweets such as invalid ice cream, from the reasoning that sugar is nourishing and easily digestible, but these were intended for people who needed to regain strength after long convalescence.

[10] "Aspirin Timeline," Aspirin Foundation, http://www.aspirin-foundation.com/what/timeline.html.

The tea was Tilly's own project, separate from the costume group, but she told us about upcoming events from that group as well. Picnics, parties, dances—we were urged to come to them all. Gabriel, excited by the prospect of opportunities for us to wear our Victorian clothing, started to tell Tilly about our collection.

"We think it's really fun to show people the real antiques," he explained. "We think it's a really good learning experience for people to see the real thing, to see all the detail that went into them. We've really learned a lot from wearing them and feeling the way clothes were meant to fit."

"You can't wear real antiques!" snipped the diminutive woman in the baggy dress. (I think the glare of her neon blue polyester was making my headache worse.) "You'll ruin them!"

We're not telling you what to do with your own property, I thought, my head pounding. *What right do you have to dictate what we do with ours?*

"We've been getting antique clothes and repairing them specifically so that we can wear them and teach people about them," Gabriel explained, speaking the words I may have said if I were feeling better. "We think people learn a lot more—"

"You don't seem to understand that when these things are gone, they're gone!" she interrupted. She rolled her eyes while she talked.

"Dance with me?" I suddenly asked Gabriel, eager to end the conversation.

He gave me a dubious look. "Are you sure you feel up to it?"

I nodded. I think I would have danced with my brains leaking out of my ears if it meant escaping Polyester Woman's uneducated wrath.

After a dance and several more cups of water, I actually was feeling better. By the time the ball was over, I was truly enjoying myself and the headache was nearly gone. My husband's tender ministrations had helped greatly, and the throbbing pain in my head had been replaced by a swelling pride in my heart that Gabriel had helped distract me from my discomfort by dancing, even though he hates to do so.

"You know," I told Gabriel as we drove back to our hotel room. "I think I figured something out."

"Hmm? What's that?"

"Well," I explained. "My anatomy teacher's always talking about how much water the large intestine uses . . . "

"Uh huh . . ." Gabriel was clearly wondering where this was going.

"He says the colon will steal water from anywhere in the body when it needs it, and the brain's mostly water, and that's why so many people get headaches when they get dehydrated, because the colon's stealing the water."

Oh dear. This sounded a lot more coherent in anatomy class.

"Uh huh . . ." Gabriel repeated, waiting to see where I was going with this.

"Well, anyhow, I was thinking that maybe the reason my headache came on so fast this time was that the corset had been compressing my intestines all day, and then when I took it off, the intestines suddenly slurped up all the extra water because they could suddenly expand."

"So . . . you're saying that next time you get a headache, we should keep your corset on?"

"Well, maybe." Honestly, it did make a lot more sense in the abstract.

"It's worth a try, I guess."

Back at the hotel, we snuggled deep into the feather bed for our last night in Port Townsend, both agreeing that the weekend was passing far too quickly. This lovely little mini break felt like a step backward in time, and we had little desire to return to the present.

The next day, we strolled through the beautiful Uptown neighborhoods, gazing on its glorious old Victorian homes from the late nineteenth century. In the heart of the historic district, a few blocks up from a corner grocery that sold sarsaparilla and on a street where the houses were adorned with bay windows and flashed glass, tears came to my eyes.

"Hey," Gabriel frowned, and his hand came up to stroke my hair. "What's wrong?"

I sniffed, trying to blink the tears away. "It's just . . ." I looked around us, at surroundings that reminded me of a vibrant version of my dreams from childhood, when I had longed more than anything to live in the Victorian era. "We're going back today. We'll never be able to live in a place like this."

Gabriel wiped at my eyes. "Don't say that."

"It's true, though."

He shook his head. "Don't say 'never.'" He kissed my gloved hand. Then a look of amusement crossed his face and he grinned. "After all, a few weeks ago, you never thought you'd be wearing a corset, right?"

The corner of my own mouth turned up at that. "I suppose that's true," I admitted, nodding.

"See?" He put his hand around my waist. "You never know what can happen in the future." He looked around us and grinned again. "Or the past!"

The sentiment that our time in the Victorian seaport was passing too quickly was one that stayed strongly with us long after we'd passed the Port Townsend city limits. As we waited for the ferry we would ride to cross Puget Sound, I smoothed down my modern shirt over my inward curves. I had been enjoying the daylong hug of my stays so much that I hadn't wanted to take them off.

Gabriel smirked at me. "Are you enjoying wearing the corset?"

I gave him a sideways glance, and returned the expression with a smirk of my own. "Yeah. Actually, I am. I never thought I would. I would have said they were crazy if someone told me I would. But . . . I am."

He chuckled as we drove onto the ferry.

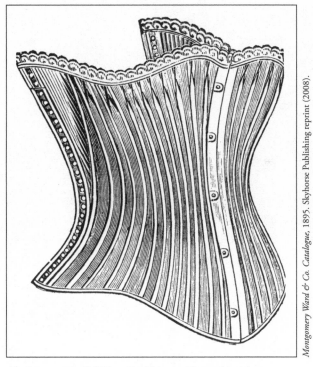

Montgomery Ward & Co. Catalogue, 1895. Skyhorse Publishing reprint (2008).

Montgomery Ward's "Venus Back" corset. Price: $2 each or $22/dozen.

4

Waisted Curves

Godey's Lady's Book (January 1890).

Victorian fashion plate.

I was entranced. Within just a few weeks, the corset went from a gift reluctantly accepted at arm's length, to something I didn't want to be without. I loved the soft feeling of being hugged all day, and of course I loved my new figure. But more than these things, I loved the sudden change in the way I was treated by the world around me.

On one of the corseting blogs I had been reading, someone posted a comment that struck a particularly deep chord with me. "When you look like an old-fashioned lady," the blogger wrote, "people treat you like an old-fashioned lady."[11] It was true.

I had lived in Seattle for years and had long since grown accustomed to all the jostling and elbow-shoving that is such a part of daily life in a big city, most

---

[11] This line is quoted from memory, and I sincerely regret that I do not remember its originator. I have looked, but not been able to find the posting again. If any readers recognize the statement and know who originally wrote it, please pass the information along to me so that I can give them due credit for it.

metropolitan residents don't notice it anymore. Suddenly, though, people were standing aside for me. People opened doors; men tipped their hats. I was still in modern clothes—cycling pants, sweaters pinned to take up the extra slack from the subtracted bulk, a polar fleece jacket I had altered a bit—but I was becoming, and being treated similarly to, a Victorian lady.

Part of the change was in myself. With the corset holding my back straight, I couldn't slump anymore. I was uncomfortable with this at first; being a naturally big girl, over the years I'd gotten used to making myself look as small as possible, as though to apologize to the world for my existence. Now I couldn't, though, and I started to realize that the world didn't need an apology for my inclusion in it.

As I stopped slumping and my shoulders went back, my head naturally followed. I took to wearing hats, and my chin came up to steady them. When I started wearing my hair in a bun, the little chignon at the base of my neck acted as a counterbalance. My beloved boots came out at every opportunity, and to keep my balance on the kitten heels, I learned to walk with long strides, lifting up my feet, which I had been dragging for far too long. After a lifetime as a shuffling, slumping little duckling, I was learning to be a swan.

I started rushing home after class, as eager to get into my corset as I had been to get out of school when I was young. Gabriel helped me on with it when he returned from his own classes, and I started to grow impatient with the lag of time between my own return and his. One day, I got tired of waiting.

I stood in front of the full-length mirror on our bathroom and held the corset up, craning my neck around in a struggle to see what I was doing. With the clasps fastened, I reached around for the laces . . . and the corset immediately fell off from the lack of tension. I frowned, but refused to give up so easily.

The second attempt was more successful. It took a while to pull the laces taught, working as I was behind my back and in the reversed image of the mirror. At last, though, I was laced and tied, sleek and curvy by my own hands. I beamed at myself in the mirror, nearly as proud of this accomplishment as I'd been the first time I'd tied my own shoes as a child.

In time, practice would make the action of tying my corset laces as easy and familiar as styling my hair into a bun. However, I still generally have Gabriel check that the bow is secure. Corset laces, like shoelaces, will work themselves loose and come untied over the course of a day if they haven't been tied properly, and there are few things quite as annoying as having to disrobe in a public bathroom to retie my laces. This tender confirmation serves to reinforce the ties that bind us together, as I'm sure it did for couples of the past.

Front of a trade card advertising Ball's corsets. (These cards were about the size of a business card and were given away to promote various products.) This particular one involves a slight visual illusion: by placing a card over the line in the illustration and bringing one's eyes very close to the picture, the uncorseted woman becomes corseted!

I loved the weekends, when I could wear the corset all day. I wanted to wear it more during the week, but worried about its compatibility with my classes. Beside the straightforward logistical problems, I fretted about what my classmates would think of me.

I was studying massage therapy, working toward certification. A big part of massage school involves students using one another as guinea pigs, and we spent as much time receiving massage as we did giving it. Since the client is undressed during full-body massage, I wouldn't be wearing anything for that portion of the class. When we switched roles from client to practitioner in each class, both time and space for the changeover was extremely limited: we usually had only five minutes for the whole class to get changed—and only two changing stalls to do it in. I was still having difficulty getting the corset on by myself; it took me at least five minutes just to do the laces, even with a mirror to help me see what I was doing. At school, I wouldn't have a mirror, but I would have a class full of impatient fellow students standing on the other side of a thin curtain, eager to change their clothes, too.

There was also the very real—and distinctly unpleasant—possibility of getting lotion on the corset if I wore it to massage class. Some of my fellow students thought it was "nice" to use an entire four-ounce bottle of lotion when giving a massage. (For anyone who has trouble visualizing that, it is the equivalent of an entire stick of butter.)

"Ah, this must feel so nice!" they'd brag, basting the helpless person under the sheet like a plucked turkey about to go in the oven. "Yummy!" (Some days I would have not one, but two showers when I got home, and I would still feel grease oozing out from between my toes as my pores desperately tried to rid themselves of the oil that had been forced into them.) I couldn't toss my corset into a washing machine like those people did with their greasy T-shirts and jeans; it would have ruined it.

There were days in school when we didn't undress, purely textbook days when relacing and grease wouldn't be an issue. However, the pressure of social stigma remained. What would everyone on campus think? What would they say?

I worried about the attitudes I would encounter within the very particular community of my school. Massage therapists are an interesting bunch—students studying to become them even more so. The individuals at my school covered a dramatic range in degree of credulity, from the grounded to the stratospheric. I don't think a single bit of science fiction, fact, or conspiracy theory has even been voiced by man that at least one person at that school wouldn't have believed. (My personal favorite was the girl who thought Earth was hollow, and that if you walked to the North Pole you could drop in a hole and fall all the way to the South Pole. One of my friends, who has a degree in geology, nearly fell off his seat laughing when I told him about that one.) If quite a few of them believed that underwire bras cause cancer,[12] what on earth would they think of a corset?

I started to feel like I was doing something clandestine after class, rushing off to engage in an activity that was hidden from the people who knew me in that other aspect of my life. Yet, the more I wore the corset, the more comfortable I grew with it. The more it taught me about grace and pride, the more I felt that this was truly myself. Somewhere, amongst the steady sweeping strides and the eyes lifted from dirt to horizon, amongst the smiles of strangers, I had stopped feeling like a duckling playing with a swan's feathers. I wasn't surprised anymore by the curves I saw in the mirror. I missed them when they were gone.

I have always said that I don't want my life to be dictated by the opinions of other people, but it takes courage to put that attitude into effect. While I was learning more about the corset, and consequently learning more about myself, I was also learning how to be courageous.

And then, one day, I decided that I was tired of hiding.

---

[12] Incidentally, the National Cancer Institute has debunked this popular myth.
   "Pregnancy and Breast Cancer Risk—Misunderstandings about Breast Cancer Risk Factors," National Cancer Institute, http://www.cancer.gov/cancertopics/factsheet/Risk/pregnancy.

Besides, I reasoned, these people pride themselves on being "liberal" and talk a lot about "diversity." Why not let them see for themselves how truly liberal their opinions are when confronted with real diversity—with something that's truly different from what they see every day?

On the last day of our module on Swedish massage, we were scheduled to have a paper-based test. We would begin our classes on deep tissue manipulation soon enough, but the day of the written test wouldn't require undressing. In a way, it was oddly appropriate that I chose the last day of Swedish techniques as my first day to wear my corset to school, because although Pehr Ling (the so-called Father of Swedish Massage) died slightly before Queen Victoria was crowned in England, his techniques were popularized in America during the time she reigned on the other side of the Atlantic. Similarly, the corset had existed before the nineteenth century, but it really came into its own in America during this period. Whether students of one Victorian concept would tolerate another was yet to be seen.

I have never had a driver's license, and it was my custom to ride my bicycle to school. I was a little nervous about cycling corseted, but after going a few blocks, I realized I needn't have worried. My posture was a bit more upright than the classic cycling position, but nothing quintessential had changed. The corset didn't interfere with my legs' range of motion, and of course, my arms were completely free. The added stiffness on my torso required a bit of acclimation as my body practiced the little hindbrain tricks of balancing that a cyclist does so quickly that conscious thought doesn't get a chance to enter into them, but overall the changeover from uncorseted to corseted riding was really no harder than a shift from off-road tires to slicks: something to get used to, nothing to worry about.

In class, the man sitting next to me that day kept staring, but it was a woman who actually said something. She looked me up and down, slump-shouldered and disapproving. "Wow, you've got the posture from hell today!" she boomed out.

Previously, my automatic reaction to such a comment would have been to slink down apologetically in my chair. I actually noticed other students within earshot doing exactly that, crouching down their already hunched shoulders in compliant submission. Some of them tittered nervously.

I couldn't slink down, though. The corset kept me upright, so I did the only thing I could do. I sat up straighter.

I nodded slowly, keeping my voice low and level. "I'm wearing a corset."

She stared throughout the length of several of my slow blinks. "Does that, like, hurt?"

"No, not at all," I asserted. "It's actually really comfortable."

My classmate stood down, took her seat, and the test commenced shortly thereafter. Further discussion would wait until several hours later, when the exam had long been completed and everyone was munching snacks that had been brought to celebrate the end of a class module. One of the youngest members of the class—a woman who had come in late and thus missed the earlier confrontation—pointed to my midsection.

"Are you wearing a . . . a . . . *thing*?" she asked.

"A corset?" I smirked. "Yeah."

She giggled, poking the metal busk through my dress. "My grandma had one of those." She giggled again. "Can I see it?"

I paused for half a beat. "Sure . . . " The request caught me off guard, but I didn't see any reason to deny it. "Why not?"

We went into the women's bathroom and I undid my dress far enough to show her the corset. "Damn!" she said, approvingly. "Can I, like, feel it?" She held out her hands in a circle, parallel around but not touching my waist.

"Sure, go ahead."

She put her hands around my waist and squeezed the corset slightly. "Damn!" she repeated. "I gotta get me one of those."

She asked me where I'd gotten it, and I related what I'd heard from Gabriel about the website[13] where he'd made the purchase. While I was giving her the information and still had my dress down, another of the younger class members entered the lady's room. She also wanted to feel the corset and find out where I'd gotten it, so I patiently repeated myself as she squeezed my waist. The first girl was still giggling when we returned to class together.

Well, I assessed in the privacy of my thoughts. *Two for, one against. Not a bad score, really.*

Massage and the Original Swedish Movements, by Kurre W. Ostrom, 1895.

Illustration from nineteenth-century massage manual.

---

[13] Check it out yourself!
      Timeless Trends Corset Designs, http://www.timeless-trends.com.

5

Stayed Slumber and Sizing Down

From *A Widow and Her Friends* (1901). Illustration by Charles Dana Gibson.

As much as I loved wearing my corset during the day, it took me a few weeks to creep up on the idea of sleeping in it. It had been my custom for years to sleep wearing nothing at all; the idea of sleeping in the tightest garment I'd ever owned seemed crazy. Not to mention, uncomfortable. But mostly crazy.

Still, as I'd told Gabriel, before I'd started all this, the idea of myself wearing a corset at all would have sounded mad to me—and once I'd tried it, it wasn't as uncomfortable as I'd expected. Quite the contrary, in fact, once I had gotten used to it. I'd grown to look on it like a case of a person who'd gone barefoot her whole life and had suddenly been given a pair of sturdy boots. At first the unfamiliar items would seem constrictive and uncomfortable, but after a while, the wearer would find it hard to go back—and, most likely, wouldn't want to do so.

Of course, it would be distinctly odd to wear shoes to bed. That was where I hovered for a while with the corset: it was pleasant for the day, but it was a "day thing" in my mind, and it was sort of nice to take it off at night. In the mornings, I was finding myself reluctant to get out of bed, because I knew the first half hour or so after I had squished myself into the corset would be the worst part of the day.

As I had seen in models in anatomy class, and in actual bodies in the cadaver lab I had attended, the lower portion of the human torso is mostly filled with intestines. On their own, these are latex-thin (a very reasonable analogy is sausage casings, which are made from animal intestines). The only appreciable bulk involved is their contents, which are rather amorphous. (This is why a corset can do what it does on the abdomen and not, say, the leg.) Over the course of the day, these intestinal contents would settle into the shape of the corset, and as things evened out, wearing the corset would become comfortable.

My research had lead me to the conclusion that the more a person wears a corset, the faster the waist diminishes. Certain nineteenth-century texts referenced women loosening their corsets for bed (implying that at least some women did sleep in them) or wearing their older corsets at night to save the nicer ones for day wear. The bloggers on the websites I had read who slept in their corsets all agreed that it was the best (most said the *only*) way to achieve a small waist. I dithered, but at last decided to give it a try.

The first night I slept in my corset, I tossed uncomfortably for hours after lying down. When I finally did attain sleep, it was fitful at first. But after an incredibly vivid nightmare of violent strangulation, I awoke at midnight, clawing at my laces. Gasping for breath, I yanked at the ends of the laces, pulling them far out as soon as I managed to untie the bow. I didn't retie them, but left them hanging loose down my back as I fell into a deep slumber.

In the morning, Gabriel curiously examined the loose, slightly tangled cords. "How did that happen?"

I was embarrassed and didn't want to answer at first. "I . . . guess they must have gotten caught on something while I was sleeping," I lied, lamely. He looked surprised, but didn't ask any further questions.

The second night was easier. I woke up a few times, but resisted the urge to undo my laces, and managed to get back to sleep. In the morning when I got dressed, I was pleasantly surprised not to have to go through the initial morning *squeeze* to which I had grown accustomed. Since the form had stayed in place, my intestinal contents had never oozed out into an amorphous blob, and there was no displacement to deal with. I was comfortable in a way that I had come to associate with evenings, after internal contents had settled. It was a pleasant comfort and it inspired me to continue sleeping in the corset.

The third night was easier still, and the progress continued until I was sleeping normally, more or less. I found the advice of the bloggers had been quite true, although I was in no way prepared for how quickly my waist started to shrink. After a week of sleeping in the corset (a mere month after I'd first worn it at all), I could wear it so tightly laced that the two halves were overlapping in the back, and still have enough spare room to thrust both arms down behind the busk and wave them around. I had started with a natural thirty-two-inch waist, and this corset measured twenty-eight inches. Taking the spare room (enough for both my fists) into account, that was a reduction of more than four inches in a month. There had been no surgery involved, nor any special diet. I was eating smaller portions because the constriction on my abdomen meant I had less room in my stomach, but I was eating until I felt full at every meal. (Actually, a lot of what I had been eating was cheesecake. There had been quite a large quantity of it left over from my birthday. So, no . . . No special diet here.)

It took a while to become accustomed to how quickly I now achieved a full feeling at mealtimes. I would top up my bowl with what seemed like an average portion, then run out of room halfway through. Even when my stomach felt full, my eyes would tell me I hadn't eaten enough, and I would continue trying to make myself eat, a remembered echo of my mother's voice scolding, "Finish your dinner/lunch/breakfast/snack! You haven't eaten enough! If you don't eat it all, you'll be hungry later!" Trying to heed this advice and evade this dreaded bogeyman of getting hungry later, I would stuff myself as full as I could, then suffer from stomachache and heartburn afterward.

One day, I had a striking realization. It should have been obvious—ridiculously so, in retrospect. It just ran so blatantly contrary to the advice that had been drilled into me from childhood that it came as a bit of an epiphany. *If I get hungry later,* it finally dawned on me, *I can eat more later!* This is the first world, not the third; I'm never far from food, and I can get it when I need it.

It was a relief, really, to realize that something that had been hanging over my head since childhood had never really been a threat. So what if I get hungry later? I'll eat later—when I'm hungry! What on earth have I been so worried about?

This thought found its way into the portions I placed on my plate at mealtimes. I would spoon out a given serving of food, and my eyes would tell me it was nowhere near enough. *But this doesn't have to be the end,* I would remind myself. *There's more food if I need it. If I'm still hungry after I eat this, I can get more.* As often as not, I wouldn't want to get more.

I practiced chewing slowly, counting my bites and savoring the flavor of the food instead of forcing it down as though it would be taken away any minute. As I took more care with my meals, they became better-rounded, with more salubrious proportions of fiber and protein to starch.

The stomachaches went away, as did the heartburn. One night as I was relishing my cheesecake dessert, enjoying the sensation of being pleasantly full but not stuffed, I looked over at Gabriel.

"You know," I told him, pondering. "My mom and my brother both have something called acid reflux, but that's really just a fancy name for bad heartburn. Their doctors give them prescription drugs for it, and they've got all kinds of side effects. Then they take more drugs to deal with the side effects, and with the side effects of the side effects . . ."

I let the chocolate cheesecake melt slowly over my tongue, savoring its richness, then I continued.

"But since I've been eating smaller portions and eating slower, my heartburn's gone away." I swallowed the creamy chocolate and cocked an eyebrow, thinking of my mom's overflowing medicine cabinets. "Do you think their heartburn would go away, without the drugs, if they just started eating less?"

Gabriel nodded. "Oh, I'm sure it would." Then he shrugged. "But do you think they're going to do that?"

"No," I sighed. "You're right." I shook my head. "It's too bad, really."

When my mom moved into her own house after my grandmother died, I spent several seasons planting her yard with a myriad of fruit trees and bushes, thinking that the fresh fruit would be good for her diabetes. My reward had been hearing how her friends at work loved the cherries, apples, and Asian pears and how the neighborhood birds loved the mulberries—never any comments about her eating any of it. Her refrigerator remained full of highly processed, microwavable foods, and meanwhile her diabetes continued to get worse.

I had long since given up on trying to change my family.

But at least I now knew I could change myself for the better.

As my waist dramatically reduced, that first corset rapidly grew loose enough to be uncomfortable. It may seem counterintuitive, but a loose corset can actually be just as uncomfortable as an unreasonably tight one. The first time I had put on my corset, it seemed to have been suffocating me, but as we grew accustomed to each other, I found that I enjoyed the support it offered. I could stand up straight, with a lovely posture (which is rare in modern times), comfortably held in snug support. When I sat, I had a ready-made brace at my back fitted to my exact contours, regardless of how awful the chair behind me might be.

However, as my waist reduced and the corset became looser, it provided increasingly less support. I still had to remain upright, or else be slumped uncomfortably against bones of sprung steel, but the stays were too slack to provide their intended support. My back muscles grew tired, holding that agonizingly perfect posture on their own, and I became fidgety.

It was time for a smaller corset.

Gabriel showed me the website from which he had ordered my first set of stays. They had a number of lovely choices, all of them tempting. After some delightful dithering, I chose a twenty-four-inch model in green silk brocade, embroidered with gold thread. I watched the mailbox, eager for its arrival.

When the new corset came, it was the first day all over again. I had grown used to seeing my curvy image in the mirror, but the new figure brought those curves to new levels. The first corset had given me a form that could still (with imagination) be attributed to lucky genes or intense exercise, but this was starting to look unreal.

The first time Gabriel helped me on with the new corset, I flashed a coquettish grin at myself in the mirror. I slid a hand down the curve of my gold-touched emerald flank and gave my silken armor a playful slap, then insisted we go out for a stroll.

My head was very high indeed as we walked along the streets of Seattle's University District and into the adjoining neighborhood of Wallingford. I had on my lovely kitten-heel boots and I was almost dancing. The cheerful smiles I saw at every glance may have been in response only to my own joyous countenance, but to me they all seemed to be admirers. I reveled in the pride in Gabriel's eyes as he looked at me, and the feeling as he slid his arm around my waist was very much like when we first fell in love.

As we turned back toward home, he made me laugh at some little joke that has since been lost to time. I giggled at first and the involuntary shaking of my belly muscles shook against the sides of the corset and tickled me all the way through. That sense of core-deep tickling only made the laughter stronger, and soon I was cracking up with mirth, one hand over my corseted stomach as I shook with laughter that made me sway, since I couldn't double over.

When I finally caught my breath enough to explain the delicious feeling coursing through and over me, Gabriel responded, "Maybe that's where the phrase, 'Tickle your fancy' comes from. I bet that's why nineteenth-century men were always trying to make women laugh." He raised his eyebrows at me, teasing. "Trying to tickle their fancies!" He reached for the soft spot under my arm, as though to tickle me in earnest, and I was laughing all over again.

I enjoyed having a supportive corset again, but because my new stays were so tight, I started to have real issues with my underwire bra. Since this corset was still a ready-made, off-the-rack model, its reduced size (compared to my first corset) meant that the upper portion of the corset was proportionally smaller to the waist. While I was fine with the reduced waist, my ribs were not compressible. They could—and did—move up a bit, but there was a limit to this mobility. The result was that the tender flesh under my breasts was caught between grudging bone and two layers of unyielding steel: the wire of the bra and the stays of the corset, which pressed that wire into my body. When I took off the bra and corset for showers, the mark of the underwires would be printed into my soft skin as angry red curves.

It was a bothersome problem. The obvious solution would have been to simply go out and buy a new bra that didn't have an underwire, but they were nowhere to be found. Fashion had proclaimed the push-up bra to be "in" that season, and soft-cups had completely vanished from store shelves. Anything beyond a preteen's training brassiere was padded like a bedlamite's cell and wired for liftoff.

Ever the problem-solver, Gabriel responded to my complaints by taking the matter as a personal challenge. My husband is a resourceful man, with a decidedly historic view of the world. When I saw what he came up with as a solution to my underwire issue, I rubbed my chin, shifting an amused look between him and the garishly colored cardboard box he had handed to me.

"Angle-action bra." I read the swoopy, 1950s script slanting above a grinning, flip-haired model. "Why are there bull's-eyes centered over the nipples?"

"That's the reinforced stitching!" Gabriel told me cheerfully.

"And the fact that the cups are pointing away from each other?"

"That was the style back then."

"Uh huh . . ." I removed the new/old-stock cotton brassiere from its box, a reasonable opinion forming in my mind as to why it had gone unsold for half a century.

"No underwire!" Gabriel beamed.

It did have that going for it. Even if the bullet-style, 1950s bra looked a little absurd over my emerald brocaded corset, it did increase the comfort level. It would fulfill its function until I could find something better—and I had my sights set beyond bras.

I had been discussing the idea of a custom corset with Gabriel since I had realized how much I enjoyed wearing stays. After just a month with my second off-the-rack corset, it (like the first) could now close completely in the back, and I sensed my waist could still be smaller. The bloggers on the websites I had been reading discussed the superiority and comfort of custom-made models, and I was drawn by the idea of a figure that would be made to my own form, a lovely thing of silk-satin with custom contours that would compliment while they complemented.

The thing stopping me was the price. In books and old advertisements, I gazed at the corset costs of yesteryear, jealous of shoppers a generous century previous. Prices were listed from pence to guineas, but never more than ten pounds sterling. When prices were in American currency, the standard was about the equivalent of the contemporary price of five dozen eggs.

If only . . .

Chrisman Collection, packaging (circa 1950s).

Biflex "Angle-Action" bra box.

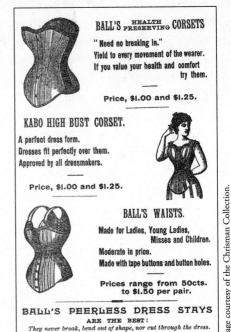

Image courtesy of the Chrisman Collection.

Back of a trade card advertising Ball's corsets.

There was a single store in Seattle that sold custom-made corsets. Gabriel took me there and we pored over the design styles, fitting their various options against the ideal corset in my mind, growing giddy with excitement. When they quoted me a price for their lovely figures, though, I despaired. It was nearly a month's rent.

Later, I quoted the price and shook my head, pacing beside Gabriel in the Northgate Mall. In rainy weather, the mall was our go-to place—to walk, though, never to buy. We were both students at this time, but even when not in sway to the various restrictions that academic life places on finances, my husband and I are very particular about how we spend our money. There are any number of adjectives, from the proud to the pejorative, that I might use to describe our attitudes toward finances, but I will admit they are a bit unusual for early twenty-first-century Americans. Gabriel will happily scrimp and completely avoid many expenses that a lot of people might consider essential, then gleefully splurge on an item or activity he considers worthy. (He terms this "budgeting the luxuries first," a description he borrowed from Robert A. Heinlein's book, *Time Enough For Love.*) My own innate tendency is to avoid spending money at all, if possible. (It is probably fair to trace this characteristic to my Depression-era grandmother, who helped raise me.) Fairly early in our marriage, Gabriel had come home one day and found me cleaning the floor with a homemade mop that I had created by attaching some old rags to a bamboo gardening stake rather than purchasing a cheap mop from the store. He expressed his hearty approval of my frugality, then bought me opal earrings for Christmas.

Discussion about the cost of a customized corset brought up the same dichotomy of attitudes. "I just can't justify that," I said, referring once again to the price. I shook my head sadly, the lovely picture in my head of my perfect corset fluttering away on swansdown wings.

"You would get a lot of use out of it, though," Gabriel pointed out. "Think about it: it's something that would last for years, and you'd be wearing it every day. This is something that's meant to become a part of you, after a while."

"Yeah, but . . ." I shook my head. The price was unbelievable. "You're talking to someone whose mom used to borrow my piggy-bank money to buy groceries when I was a kid. I just can't justify spending that much on something frivolous."

"It's not frivolous!" Gabriel told me. "It's necessary!"

I laughed at that.

"Budget the luxuries first!" he quoted. My husband grinned and squeezed my hand as we walked. "You've come as far as you can with the off-the-rack corsets, and this one will be too big soon."

I nodded. I had it only a month, but the green corset, like its blue-roses predecessor, was rapidly outsizing my shrinking waist.

"And just think how comfortable it would be!" Gabriel continued. He kissed my hand. "It's not frivolous. Like I said, it's something you'll be wearing every day. It's worth it to have you comfortable and beautiful."

I blushed.

"In the end, though, it's up to you," he concluded.

We walked in silence for a while, pondering. It wasn't the first time we'd had this same conversation. I had fallen in love with those curvy, silken images, but this was so much money. And yet . . .

As we passed by a bustling coffee stand, I looked at the crowd of people seated nearby, sipping their lattes. The prices on the menu ranged between three and five dollars—more for extras like whipped cream and flavored syrup. "I guess, if someone bought one three-dollar latte every day—"

"Lots of people do that," Gabriel agreed. "Heck, that's the low end. Around here, plenty of people buy a couple coffee drinks a day."

"Yeah," I nodded, trying to be discreet as I watched a barista totaling a customer's order—a very standard one, for Seattle: a twenty-ounce Frappuccino, plus one pastry. It came to over six dollars.

"But let's just say a person spent three dollars a day on coffee."

"Most people do that," Gabriel agreed.

"Over the course of a month," I calculated, "that's around ninety dollars. Times twelve for a year . . ." I cocked my head. "That's more than the corset would cost, right there."

"Right," Gabriel nodded. "And you don't drink coffee."

Hardly ever, anyway. "And I don't have a cell phone[14]—"

"—which are expensive," Gabriel agreed.

---

[14] I am constantly puzzled by people who ask, "How do you live without . . . ?" and complete the question by naming an item that did not exist throughout most of human history. Cell phones are hardly on the same level of human needs where one would rank food or oxygen. They hadn't even been invented yet when my older brother was born, and even by the time I finished high school they were still fairly unusual. It was my high school's policy in 1998 that if a student answered a cell phone call during class, the phone could be confiscated for the rest of the entire school year. The few teenagers who had their own cell phones were generally intimidated enough by this policy that they dared flout the restriction only in the last few days of class. Now, when I tell teenagers about that rule, they stare at me as though I were describing use of a whipping post or pillory. Somehow, in just a few short years, the cellular telephone has become so commonplace that most people would not dream of being deprived of one. For my part, though I value my privacy when away from home, I value mindfulness about where I am and what I am doing. I always think it is terribly sad when I see two people obviously well acquainted with each other who have come to a beautiful setting together, yet are each ignoring the human being closest to them in favor of interaction with an electronic device.

"And I don't drive. How much do you suppose most Americans spend on gas alone?"

"Just on gas?" Gabriel shrugged and shook his head. "Tons. Plus with a car, there's car payments, insurance, repairs . . ."

"But I ride my bike everywhere."

People often tell me I'm crazy for never even applying for a learner's permit. I often think they're crazy when I hear about the tally of their auto bills.

"Hmm . . ."

"Think about it," Gabriel urged. "You've got to spend money on yourself sometimes." He squeezed my hand. "In the end, though, it's your decision."

The debate went on in my mind. My thoughts filled with swansdown and silk-satin, and I pored over ads old and new, coveting the images. I dreamed and I saved, and the borders of my notebooks filled with sketches of corsets.

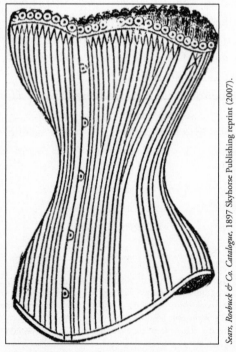

Sears, Roebuck & Co. Catalogue, 1897 Skyhorse Publishing reprint (2007).

Sears, Roebuck & Co.'s "High Grade Special Corset": $1.25.

6

A Museum Visit

Godey's Lady's Book (September 1889).

Victorian fashion plate.

After meeting the costume group who had been playing tourist in Port Townsend, we were added to their emailing list and announcements came to us of various events. Many of these we declined for reasons of cost or practicality; even when these events were free, they tended to be fairly remote. For May, though, an invitation was issued that would have been difficult to refuse: they were holding high tea in a Victorian mansion, and Ellen was offering us a ride.

Ellen was the tall, ebullient matron from the group who had clasped us to her bosom at first meeting. Even in the confines of a compact car, she seemed to be perpetually projecting her booming voice over an unseen audience. At times it was difficult to tell whether she was addressing her immediate companions or the blinking Bluetooth device that she never removed from her ear. Jammed into her auditory canal, this plastic anachronism flashed a steady pattern of garish, digital blue against the several pounds of ostrich feathers glued to her hat.

Throughout the long ride to the mansion, Gabriel and I both squirmed uncomfortably in Ellen's backseat. For reasons known only to the car's designer, it had been made with the seat angled forward, the seat and its back forming a distinct V-shape. It seemed calculatedly designed to force its occupant into a slouch.

"Enjoy those seats!" Ellen boomed, smiling at us in the rearview mirror. "This car is so comfortable!"

Maybe for Quasimodo.

The only way for a human body to fit into those seats was to fold itself into the shape of a hunchbacked primate. Gabriel and I had both been practicing proper posture for months and neither of us wanted to slouch, but more than that, we couldn't. My corset wouldn't let me, and Gabriel's fitted Victorian suit was every bit as restrictive. In the proper circumstances, both these garments were wonderfully supportive, but this context was about as proper as a cave.

At some point in the very long drive, the subject of corsets came up. "Fine for the women who had everything done for them!" Ellen boomed. "The ones who didn't have to work. It's not like you can scrub a floor in a corset!"

I opened my mouth to tell her of my research, of the photos I'd seen of corsets marketed specifically toward servants, the nineteenth-century citations in Valerie Steele's book[15] of men complaining that they couldn't tell the servants from the mistresses anymore because their figures all looked alike. I wanted to tell her that I scrubbed my floor in my corset every week.

"Actually—" I began.

"And the men's clothes!" She bowled over my protestations. "Men always have it so easy!"

"Actually—" Gabriel tried to interrupt.

We had discussed the matter so often, I knew exactly what he wanted to say. The men's clothes were just as restrictive as the women's. The suits were tailored specifically to hold the shoulders back in proper posture, and the trousers were tailored to stand, not to sit.

"Coffee break!" Ellen cut off Gabriel's interjection. She pulled into a drive-through Starbucks and ordered a venti drink with flavored syrup. "What do you guys want?" We gave each other frustrated looks and declined to order.

We arrived at our destination too early for the scheduled tea. While Ellen searched for a parking spot, we asked to simply be dropped off on the small town's main street and allowed to find our own way to the mansion. Free of the

---

[15] Steele, *The Corset*, 47.

torturous seat, Gabriel and I stretched our backs and rolled our shoulders, glad to have regained the posture of *Homo sapiens.*

We wandered through the town's quaint shops. I smiled at sweet little temptations, but kept my purse firmly closed: I was saving for my custom corset. After exhausting the possibilities of window shopping, we strolled up the hill toward the advertised event. There were two museums on that hill: the quilt museum in a Victorian mansion, which we had come to see, and a more conventional, smaller museum. The latter was housed in a humbler, modern building and outlined the history of the area. We found that we were still early for the event at the first museum, so we meandered our way up the hill toward the second.

The curator at the little museum was delighted to see us. (The museum was small enough that I think she would have been happy to see any visitors at all.) She listened with rapt attention as we explained the histories of our outfits, and told us we looked as though we should be in one of her displays. We enjoyed the compliment and gladly accepted her invitation to view the museum for free in exchange for a simple promise to tell more people to come visit.

The museum was a standard format, but it was our favorite kind. There were no artifacts of great men involved, no prototypes of inventions that changed the world. It was simply a collection of small tokens of people's everyday lives—not grandiose personages at whose words the earth shook, just simple people like us. They were born, did their duties, and cherished the happiness life gave them, and then departed, leaving these faint traces of themselves, now gathered here as reminders.

Peterson's Magazine (April 1890).

We lingered over the clothes they had worn and the dolls they had played with as children. An exhibit of wax cylinder recordings particularly caught our eyes. Gabriel had recently learned of a digitized collection of these early audio recordings, and we

Fashion plate from 1890 showing children's clothes and toys.

had been enjoying listening to downloaded versions of the songs whose original medium was now too fragile to be used. I peered at the thick wax cylinders, which had pre-dated phonograph records, the small metallic horns that had once conveyed music to rapt listeners. As we wandered through the museum and I watched my husband beside me in his fine clothes, the lines of a particularly favorite song played themselves in my mind:

> *When I was the dandy, and you were the belle,*
> *We went out walking on Sundays*
> *I wore a tulip right in my lapel and you wore the bonnet with red roses on it*
> *Oh how proud and happy I used to be to have the crowd see you out walking with me,*
> *My dear*
> *When I was the dandy, and you were the belle,*
> *In those dear old sweetheart days . . .*[16]

From About Paris (1895). Illustration by Charles Dana Gibson.

---

[16] Dave Dreyer, Lou Handman, and Herman Ruby. "When I Was the Dandy and You Were the Belle," performed by Walter Van Brunt. Edison Blue Amberol, 1924.

After our tour of the museum, we bid good-bye to its cheerful curator and wandered back to the mansion. The beautiful old building had been converted to a museum, but this one was entirely devoted to quilts. The keeper of this collection was handing out white cotton gloves at the door.

"The tea is happening in those two rooms over there." She pointed. "If you go in any other rooms, you have to wear these. Oh!" She stopped at my quizzical look as I dubiously reached with my own gloved hand for the gloves she was handing me. "You brought your own!" She smiled at me.

The tea was potluck style, and we were designated the dining room and adjoining sitting area. These were both filling rapidly with polyester-clad women on the downward slope of middle age, their thronging mass punctuated occasionally by a put-upon-looking husband. Besides Gabriel and myself, the only other group member who appeared to be younger than forty was a woman stiffly seated in the corner. After an abortive attempt to engage her in conversation, a great deal of being subjected to petty gossip by the older women, and yet another chewing-out from Polly Esther (the short woman who had scolded us in Port Townsend) about how horrible she thought it was to wear real antiques, I evaded the tea party and went to explore the rest of the museum.

The museum curator had ceased passing out gloves and had caught me on my way up the stairs. "I have to ask," she began, her voice low. "Is your waist really that small?"

This is always a somewhat strange question. It seems to imply that I paint invisibility makeup over triangular sections of my torso, the way that other women paint on lipstick or mascara.

"Well," I offered. "I am wearing a corset."

"Wow!" She looked me up and down. "Do you mind if I ask how big it is?"

"Twenty-four inches."

"You're kidding!" She stared in openmouthed admiration. "And, how big is your waist without the corset?"

"Well, it shrinks when you've been wearing a corset awhile," I explained. "The more you wear a corset, the smaller your waist gets. I had a natural thirty-two-inch waist before I started this."

She was clearly intrigued. "And when did you start wearing the corset?"

"March twelfth." I smiled. "It was a birthday present."

"March! Just in March?!"

I nodded. It was early May at that point.

"You've gone from thirty-two to twenty-four inches in three months! And it's just the corset that's done that?"

Again, I nodded.

A new group of people came through the door, clearly seeking the museum itself, not the tea. They dithered over the admissions sign and the curator looked quickly at her basket of gloves.

"Oh! I've—" She held up a finger to me. "Wait right here!"

She returned in a short moment, several blue-jeaned teenage girls in tow.

"You've got to see this woman!" she was telling them excitedly. She presented me to them with the air of someone unveiling a masterpiece. "Her waist went down from thirty-two to twenty-four inches, just from wearing a corset!"

I did my best not to laugh at the curator's sweet enthusiasm. The girls in their T-shirts were clearly not as struck as she was, but they were polite enough. After a few minutes' conversation, the museum keeper saw that more visitors were entering and rushed off to glove them, bidding me a fond adieu, with many thanks for talking with her. As she bustled off and I ascended the stairs, I giggled privately at her ardor.

Most of the quilts in the mansion were highly modern and not to my taste, but the building housing them was lovely. I particularly fell in love with a beautiful tower room overlooking a soaring view. When I ventured downstairs again and found a teenage girl caught between two gossiping matrons with the air of a fox-cornered rabbit, I took her back up to the tower room with me.

Her mother was considering joining the costume group and they had arrived late, she explained. "But," she confessed, taking off her broad-brimmed hat, "I'm really more into sports."

We passed a cheerful hour chatting, enjoying the gorgeous room, and avoiding the crowd downstairs.

Eventually, Gabriel infiltrated our hideout. He had fled the mansion when I'd come upstairs and had been spending the intervening time speaking with members of an antique cars club outside. They were leaving, though, and it seemed like a reasonable opportunity to ask Ellen if we might head home.

On the ride back to Seattle, we managed to wedge enough of ourselves into the conversation to bring up the points we had wanted to discuss earlier about antique clothing.

"People talk a lot about corsets," Gabriel explained, "and how restrictive they were, but people don't realize that the men's clothes were just as restrictive."

He tried to point toward his back to illustrate his point, but this simple action was defeated by the Car Seat of Doom.

"The tailoring," he continued, abandoning illustration, "forces you into an upright posture. So you have to stay upright, you can't slouch. That was part of the point of the clothes—you showed that you were an 'upright citizen' by being upright, and the clothing enforced that."

"And corsets aren't nearly as restrictive as people think they are," I put in, speaking up for the women. Ellen started to object, but I refused quarter. We were nearly home, and I wanted to make this point. It was important to me. "I wear a corset every day: I eat in it, I go to class in it—"

"She rides her bike to class in it!" Gabriel added.

"You ride your bike in a corset?!" Ellen asked incredulously.

"Yes, I do." I asserted. "Six miles every day."

"Well." Ellen shook her head as she made the turn off the highway to our apartment. "Just don't talk to (she named the woman I had come to think of as Polly Esther) about corsets!"

Sears, Roebuck & Co.'s "Yukon" ladies' bicycle, 1897. Price: $56.

Sears, Roebuck & Co. Catalogue, 1897 Skyhorse Publishing reprint (2007).

7

Twenty-Four-Seven

From *A Widow and Her Friends* (1901). Illustration by Charles Dana Gibson.

By May, I was wearing my corset to class almost every day. I had started with the decision to wear it on the days when we should have been working strictly from textbooks, but this proved irritatingly hard to predict. Theoretically, we had a schedule for hands-on days versus study days, but our deep tissue massage teacher could not count organization amongst her virtues, and she was just as likely *not* to change the schedule around completely on any given day of class. Her students learned to haul around our full kit (linens, bolsters, lotion, textbooks, etc.) every day, irrespective of what the syllabus listed as the activity.

The first few times I was caught off guard by one of these last-minute schedule changes, I carefully rolled up my corset when I got undressed, and slipped it into my bike pannier to deal with after I returned home. No matter how carefully I packed the pannier, though, I worried about damaging the corset. I was a cautious rider, but I'd had crashes in the past, and whereas I would heal after being tumbled across the road, the corset wouldn't. Besides that, I felt sloppy without it.

Once I'd gotten used to the corset, going without it felt absolutely slovenly—like a grown woman running about with no bra. I won't deny that vanity came into play as well: I was starting to grow accustomed to my reflection having a defined waist; when the corset came off, everything went right back to where it had been before the stays. Beyond these things, leaving my stays off for any considerable length of time had a peculiar side effect: it made me fall asleep.

I had read theories online and in articles about why corsets make their wearers more alert. Generally, the ideas revolve around blood supply and the corresponding availability of oxygen to various organs. Blood cells replace themselves after trauma or as they wear out, but the overall amount of blood within a body should be fairly steady. If it is pushed away from the stomach and intestines, it becomes available to other organs, notably the brain. (It's a bit like what happens after most people eat a large meal, but in reverse. Instead of the blood rushing away from the brain to work on the digestion, it gets pushed away from the digestive system and puts its oxygen-bearing cells to higher functions.) When I took my corset off, though, all that blood rushed into my stomach. Like a glutton after Thanksgiving, I found my attention drifting as my chin slowly nodded downward.

This was where I reached the limit of my frustration regarding this particular situation. I could grudgingly tolerate feeling slovenly, but I drew the line at falling asleep in public. *Massage class or not, if I'm not actually on that table, I'm wearing my corset!* I decided.

By this point, I'd had considerably more practice in lacing and unlacing myself unassisted. It was nice to have Gabriel help me in the mornings, but knowing that I didn't need him to take the corset off alleviated much of the initial claustrophobia I had experienced with the garment. Enjoying being corseted is not the same as liking to be tied up. I was reassured by the knowledge that I could get into and out of my stays alone.

From my initial experiments in tying my own laces, I had grown rapidly more proficient at it. Now, I could get into the body in under a minute, and out of it in even less time. The quick changes in the curtained-off areas at school seemed far less intimidating at that rate.

This left only the lotion as problematic. In all fairness, greasy substances had been an issue throughout my time in massage school, even before I'd started corseting. My skin leans very slightly toward the dry end of the scale, but it is quite comfortable with its own sebaceous secretions. Harsh cleansers leave me raw; goopy lotions give me acne. Since starting massage school (with the attendant oil bastings at the hands of my fellow students), I had been suffering from monstrous breakouts over portions of my skin that had never before seen a pimple throughout my entire existence. I had gamely borne the oil dousings for months, but now I had finally started to protest. The other students thought I was being ridiculous, and it was a constant battle not to be slicked down like a Prince William Sound sea otter circa 1989, but I kept up the fight.

During a palpation test for kinesiology, my teacher commented on how easy my pectoralis minor (a muscle that lifts the first rib) was to locate. She said that my palpation partner for the exam had an easy time of it; most of the other students in the class had a hard time even feeling their own pec-minors, but I could see mine when I took a breath. The more I wore the corset, the more developed my upper respiratory muscles were becoming. (With the diaphragm compressed, the lungs move up, instead of down, for a deep inhalation.) I was often short of breath when I first started corseting, but as these muscles strengthened, I realized the issue was purely transitory. (The modern slouch-shouldered posture had actually been impinging on my breathing just as thoroughly as any corset by causing my upper respiratory muscles to atrophy and crushing my lungs from above. Now they were finally serving their function.) I was breathing differently than when I'd lived hunched over and slump-shouldered, but I *could* breathe— and that's what mattered.

Peterson's Magazine (August 1897).

Mrs. Elizabeth Northrop was a soprano soloist with John Philip Sousa's band. This was a woman who depended on lung power for her job, and look at her figure!

Modern medical texts have very narrow views laying out the "right" and the "wrong" way to breathe, but their nineteenth-century predecessors were more open on the matter. Dr. Austin Flint's 1893 edition of *A Text-Book of Human Physiology*[17] describes not "right" and "wrong" ways to breathe, but simply different breathing patterns. Three different types of respiration are explained: "the abdominal type" (breathing from the belly), "the inferior costal type" (breathing from the lower chest), and "the superior costal type" (breathing from the upper chest).

Flint describes the abdominal type of breathing as most often seen in babies under three years old. (Incidentally, this is the breathing pattern most modern people have.) He explains that men (of his time) mostly engaged in the inferior costal type of breathing, while the superior costal type of breathing appeared in females "a short time before the age of puberty."[18] He attributes this "to the mode of dress now so general in civilized countries, which confines the lower part of the chest and renders movements of expansion somewhat difficult."

Peterson's Magazine (November 1897).

Another powerful singer shows off her corseted figure: Alice Nielsen, opera prima donna.

He goes on to cite an 1887 study by Thomas J. Mays: "[U]pon eighty-two chests of Indian girls at the Lincoln Institution in Philadelphia, between ten and twenty years of age, who had never worn tight clothing, the abdominal type of respiration was found to predominate . . ." He ultimately concludes, "It is certain that females accommodate themselves more readily than the male to the superior costal type; and this is probably a provision against the physiological enlargement of the uterus in pregnancy, which nearly arrests all respiratory movements except those of the upper parts of the chest . . . it is observed that females are able to carry, without great inconvenience, a large quantity of water in the abdominal

[17] Austin Flint, *A Text-Book of Human Physiology*, 4th ed. (New York: D. Appleton & Company, 1893), 126–27.

[18] Ibid., 126.

cavity; while a much smaller quantity, in the male, produces great distress from difficulty of breathing." In other words, evolution has designed women to be capable of breathing from our upper chest; it's part of our legacy as the child-bearers of the species.

I enjoyed how much more aware I had become of my own body since I had started corseting. While the other students in my class tried to remember the location of the spleen and whether the liver was on the left or the right, I knew exactly where all my organs were. I knew the location of my spleen because I could feel it get tender when I caught a cold, and as for the liver, I had seen it in too many articles of corseted anatomy to be ignorant of its location. Knocking on different parts of my corset, I could hear the difference between the solid liver and the hollow organs; it was in no way mysterious.

It was about this time that I started to alter my clothes to fit my altered form. I had taken to wearing a frilly blouse tucked into my skirt, but as my waist drew in, I became increasingly dissatisfied with the way the shirt bagged at the sides. At first I simply took it in with a few basting stitches, pinning it on inside out and sewing up the excess. The extra fabric added bulk, though, and after a time I grew bold enough to snip it away, replacing the wide basting stitches with neat seams. Before long, nearly all my garments came under the shears in one way or another; I altered them if I could or simply gave them away if they had passed out of suitability. A lot of modern clothes were simply unfeasible to alter: the hips were too low on pants with a fly, and any shirt that pulled over the head couldn't be taken in adequately. (If the waist were suitably altered, its reduced diameter would never fit over the shoulders.) All of my jeans went away, as well as most of my T-shirts, the lion's share of my shorts, and a good deal of my sweaters.

Summer dresses were generally acceptable; they tended to have ties at the back, and I simply drew them as close as the fabric would allow. Even this left waist-bagginess over time, however, so the needle and thread came out again, drawing seams tighter until they fit like a Victorian glove.

The effect when I went out in public was dramatic. Whereas before people did double takes, now they simply stared. I had lived in a big city for a long time; I was used to jostling and shoving—but it suddenly no longer applied to me. It was as though I had my own private little pass-bubble through the elbowing crowds. The corseted figure seemed to strike at something hardwired into the human subconscious, the upright posture with the accentuated hips and bust seemingly shouting, "Alpha female, coming through!" People would suddenly cease glaring at their push-shove neighbors to smile at me and make room for my passage.

Of course, some responses were less classy than others. One day, as I was walking along the sidewalk with Gabriel, a woman moving in the opposite direction simply screamed at me, "You've got the smallest waist in the world!"

Was that a compliment? I wondered. Generally I don't associate compliments with screaming strangers. Was I supposed to respond? How do you respond to that? "No, actually the *Guinness Book of World Records* lists record-holder for the world's smallest waist as Cathie Jung"? It didn't seem quite appropriate, and anyhow, the woman was already shouting at someone else halfway down the street.

Words like "lovely" or "beautiful" have a ready response in cultural dialogue. They are clearly compliments, so it is easy to thank people for them. But I never know quite how to respond to odd statements in ambiguous tones—and there are a lot of odd people handing those out in this world.

From *About Paris* (1895). Illustration by Charles Dana Gibson.

8

Meeting Mom

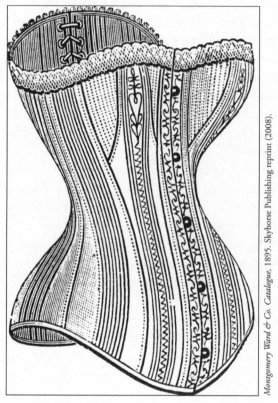

Montgomery Ward & Co. Catalogue, 1895. Skyhorse Publishing reprint (2008).

Corset advertisement from 1895 Montgomery Ward &
Co. 1895. Price : 50 cents.

From the first time I'd worn the corset, I'd dreaded presenting myself to my
mother in it. My mother, who, when I became a teenager, had started declaring
anything below a size extra-large—or, by her preference, double extra-large—to
be "too tight." (I'd had my own job earning my own money from the time I
turned sixteen, but I didn't gain freedom to buy clothes that actually fit until
I went off to university.) High school class of 1966, she is the sort of woman
who had burned her bras. She is also the type of woman whose arms are covered
in tattooed images of her pet parrots.

When I had longingly dreamed of the Victorian era as a child, one of her favorite admonitions with which to scold me had been, "If you'd lived back then, you would have had to wear a corset!" This was generally coupled with, "If you'd lived back then, you'd be dead now!" When I was twelve, we visited the Flavel House Museum[19] on a trip to Astoria and I'd asked her to leave me there.

Mom is rather averse to deviations in her routine, and she'd seen me the weekend before my birthday. I had a few months before she visited again. Whether this helped or hindered my presentation of the corset is debatable. It meant that I had more time to work up my courage, but it also meant that my figure had had time to change dramatically.

"You'll stick up for me, won't you?" I asked Gabriel, nervously finishing the last wipe-down of the apartment after a morning of frenzied cleaning. "If she starts being nasty about the corset?"

"Of course." He kissed my shoulder. "Don't worry!" He gave me a pat. "She'll be fine with it."

I glanced at my bureau. "Maybe I should put on something looser, after all." Something that would hide my figure. I had been debating this for weeks. Not many loose clothes had survived my repeated wardrobe purges, but I had saved some pants for bad-weather cycling, and I had kept a few baggy T-shirts, like one bought on vacation in France, purely for their sentimental value.

Gabriel shook his head. "It'll be fine."

"Easy for you to say." I turned down one corner of my mouth and took a deep breath.

When I opened the door for her later that day, my mother frowned, staring. "Have you been sick? You've lost a whole bunch of weight!" (I can't remember a time in my life when my mother didn't consider the slightest downward alteration in my weight to be a sign of mental and/or physical illness. I also can't remember a time when she wasn't complaining about her own weight.)

Moment of truth. I took a full breath. "No. I'm wearing a corset."

She blinked, her chin jerking backward. "Does that hurt?"

"No." I shook my head emphatically. "Not at all."

At that moment Gabriel's mother arrived. "Hi!" She thrust a package into Gabriel's hands and wrapped me up in a hug. "Wow, you look great! The ferry was packed . . ." She launched into her usual detailed account of the trip to Seattle from her home on Bainbridge Island. This flowed seamlessly (as it always does) into a recounting of all the various details of life that had passed since the

---

[19] An 1885 Queen Anne–style home, which has since been converted to a Victorian museum.

last time she'd seen us. She didn't pause for breath until she had covered every element of minutia.

Bless her.

In the kitchen later, Mom was looking me up and down. "Can you breathe in that thing?"

No, Ma—look, I'm flopping around on the floor, gasping for breath.

I took the teapot down from its place on the top shelf. "Yes, I can breathe just fine." I took a full breath to illustrate my point.

She shook her head. "That thing's got to hurt. How do you pee in that thing?"

I was irritated by her repeated use of the word "thing," as well as by the absurdity of the question. How do I pee? How does she think I pee? I pulled up my skirt and flashed her. "Like this!" That ended the discussion—for that day, at least.

My mother turned the phrase "Have you been sick? You've lost a bunch of weight!" into her standard greeting to me for the next twelve months. No matter how many times she saw me in my corset, each new encounter was met with fresh resistance to belief. (She also refused to refer to it as anything other than "that thing.") Every time, this was followed by the same questions about breathing and reiteration of her belief that it had to be painful to wear. Mercifully, she didn't ask me about elimination again, although she did demand the answer to an even more intimate question right in front of the clerk as we checked out of a grocery store.

Of course, it was a grocery store in my own neighborhood, with a clerk who checked me out all the time. He smiled at me in his usual, friendly way.

"You know," he said, a little embarrassedly, "I've been wanting to ask you . . ."

He looked down sheepishly.

I smiled encouragement, nodding a little.

"You always look so nice when you come in here." He traced subtle curves in the air. "So . . . Victorian. I was wondering . . . Do you wear . . . Do you wear a *corset?*" He nearly whispered the last word, as if it were a secret.

As I was nodding, Mom broke in at top volume. "She says that thing is comfortable, but I can't believe it doesn't hurt!"

The grocery clerk looked embarrassed, but he did manage another question. "Do you wear it all the time?"

"Mmm-hmm." I began my usual explanation. I'd had this question asked often enough by this point to have a rote response worked up. "I wear it pretty much twenty-four-seven; the only time I take it off is for showers—"

"And sleeping!" my mom interjected.

This annoyed me. That I slept in my corset was generally the hardest thing for strangers to believe, and here was my own mother telling the world that it wasn't true.

"Actually," I said pointedly. I had told her this before. "I do sleep in my corset."

The clerk smiled.

"You sleep in it?!" she asked disbelievingly.

I have no idea why my mother acts incredulous over facts I've already told her multiple times on previous occasions.

"Yes."

"What about . . . in moments of intimacy?"

Oh gods. Things you don't want to hear your parents say. Most especially, things you don't want to hear your parents shout in the middle of the grocery store.

"That's none of your business."

I hurried her out of the store. This was *my* neighborhood; Mom lived in a different city on the other end of the county. She didn't have to ever see these people again, but this was the closest grocery to my apartment.

Outside, she started complaining. "You get so offended at everything!" She shook her head, making a *hmph!* noise. "Can't I just talk to you about things? You used to talk to me!"

Not about *that*—and especially not about *that* at broadcast levels in my neighborhood supermarket.

"You just get so offended at everything!" she repeated.

The battle on the home front clearly had a long way to go.

Peterson's Magazine (1890).

An Impending Storm. Illustration in nineteenth-century magazine. Conflict between generations is nothing new.

9

Serving at Table

Montgomery Ward & Co. Catalogue, 1895. Skyhorse Publishing reprint (2008).

"Imperial Pattern Carlsbad China" set: *Montgomery Ward,* 1895.

Tilly, the woman whose luxurious chestnut tresses I'd admired at the Victorian Festival, reissued her invitation for us to wait at table for the senior tea she was organizing. It was the major fund-raiser of the year for a little activity center serving an elderly community, and she wrote to us of how appreciated our help would be if we could find the time to assist in it. She told us how much she had enjoyed meeting us and how eagerly she looked forward to seeing us again. As an added enticement, she told us of the vintage fashion show that was scheduled to accompany the tea.

The senior center was in a different county from the one in which we lived, and the buses serving the area were infrequent. Nevertheless, after some discussion, we decided that this was a worthwhile opportunity to be involved with in the community (even if it wasn't our particular community). Besides, the fashion show sounded like an event that would match our interests perfectly.

"I'm actually really looking forward to it!" I told Gabriel as we waited at the bus stop next to a busy highway. I knew it was difficult to hear over the noisy traffic, but I still lowered my voice conspiratorially for my next comment. "I'm hoping they have some better stuff than the last one we went to."

Gabriel nodded. "Yeah, I hope so."

The last "historic" fashion show we had seen had been a bit heavy on plastic clothes and thrift-store finds for our tastes.

"I just really prefer seeing the real thing—the actual antiques," he said.

"Me too," I agreed. I rocked a bit on my heels. "Remind me again, why did Tilly want us to go to the senior center four days before the tea?" The event where we'd be volunteering was still half a week in the future.

Gabriel shrugged, both palms skyward. "I don't know."

"She said we'd be picking up our tablecloths," I remembered from the email. "What do you suppose that's all about?"

Gabriel shook his head, palms up again, a nonverbal expression of the statement, *I have no idea.*

"Maybe we're putting them on the tables tonight?" he ventured dubiously.

I frowned. "But we're supposed to get there on Saturday two hours before the tea. That seems like enough time to put down a tablecloth . . ." I shrugged. "I guess we'll find out soon enough."

Gabriel nodded. "Well, whatever it is, we'll be doing it there. It's not like she'll expect us to drag a tablecloth home, and then back there!"

An hour-and-change bus ride later, we learned that this was exactly what we were expected to do. In the senior center's back room, I looked down at the expansive yardage of lace draped over one of my arms, while I squinted at the closely printed list in my other hand. "We're bringing two teapots?" I asked, thinking of the cramped bus ride.

"Each!" asserted one of the veteran tea-servers.

That means four, between Gabriel and me. Good g—

"Can anyone take on another table? Some of the volunteers didn't come tonight!"

I froze and stood as silently as I could. I think I may have stopped breathing, so intent was I that I not show any motion that could in any way be construed as volunteering to take on another list of items to bring. My eyes darted over the list of things to which we had already been unwittingly committed. Two teapots, two sugar bowls, two creamers, eight glasses, eight forks, eight spoons, eight knives, one centerpiece . . . All of this times two, since Gabriel and I had each been saddled with a table. *To serve at, fine, but no one said we'd be lugging all this from Seattle. We don't even own four teapots, and as for sixteen glasses . . .*

"We should bring matching plates and serving platters, too!" someone insisted. "It looks so junky if things don't match!"

"That's a great idea!"

No, no, please no!

I looked helplessly at Gabriel, who wore a deer-in-headlights expression to mirror my own. No help from that quarter, I cast my eyes beseechingly at Tilly.

We managed to get the plates and platters voted down, albeit by a slim margin. (It earned us some dark looks from their proponents.) After the volunteers had parted ways, each with a lengthy tablecloth in tow, Tilly turned a sympathetic look upon us. "You guys weren't quite sure what you were in for, were you?"

I did my best to smile at her. She looked so small and frail standing there in a flimsy modern dress. The chestnut curls I had admired at the ball were gone (they had been a wig); her dust-colored hair was thin, and bobbed. I looked down at the tablecloth I was still holding.

"Could we leave this here until Saturday?" I asked. "We came on the bus."

Tilly looked as though I'd suggested we come to the tea naked.

"It needs to be washed," she instructed. "And ironed."

I looked down at the pristine, unwrinkled tablecloth and withheld a frustrated sigh.

Montgomery Ward & Co. Catalogue, 1895. Skyhorse Publishing reprint (2008).

"Table Cover": *Montgomery Ward,* 1895.

We scrabbled to find the massive quantities of listed items over the next few days. I repeatedly apologized to Gabriel for having involved us in what was effectively turning out to be an elaborate scavenger hunt. We'd both been perfectly willing to donate our time, but acquiring all the items we were expected to bring meant quite an investment of cash for things that would be of no use to us after the tea was over. (We'd been slowly getting rid of our own dishes for the past several years, trying desperately to squeeze a little more living space out of our microscopic studio apartment.)

"How are they even expecting to fit all this stuff on a table with eight people at it?" Gabriel asked as he stumbled his way around a pile of glassware. "Where are they going to put the food?"

I held up my hands in a helpless expression of ignorance, mimicking his gesture from days earlier when we'd waited for the bus. "Beats the heck out of me. And how are we supposed to carry centerpieces on the bus?"

Once we'd filled our backpacks to bursting and piled everything we could conceivably carry into miscellaneous bags, we were toting enough bulk to make veteran Sherpas stagger. We decided that the only possible way to add center-pieces to this lot was to tote along empty vases and find somewhere to buy flowers once we'd reached our destination. (Yet another unexpected expense to tax our tiny students' wallets. It might have been cheaper to go to a spa for the day and forget all about the volunteering.)

The morning of the tea, we crammed our way past rows of glaring riders and shoehorned ourselves into seats. With dishes rattling, flatware clacking, and our fellow passengers muttering, we disembarked over an hour later, apologiz-ing our way down the corridor of the grumbling vehicle.

Once I'd relieved myself of my half of the kit, I left Gabriel to set up our tables, centered around the notably empty vases. I set out to commence Operation Find Flowers.

The city was strange to me and I had no idea where to locate a grocery store, let alone one that specifically had a florist section. I wandered through neigh-borhoods, which seemed to consist primarily of senior living communities and churches, all the while the thought strong in the back of my head that when I finally did find the elusive grocery store, the flowers they (theoretically) had for sale had better not cost more than the contents of my wallet, which was not a large sum.

After a great deal of fruitless wandering, I started to grow legitimately con-cerned about returning in time to serve at the tea. If I were to get back punctu-ally, I would be faced with two choices: subject the little old ladies at the tea to yawningly empty vases, or pinch some flowers off the neighborhood landscape. I opted for the latter.

Stealing flowers from a senior community to benefit a senior center was a little too ironic for my taste, and besides, the really good flowers were flush up against their picture windows (hardly discrete). Since it was Sunday, the churches were full of people and theft from their shrubbery would have involved a very high likelihood of being caught, not to mention the deeply perverse moral problem in contemplation of theft from a church. (With my luck, the sermon would have been on the Eighth Commandment: "Thou shalt not steal.") In the end, I pruned some rhododendrons from a bush outside a rather large and garish casino, reasoning that a) it was 10 a.m. on a Sunday, and very few people were likely to be there; b) a casino with poor enough taste to set itself up amidst a plethora of churches deserved to pay some sort of penalty; c) the seniors deserved the flowers more than the gamblers; and d) the shrubbery needed pruning anyway.

Gabriel had almost finished setting up the tables by the time I got back. As I was helping him with the final touches, we reiterated to each other how excited we were to see the upcoming vintage fashion show. All these inconveniences, we thought, would melt from memory, replaced by all the exciting antiques we were to view.

We had both worked in food service positions in the past; carrying trays and refilling teapots represented no vastly challenging activity. We were glad, though, to see that the program specifically stated that service would be paused during the fashion show. This was to avoid distractions from the presentation, but it was an equal boon to us: we would get a chance to watch those lovely antique fashions, unhindered by our serving responsibilities.

The first few outfits were a disappointment. "We put this together from stuff from the Goodwill," the announcer proudly explained to the accompaniment of recorded music amplified over the public address system. I tried not to cringe at the plastic pearls, the rayon and polyester. "This is like something that would have been worn . . ."

I think I managed not to visibly shudder—at least not so obviously the seniors would have seen.

The next outfits were worse. *Polyester on parade*, I thought inwardly, being very careful to keep my facial expression bright and smiling. At one point, Gabriel caught my attention from his position standing behind the next table, and we exchanged a brief, very subtle communication by eyes alone. Neither of us is psychic, and words can't be expressed by such a discreet exchange, but it was enough to share a sentiment. *The horror!*

It wasn't simply the disingenuous nature of the garments. The commentary that accompanied them was rife with stereotypes, myths, and outright fabrications presented as truth. "Broken bones were common!" boomed the announcer about—bizarrely—an elasticized girdle. The clothing only got worse as the presentation continued.

By the time the show was over, our ears were sore from the volume of lies that had been poured into them, both literally and figuratively. The PA system had been cranked up far too loud, apparently on the theory that age equates with deafness and anyone for whom this is not the case should be aided in their lack of disability. We shrugged to each other, sighed, and cleaned our tables.

We told Tilly we'd donate most of what we'd brought to the senior center, so we wouldn't have to drag it back through another bus ride. As we departed, I cast a last glance at the chestnut wig that once again covered her thin, bobbed hair. Truth proves ever elusive.

"Feather Bang" false hair: *Montgomery Ward,* 1895.

Montgomery Ward & Co. Catalogue, 1895. Skyhorse Publishing reprint (2008).

10

Figure Facts

Photograph of unknown women, taken in Edinburgh.

A vast number of misconceptions exist in the world about any number of things. I suppose it should come as no surprise that people are most likely to believe the grossest absurdities about subjects of which they have the least knowledge, but it is sad when they try to indoctrinate others with these falsehoods. When I taught English in Japan, I used to cringe at hearing other gaijin[20] lecture the locals about Japanese culture. It was even worse than when I studied abroad in France and the natives there would deliver sermons about what it meant to be American. At least in France I could be mildly amused at their ignorance; when it was my own countrymen making asses of themselves, it was just embarrassing.

The vast majority of nineteenth-century writings against corsets were written by men. Given that males had mostly given up wearing stays in the eighteenth century, it seems vastly unfair for them to pick on what women chose to do with their bodies. (Pun intended! Remember that "body" is another word for "corset.") Evidently, nineteenth-century women held the same opinion; they were wont to write essays ordering the males of the world to stay out of women's business.

Contrary to modern popular belief, nineteenth-century women's fashion was not some masochistic Machiavellianism, dictated to powerless females by their masculine overlords. Quite the contrary: women chose their fashions because they—the women themselves—liked to wear them, and their collective opinion seems to have been that men should stay out of the matter. If objections were raised to women deviating appreciably from the standards of the time, they generally came just as much—if not more—from other women than from men.

When certain suffragettes started wearing the notorious "Bloomer costume," Susan B. Anthony herself objected, saying that when such clothing was worn, audiences would be paying more attention to the costumes than to the political views of those wearing them.[21] Named for Amelia Bloomer, the Bloomer costume included straight pantaloons worn underneath a short skirt. It was also called the Turkish costume, after the belief of the time that the pantaloons resembled those worn by women in Turkish harems. When pondering this style of dress, it is interesting to consider several contradicting elements of the psychology surrounding it: The style was quite aberrant, and the few women who adopted it tended to be followers of the hygienic movement, suffragettes, or—most often the case—both of these. They argued that the outfit was more hygienic than the fashionable long skirts of the time because it could not drag on the ground and pick up dirt. The secondary argument promoting the style—and the one far more publicized by modern feminists—was that

---

[20] Japanese term for a foreigner.
[21] Sally G. McMillen *Seneca Falls and the Origins of the Women's Rights Movement* (New York: Oxford University Press, 2008), 131.

wearing trouser-like garments, as men did, gave women greater freedom. The irony of this argument lay in the fact that mainstream women of the time considered the Turkish costume a mimicry of outfits worn by Eastern harem girls, whom they saw as little more than slaves. (The actual condition of women's rights in the Middle East, or their actual traditional dress, is not important to this case; what was important was how these were imagined by the women of the West). Curiously then, this style was espoused by its proponents as promoting freedom, while being denounced by its critics as copying a style of oppression.

Another interesting element to consider about the Bloomer costume is the short skirt that overlaid the pantaloons. In the nineteenth century, only very young girls wore short skirts, just as only very young boys wore short pants. In both sexes, their lower garments grew longer as they matured. For a grown woman, then, to wear a short skirt was for her to appear in the costume of a child. (It would have been equally shocking for a mature man to appear at a formal occasion wearing short pants.) It should come as little surprise, then, that the more mainstream members of society found it difficult to treat adopters of this costume seriously. It effectively seemed to be a child's clothing, juxtaposed against the clothing of the opposite gender. Imagine the hilarity that would ensue if a modern, twenty-first-century man were to appear at a political meeting wearing corduroy overalls along with the skirt from a belly dancer's costume! Furthermore, imagine the reaction if he were then to become upset that he were not being taken seriously!

Other suffragettes were even more outspoken against the costume than Ms. Anthony. Jane Swisshelm "found such attire 'immodest, inconvenient, uncomfortable, and suicidal' and felt that wearing it would ruin her reputation."[22] In addition, Paulina Davis "refused to wear bloomers in public, for 'if I put on this dress, it would cripple my movements in relation to our work at this time and crucify me ere my hour had come.'"[23] It is interesting to note that these celebrated suffragettes were referring to bloomers— uncorseted fashion—in terms of something that was "suicidal" and would "cripple" them, while they, the most emancipated women of their time, preferred to wear figures.

Women were choosing their fashions, and they were choosing their corsets. When allegedly scientific arguments were presented against stays, they often centered around perceptions that corsets detracted from women's "proper"

---

[22] Ibid.
[23] Ibid.

maternal duties. Often, their logic was so stretched as to be amusing: In France women wore tight corsets. France had a low birthrate. Therefore, wearing tight corsets resulted in a low birthrate. Of course, the false logic of this rather fuzzy argument totally overlooks the fact that France was famous for its pervasive availability of birth-control devices. It was so closely associated with birth control, in fact, that terms like "French cups" or "French sleeves" were well-understood euphemisms for contraceptives. A similar (and similarly odd) argument maligning corsets as harmful to fertility held that because stays were worn tighter in the 1880s and '90s than in preceding decades, and tended to be worn tighter by upper-class women than by lower-class ones, figures were responsible for the decreased birthrates among the upper classes within those years. Left out of this version of the argument is the fact that birth control had recently become widely publicized following an 1877 trial of two individuals for disseminating information about it,[24] and that contraception was much more readily available to the upper classes.

People sometimes ask me about what women accustomed to wearing corsets did during pregnancy. I have never been pregnant myself, so this is always a somewhat awkward question to answer. Truly, the only woman who could give a fully authoritative response would be one with direct personal experience—and that's not me. I generally refer people to the past existence of maternity corsets, which had extra lacings in various places that could be let out as the fetus grew while maintaining the back support that becomes even more important as a woman's figure takes on the dramatic increase in weight that accompanies a pregnancy. (A particularly common complaint I've heard from pregnant women is how much their lower backs

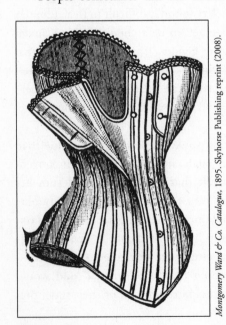

Montgomery Ward & Co. Catalogue, 1895. Skyhorse Publishing reprint (2008).

Nursing corset.

---

24 This was the trial of Charles Bradlaugh and Annie Besant, who were brought to court on charges of obscenity for publishing a pamphlet on birth control.
Sally Mitchell, ed. *Victorian Britain: An Encyclopedia* (New York and London: Garland Publishing 1988), 618.

ache. One of the pregnancy massage techniques we learned in massage school was the incredibly simple move of standing behind a pregnant woman, cradling her belly, then lifting up slightly so that the massage practitioner is holding the weight for a moment and the client's back gets a brief respite. Whenever I've done this for a client, she has loved it. One of them asked me half-jokingly, "Could you please just follow me around this way until I have my baby? Maybe then I could get some sleep!") The Victorians did have a tradition for pregnancy called a confinement, when a pregnant woman would stay at home and lounge about in whatever state of undress suited her, and the length of confinement varied widely depending on a woman's individual health and economic status. I shall leave that book to be written by someone with personal experience.

Women's bodies and what we do with them create controversy. It is curious that otherwise rational people—individuals who would never give credence to tales of Pop Rocks killing child actors or of haunted truck stops—are eager

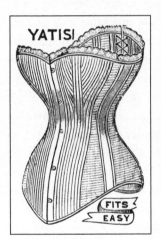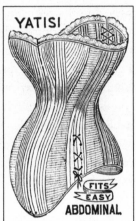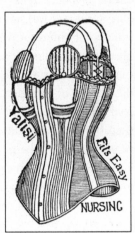

The 1895 *Montgomery Ward & Co. Catalogue* offered its Yatisi corset in various styles. Shown are the fashionable model; the Abdominal Yatisi corset, "introduced specially for married ladies" (note the extra laces at the sides to allow the abdomen to expand during pregnancy); and the Yatisi Nursing corset (note the pivoting bust pads).

to believe the most fantastic legends about corsetry. An obnoxiously pervasive example of this is the myth of rib removal. My high school German teacher had told my class this one, with all the heavy-handed persuasive powers of an authoritative German who is utterly convinced of the idea she is espousing. "Doctors used to take out the two little ribs at the bottom of a woman's chest," she said, tracing the bones on her own torso. "That's how they got their waists so little. You can't make a waist that small without taking out ribs. All you have to do is look at pictures to know that!" (In retrospect, I can think of absolutely no reason why she should have been discussing corsets at all in what was purportedly a grammar class. Frau Schmidt dearly enjoyed tangents.) As an earnest young scholar with a deep respect for my teachers, I had believed this as I had believed all instruction, from the information that d = 2r, to the fact that Pluto is the ninth planet. When I went back as an adult to reexamine it, however, it made even less sense than my old literature teacher's opinion that there is artistic merit in Melville's *Billy Budd*.

Early surgery was strictly of the slash-and-burn variety. Used as a last resort in situations where the only alternative was immediate death of the patient, it chiefly consisted of the sawing-off of already mangled limbs, followed by cauterization by hot iron, boiling oil, or other such crude methods. Over the course of centuries, surgeons had been slowly pulling their profession out of its medieval origins and tactics, but the ability to anesthetize a patient during surgery was not achieved until 1846, with the first ether experiments (the use of chloroform in surgery was adopted the next year). Even after this breakthrough allowed surgical patients to be rendered unconscious, any cutting of the body remained an incredibly risky procedure for decades, due to the danger of infection. Wounds were treated with various substances from cold boiled water to bread poultices, and staphylococcus bacteria and streptococcal infections could cause death from minor cuts, let alone major thoracic surgery. It would be nearly twenty years before Joseph Lister (working from knowledge of Pasteur's germ theories) popularized the idea of sterilization of medical environments. It would take longer still for his efforts to take root in the conservative medical community: acidic sterilization of tools and durable materials was finally in widespread use by 1880; bandages, medical gowns, and soft goods that could not withstand acid would not be disinfected (by steam) until the 1890s.

The last two decades of the nineteenth century brought changes in medicine which were, for their times, giant leaps forward. Skin grafts and appendectomies were pioneered, and for the first time in history a woman stood some chance of surviving a cesarean section. However, surgery remained fraught with risk and potential complications. (Blood transfusions, necessary to replace vital fluids lost during surgery, were not successful until after the discovery of blood-type groupings in the twentieth century.)[25] Serious work in plastic surgery was not considered until the time of the First World War,

---

[25] Mitchell, *Victorian Britain*, 774–76.

when it was developed as a way to reconstruct the shattered features of severely wounded veterans.

Consider, therefore, the surgical situation in the Victorian era: there will not be any replacement for blood lost during the procedure; sterilization, if it is used at all, is a new concept, and the entire operation will likely be done by a combination of gaslight and what sunlight can be let into the operating room through windows and mirrors. Under the circumstances, one would be forgiven for balking at the idea of any surgical intervention, even for a need as pressing as a ruptured appendix. The idea of considering it for an elective procedure would have been madness.

Moreover, there is absolutely no evidence to support the idea that cosmetic rib removal has ever been performed, past or present, madness or no. In her book, *The Corset: A Cultural History*, Valerie Steele describes how, in her many years of very active research (she is the chief curator and acting director at the Fashion Institute of Technology), she has never found any credible documentation of such surgery ever taking place.[26] She even interviewed modern physicians on the subject of whether such an operation could be performed with modern surgical technology. While the medical professionals grudgingly admitted that, in theory, such an operation might be possible, they were very explicit in pointing out that because of the proximity of the floating ribs to the lungs, such an operation would be extremely dangerous, even with the most modern of techniques.[27] Any surgeon who would attempt such a risky procedure for cosmetic reasons would not only put his patient's life in danger, but also jeopardize his medical license and professional reputation.

Critics of corsetry seem to be obsessed with bones, likely because of the linguistic confusion surrounding the matter of millinery ribs and bones versus the osseous variety. After reading about the so-called "corseted skeletons" in museums—deformed skeletons alleging to be examples of damage caused by corsetry—I brought up the subject with an old college buddy of mine who was visiting from Montana.

Tom and I had met when he'd been the president of the University of Washington's archery club and I'd been a club member; back in the days when I'd been double-majoring in international studies and French, and he'd been multiple-majoring in (as it seemed to me) every branch of science known to man. His current laundry list of credentials includes university degrees in biochemistry, cell and molecular biology, conservation biology, geology,

---

[26] Steele, *The Corset*, 73.
[27] Ibid., 74.

and paleobiology. He's now a research scientist at a laboratory in Bozeman, Montana. Specifically, he is a taphonomist, which means that bones (and the ways in which they can be changed) are his specific area of study.

"And everything I've read about it," I told him eagerly, "says that the reason the nineteenth-century skeletons look different isn't that the corsets changed them; it's that the skeletons were boiled, then hung when they were mounted. So the warping was actually done by the preservation process!"

He looked as though I'd just eagerly informed him that mammals breathe air. "Well, yeah!" He tilted his head, and shrugged. "I always ask what people are going to do with specimens when they ask me to clean them. It totally makes a complete difference in how you prepare them."

Tom has cleaned, prepared, and studied more bones of more species of animals than most people would care to even encounter. One of his favorite methods of removing flesh from specimen bones is that of using dermestid beetles to eat away the unwanted tissue (a technique popularized around the mid-twentieth century), but he uses a great variety of cleaning techniques depending upon the specimen and the situation. The nineteenth-century technique of boiling specimens is one that is still very much in use by modern scientists, and Tom's extensive experience with it is ongoing. His roommates have learned not to ask what he is cooking when they come home to find a large pot of something bubbling away on the stove.

"When you boil a skeleton," he would explain to me in a later discussion of the same topic. "All the soft tissue goes away, including the cartilage that holds the rib cage together. So the ribs fall off the vertebrae and the sternum. What this means is that when people rearticulate the skeletons, the people putting the bones back together make any deformities you see in the skeleton."

It's useful to have a research scientist as a friend. When I became thoroughly weary of hearing the tired old yarn about corsets breaking bones, I wrote to Tom and asked if it was even physically possible for a corset to break human ribs. He responded by sending me a sizable heap of papers documenting various studies that have been performed to determine the strength of human rib bones. The overarching theme of all the research conclusions was that ribs are remarkably strong: they can generally be fractured only by extreme trauma, such as in an automobile collision. To give one example of the groupings of data: a master's thesis[28] lists the strains necessary to break ribs taken from

---

[28] Joseph Michael Cormier, "Microstructural and Mechanical Properties of Human Ribs" (master's thesis, Virginia Polytechnic Institute and State University, 2003).

human cadavers. In experiments, it required between 39 and 187 newtons of force to break the ribs taken from a sixty-one-year-old woman (different ribs broke at different levels of force—some ribs are stronger than others within a given individual), and between 85 and 265 newtons of force to break ribs from a sixty-seven-year-old woman. In layman's terms, this is roughly equivalent to a force between having a nine-pound bowling ball dropped on these women's ribs and having a small anvil dropped on them! (And remember, these women were in their sixties. Younger, premenopausal women have even stronger ribs.) It would be very hard for a corset to exert the same sort of pressure as a falling anvil!

Corsets can't take that sort of pressure, and they certainly can't apply it— they're just not that strong. The corset would break long before the bones would. Corsets are made of cotton coutil, a fabric about on par with jean denim, and the thread used to stitch them is weaker than the body of the fabric. If any readers remain insistent upon the old myth that corsets break human bones, I would invite them to recall the last time they tore a pair of jeans. I highly doubt they were exerting the force of a falling anvil upon them.

Of course, as Tom pointed out, "All this data goes out the window for people with osteoporosis. They can sneeze and break a rib."

But the anecdotal stories of corset-induced broken ribs never seem to be about osteoporotic old ladies. (The cadavers in the study weren't exactly in their prime, either. They had died in their sixties, long after menopause, which significantly decreases bone density.) The tales are always of the friend-of-a-friend variety, something someone heard from their friend, who heard it from a cousin, who heard of a proud young lady in the next town who had, from sheer vanity, overtightened her corset and broken a rib and died in consequence. Evidence to prove these stories true never seems to accompany them. Admitting that someone, somewhere, at some point in a long history might actually have been feeble enough—and stupid enough—to break a rib through corsetry is a bit like conceding that, in theory, an alligator could live for a short time in a New York sewer: hardly a reason to believe that it is a commonplace occurrence.

The body's rib bones are extremely strong, and the concept of a piece of cotton breaking healthy examples of them is absurd. Equally without merit is the idea that any respectable doctor—past or present—would remove them for cosmetic reasons, and there is absolutely no evidence that it has ever been done. This is not to say that modern medicine does not have some strangely eager tendencies to perform surgery on other portions of the anatomy, however.

I would very soon find myself wishing that more of my bones showed the same strength and fortitude of my corseted ribs.

Chrisman Collection (circa 1910).

Gabriel's great-great-grandmother, Mrs. Abbot Usher.

11

Broken Bones

From Blunders of a Bashful Man (1881). Illustration from a Victorian comic novel, originally published anonymously in 1881 by J.S. Ogilvie Publishing Company.

By the end of May, I was starting to get the hang of my high heels, and I was wearing my corset nearly twenty-four-seven. I slept in my corset, biked in it, ate in it, did nearly all of my daily activities in it (the only two exceptions being showers and judo). In early May, the scope of those daily activities suddenly suffered a dramatic collapse when I broke my foot in two places.

I had been part of a certain Seattle judo club for about two and a half years at this point. I do not have a naturally athletic nature and, like most people of a sane disposition, I do possess the standard mammalian aversion to pain. I had joined the club out of a desire to learn how, if I ever should be accosted by a greasy thug in a dark alley, to at least attempt to inflict a few bruises upon him, rather than having to rely strictly on the scream-and-whimper method of defense.

By this point in the narrative, judo practice was the only public activity for which I left my corset at home. In wrestling, the more flexible a person can be, the more optimally they can fight, and the corset would have added a stiffness that I simply couldn't have dealt with—plus, I was poor enough at the sport to begin with. (Sports had never been my strong point, and when I started doing judo I was an absolute coordination catastrophe. It had taken me several months to learn to do a somersault, the most basic fall and something most people go into the club knowing, or at least pick up on the first night. A lot of sweat on my part and a tremendous amount of patience from the guys in the club had gradually improved my reflexes, but my progress was slow in the extreme.) Thus, the one time when I did remove my silk-and-steel armor, my protective shell, was the one time when I knew for certain I was going to be physically attacked. (All in good sport, of course.)

In the two and a half years I had been doing judo, I could not remember a time when I hadn't had extensive bruises in colors bold enough to rival a Gauguin painting. I had broken the little toe on my left foot twice and sprained an ankle after missing the crash pad and smashing my foot against the dojo wall during throw practice. By this point, I was extremely tired of being bruised and broken. Still, I enjoyed the camaraderie of the group, and it takes a lot for me to quit something.

On May 31, 2009, at approximately 7:20 p.m., I was sparring with the largest man in the club. A Seattle police detective by profession, he stood a full head taller than myself and outweighed me by an unguessable mass of sheer muscle. I side-swept him, hooking my right leg around his to sweep it out from under him while knocking him off balance. He counter-swept my posted leg, and we went down together.

An ideal situation would have been a clean takedown with one of us still standing. By secondary preference, I should have rolled fast enough to land my right foot flat before my sparring partner hit the mat. What actually happened, though, was so far from ideal that it wouldn't even recognize the word.

It was too fast for conscious thought or decision, just a flash reflex that knew I was falling incorrectly and I had to protect my knee. So I twisted my leg and my foot with it in midair. The result was that my foot had just come perfectly vertical above my toes on the mat, like a ballerina en pointe, when Bill—all six-foot-three, two-hundred-odd pounds of him—came crashing down on top of my heel, effectively folding my foot over on itself.

I wasn't even aware at the time that I'd screamed, but afterward one of the club members described the noise I made as "the most awful sound."

Several thoughts had entered my head during this moment, so quickly each successive idea overlay and jumbled into the others, like broken glass thrown at high velocity against concrete. The first was brutal animal pain, primitive beyond vocabulary; then came the knowledge of a single word: broken. Against this smashed the first coherent thought, "I can't have broken my foot! I won't be able to wear my high heels!"

Instantly, I was surrounded by every club member who was there that night. "What'd you hurt? Tell us!"

I rocked slightly toward the wall, stuffing my fist in my mouth and biting down hard, trying to overwhelm a pain I couldn't control with one that I could.

"What'd you hurt?"

I couldn't answer, couldn't think words, but all around me the question was insistent.

"What'd you hurt?"

"Foot! Foot!" The word came out explosively. My grammar was gone.

Gently and competently, they stretched out both my legs straight. "Which foot?"

The pain had driven out words like "left" and "right." I pointed.

Strong hands laid my trembling foot flat against the mat. "Can you wiggle your toes?"

I tried, gasped in pain.

"Are there shooting pains going up into your knee?"

I shook my head. The pain was all in my foot.

"Can you feel this?" Someone had grabbed a Phillips screwdriver from the tool can and was carefully poking my foot.

I gasped, nodded.

"Can you feel this?" Another spot was prodded. I winced, glaring. "That's good! If it's numb, that's bad."

"Well," came the analysis, "it looks like you've broken it. You'll need to get it X-rayed, though."

I was carried to the side of the dojo, and Lana brought me her cell phone to call Gabriel. I lay on the mat, waiting for him to come get me, and muttered Rudyard Kipling's "If" under my breath, trying to force some of the pain out of my brain by willing my mind to remember familiar lines. Whereas at first the pain had driven out all words, now I was trying to use words to drive out the pain. "If you can keep your head . . ."

The guys took turns wandering over to check on me, and one of them would periodically poke my foot with the screwdriver to make sure it wasn't going numb. I tried to hide my increasing annoyance. "I feel it!"

"Good!" came the upbeat reply. "When you don't feel it, let us know."

When Gabriel arrived, he and Lana carried me outside and helped me into the DeLorean while Greg maneuvered the dojo doors and one of the other guys brought along my shoes and gym bag.

"Let us know how you're doing!" Lana instructed as she closed the car door for me. The guys gave me encouraging thumbs-up gestures as we left.

While Gabriel and I sat interminably in that modern version of purgatory, the hospital waiting room, I remember thinking that I never wanted to go through as much pain as I was experiencing ever again. I tried not to even consider what women in childbirth must suffer, but made a mental note to call my mother.

Several hours later, I was wheeled off for X-rays, then wheeled back to the room where Gabriel waited for me. At around 11 p.m., Gabriel commented that, if he'd known it would take this long, he would have brought my corset. I glared at him. I was still mad that he'd taken the time to grab his iPod on his way out of the apartment, as I'd lain in the dojo with a broken foot. Still, I had to privately admit to myself that I'd had the same thought about the corset.

When a doctor did finally come into the room, the first thing she wanted to do was give me drugs. "No," I told her. "Thank you."

She stared at me incredulous, her pen poised over her prescription pad. "I'll just write it out—"

I shook my head, adamant.

"No, thank you," I repeated.

I was in pain, but I didn't want drugs. I just wanted to get fixed and go home. I could handle pain. I didn't like it, but I could handle it.

In the nineteenth century, a large occupation of many individuals who called themselves doctors had been the selling of various "remedies." These were of widely differing efficacy and often stupor-inducing. Sensible people used them with caution, and the most adamant followers of temperance principles avoided them altogether. The specific drugs had changed somewhat since that time. The relationship of pusher to patient, it seemed, had not.

The rest of that very long night would be comprised of a series of interminable waits, separated from each other only by flitting appearances of individuals offering me drugs, arguing when I told them I didn't want any, then disappearing, never to be seen again. Mostly, we were left alone to share our own increasingly disagreeable company.

Eventually, an intern came in. My foot was broken in two places, he explained, showing me the splinter of the third metatarsal on the X-rays. I had to squint to see the tiny chip off the cuboid bone—and might not have seen it at all were it not for my diligent studies in anatomy classes, which allowed me to follow what he was saying.

He asked me what drugs I was taking. I told him I wasn't on any. He stared at me in disbelief, then quickly said he would get me a prescription. I insisted that I didn't need one and finally managed to convince him. I didn't want to go through an extended, awful experience knowing the whole time that it would only get worse in a few hours when the pharmaceuticals wore off. I much preferred to simply get the worst of things done as soon as possible.

The intern said he was going to set the broken bones. I held Gabriel's hand, and squeezed hard.

"If you can force your heart and nerve and sinew / To serve your turn long after they are gone, / And so hold on when there is nothing in you / Except the Will which says to them: 'Hold on!'"

More lines from "If."

Painful experiences always slow down time, but at length it was over. I took a deep breath and swallowed, proud of myself for not giving in to the drug-pushers. My mind was clear, and there would be no dread of waiting for false comfort to wear off. I could know the worst pain was over.

Next, they immobilized my foot in a huge cast of splinted plaster. It went all the way up my calf and ended partway up my knee, which even then struck me as a bit excessive for two little broken bones buried deep within my foot. The cast came up so high, I couldn't bend my knee properly. I was given crutches and told to wait some more.

Eventually, a doctor came along. "You're the fracture?"

"Mmm-hmm." I nodded.

He shook my hand and Gabriel's hand, apologized for the wait, and asked what drugs I was taking home with me.

"None." It was well past one in the morning, my foot hurt, I was literally tired in body, and figuratively tired of all these attempts to push drugs on me. "I don't want any."

Again my insistence was met with disbelief, and, like the others, he tried to convince me. I held true and won out. Finally, at 1:30 a.m., six hours after Gabriel had brought me to the emergency room, we were given leave to go. Before quitting the hospital on that very long night of waiting, I was told that my break was an unusual one that would have to be seen by a specialist, and they made an appointment for me for Thursday (four days in the future) at the hospital's joint clinic.

Had it not been for Gabriel's encouragement, that night would have been my first uncorseted sleep in months. As I staggered into our cramped little apartment, moving very unsteadily on my crutches, my only thought was for bed. The corset had been the last thing on my mind.

"I'll help you on with your corset," Gabriel told me, his voice tired, just as I was collapsing onto our futon.

I looked up at him, sideways. I made a disgruntled sort of moaning sound, but then managed to get out one word: "bed."

He yawned. "It'll only take a minute."

"Rrrarhaoh," I grumbled incoherently. I was too tired to argue, either with him about wearing the corset or with myself about not wearing it. I might have just slid into an unconscious stalemate if my cat Pretty Kitty had not chosen that moment to pounce at my cast. That roused me.

With my foot broken, the sight of Gabriel lacing me in was an absurd spectacle, even to myself in the mirror. (It would be repeated many times over the ensuing weeks, so I was given ample opportunity to observe how ridiculous the procedure was.) I couldn't put weight on the broken foot (the larger of the two breaks was directly in the arch of my foot), but I couldn't post all my weight on my unbroken foot, either. Standing on one foot alone puts a slight twist in the spine, which the corset cinches in place, enforcing a temporary scoliosis that lasts until the corset is removed and the spine is flexed again. The condition is completely reversible, but quite uncomfortable, and I was in enough pain already. Corsets are supposed to be laced on with the wearer's spine erect: my newest challenge was to work out a way I could keep my back straight without the ability to place both feet flat on the floor.

Sitting was no good for lacing in; even if we'd had a suitable chair for it (which we didn't—we would have needed a stool, and all our chairs had backs), human anatomy shifts when we sit, and it would have been difficult to get everything just right. Lying down was out of the question, simply because lying on my side would have presented the same aforementioned crooked-spine problem, and lying on my back or stomach would have meant lying on the laces or busk.

Ultimately, the solution Gabriel and I worked out was for me to stand between two chairs, holding their backs. I would support myself as much as possible on the chair backs (trying not to tip them over) and attempt to keep my back straight while Gabriel tied the corset. I'll admit that I have been in more absurd positions in my life, but I can't recall any that were so often repeated.

With the huge cast encasing my right leg up to the knee and the corset preventing me from bending at the spine, I felt thoroughly trussed. I was supposed to keep the broken foot elevated (any time I didn't, the blood pooling in the immobile extremity would cause excruciating pain), so most of my time during convalescence was spent lying flat on my back with the foot propped up on as many pillows as I could muster. Once I was in this position, the only way out of it was by semi-rolling, semi-flopping to the edge of my futon (we didn't have a proper bed), then cautiously posting out my crutches and levering myself to a standing position. (I couldn't shift leverage with my torso, since the corset kept me from bending at the waist.) Once I was standing, I could hop about a bit on my crutches until the blood pooling in my foot became too painful, then the only way down again was a sort of semi-controlled fall onto the futon, followed by side-to-side rocking and flopping to get my foot back on top of the pillows.

Time and time again, I considered taking the corset off. At least then part of me would have been flexible, and I wouldn't have the edges of the stays chafing and pinching the sides of my breasts against the crutches when I tried to move about. I didn't really want to take it off, though. I'd worked hard over the preceding months to winnow down my waist—it seemed a shame to waste it. If I couldn't continue practicing how to walk in kitten heels, at least I could try to keep from backsliding with the waist training.

On Thursday, my appointment with the specialist was scheduled for a time when Gabriel would be in class, so I was completely on my own in finding a way to the clinic. It was half a mile from my apartment—not at all a challenge when I was healthy, but now a rather intimidating stretch, most of all because of the intense pain caused by the pooling of blood in my foot any time it was below my heart for more than two minutes. I took a deep breath, gritted my teeth, and set off.

Maneuvering on crutches while wearing a corset was a different experience than what I remembered of crutch-walking with past injuries. Since my torso was rigid, I couldn't swing for leverage as effectively; to make up for this, I put more stress on my arms and shoulders. Then there was the pinching problem. The underbust corset I was wearing came quite close to my armpits on the sides of my body. Because it was an off-the-rack corset (not custom-fitted to my body), and because I was still relatively new to the whole corseting experience, there was a bit of bulge at the top where the fat and muscle tissue lateral to my breasts squeezed out. The crutches the hospital had provided were several inches too short for me, and their pads came right up to this bulge. As I tottered about, that sensitive tissue on my sides was pinched over and over again, every time I put my weight down. I took my weight on the heels of my hands as much as I could, but my wrists were not accustomed to bearing so much weight, and they added their cries of complaint to all the other pains I was experiencing.

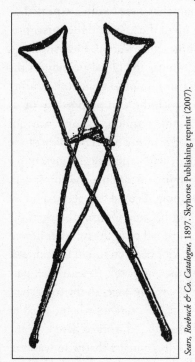

Sears, Roebuck & Co. Catalogue, 1897. Skyhorse Publishing reprint (2007).

I made it a few blocks, foot throbbing, wrists screaming, and tender flesh being chafed raw, then swung into a newsstand café for a brief moment of seated respite. I snatched a few minutes of no pressure under my arms and no weight on my wrists, then set off again. My left leg screamed at all the extra work it was doing; the hamstrings in my right thigh quivered and trembled, exhausted from holding up the monstrous weight of the oversize cast. I got a few more blocks, sat on the doorstep of a closed business, got up, and traveled a few blocks farther. In this way, slowly, ploddingly, I eventually made it to the clinic.

In the 1897 *Sears, Roebuck & Co. Catalogue*, crutches ranged from 75 cents a pair to $8 a pair, depending on what type of wood they were made from.

The line was long and tedious, and my one bright spark of amusement in the whole experience came from examining the back brace of the man in line in front of me: I wondered what he'd think if he knew how closely it resembled a corset.

At great length, I was shown to a treatment room and the archaic cast was removed by an assistant. It would have been nice to wiggle my toes at this point, after they'd been forcibly immobilized for so long. Unfortunately, my foot was still broken. It was, in fact, covered in contusions of a color that would put any reasonable person off their lunch. Mobility was not really an option yet. Instead, I just looked at it, and waited.

Eventually I heard the doctor in the room next door to where I had been placed. "Well," he was telling the unseen patient in that room, "this isn't really my specialty. I'm a shoulder specialist. You're going to have to go to—" he named another hospital in a different section of the city, "—and see their specialist there." Worry was clearly audible in the patient's voice as she tried to ask a question, but the faceless doctor cut her off.

Less than two minutes after he'd introduced himself to the patient in the other room, the "specialist" had cast her aside and was now in my room. He introduced himself and glanced at a clipboard. "This isn't really my specialty . . ." The set speech was repeated and he was out the door even while my lips were still forming a protestation. I did manage to ask his swiftly retreating back how I'd get an appointment at the other hospital, as he was telling me to do; he said offhandedly that the receptionist would do it for me, then he was gone, leaving the door open behind himself.

I looked at the brownish-yellow mottling of pools of dead blood underneath the skin of my unsupported, broken foot—now naked of its cast—then to the empty door, then back at my foot again. *How am I going to get home like this?* If I were to bump it on anything, it would break even worse.

I didn't even want to contemplate what it would do to my recovery if I stumbled and inadvertently put any weight on the naked fractures. Even the danger of someone or something bumping into it represented a legitimate hazard (not to mention the pain involved). I couldn't think of a way to get home safely, let alone to a different quadrant of the city and to the other hospital.

At first, I couldn't really believe they were sending me home that way. In his blitzkrieg-style encounter, the doctor had given every indication of washing his hands of my case, but I couldn't quite believe it. I waited, staring at the open door, expecting someone to come and do something with my foot before sending me away.

An hour and a half later, I finally decided I had been entirely forgotten. With great trepidation, and taking enormous care not to jostle my broken foot, I got off the examination table and hobbled out into the waiting room on my crutches.

I spent the next several hours being assiduously ignored in the waiting room, then, in precisely the same condition, still without a cast, I found myself pushed out the door and into a cab. I desperately tried to hold my broken foot above the jerking floor as the taxi whipped over pockmarked streets. At my apartment building, I negotiated the heavy iron security door at the front, crutched my way through the lobby, pulled myself up the banisterless three steps to the elevator. The slow old elevator got me to the sixth floor; I crutched my way to my apartment, got inside, and collapsed on the futon.

I lay there for a while, exhausted. I stared at the telephone, waiting for the promised call. I looked at my little antique watch. Its clockwork ticked like a small, impatient heart for a long, long time. The telephone remained silent.

After a while I pulled myself over to the phone and tried to call them myself. With every motion, I was terrified I would jostle and reinjure my foot, or even worse, that my cat would put her weight against it in misplaced sympathy or affection. When I'd made my way across the tiny room, I dialed the number I'd procured on a scrap of paper from the clinic.

Ring, ring . . . ring, ring.

I got the automated answering service and left a message. I repeated this process several times between lengthy waits for responses that never came. I spent five hours calling, leaving messages, and waiting. Victorian doctors made house calls. Twenty-first-century technology, it seemed, was preventing even office visits.

I was at my wits' end and feeling incredibly vulnerable. When my cat approached again I scooped her up and cried into her fur. After a while, the phone rang and I answered it quickly, but it wasn't the hospital: it was Gabriel, calling from his job in the university library.

"How did it go?" he asked, his voice confident.

"It was awful!" I sobbed out the details.

He came quickly home, and my tears abated as he wrapped me in his arms. I nestled into the curve of his shoulder, which had always fit my cheek so perfectly, and my breathing started to steady. When I finally regained control of myself, I tried the hospital's number again. This time, I got an actual person.

I assumed that the clinic had called the hospital, as they'd promised they would, but my name clearly meant nothing to the bored man on the other end of the line. "I'm calling to make an appointment," I explained, looking down helplessly at my throbbing foot. "I have to see a foot specialist."

The sound of flipping pages came through the phone. "Well," the bored voice said slowly, "I could get you an appointment with one of our regular doctors next Tuesday. How's that sound?"

Next week?! My broken foot lay bare and vulnerable before me.

"No!" My cat came over, and I cringed as she sniffed at my foot in curiosity. Gabriel shooed her away. "I have to come in today!"

What would happen if I slept with my foot out like this?

"I have to see a specialist—"

"Who decided that?" the voice at the other end asked scornfully. "You?"

I started crying again, though I didn't want to. Gabriel took the phone from me, and it was one of the very few times I have heard actual anger in my husband's voice.

"Look," he started, and my champion commenced an argument from which he clearly had no intention of backing down. Yet he was not satisfied when he finally hung up.

"There's no one there!" He threw up his hands. "Not until Monday!" He shook his head at the incompetence displayed. "Even the guy answering the phone said you shouldn't have been sent home without a cast! He said you should go into the emergency room!" He glared at the phone in angry frustration.

I thought of the long, long night at the emergency room: the waiting, the sensation of being a human being in pain but treated like a piece of annoying garbage, alternately pushed around and ignored. Not again. Then of course, there was the cost involved. *No . . .* But . . . what choice did I have? I couldn't go all weekend with my broken foot unsupported.

Gabriel looked in angry frustration at the phone, and then at my badly contused foot. He sighed, and shook his head.

"It's too bad—" I began, and stopped myself.

The thought had repeated itself many times in the days since I'd broken my foot, and it kept coming back to me. It's too bad the guys in the club who are firefighters and EMTs weren't there that night. The club's coach was a Seattle firefighter, so the group contained a higher-than-average number of members with emergency training. When I'd missed the crash pad in practice half a year before and sprained my ankle by thwacking it against a concrete wall, they'd immediately palpated, tested range of movement, assessed my condition, and wrapped up the injury, all while I was still catching my breath. Then they'd looked after me through the rest of practice (telling me repeatedly that they'd drive me home whenever I told them I was ready), brought me water and ibuprofen, let me choose which one of them I wanted to drive me home, and sent me off with well-wishes. The guy who drove me home actually carried me into my apartment building, like a scene out of a movie.

Remembering all this, I looked at Gabriel. "Why don't I email the guys in the club? See if they can help me?"

Gabriel snapped his fingers. "Now, that's a good idea!"

I squished into the corner of the futon that was our wireless hot spot—our apartment did not have its own Internet connection, but we lived close enough to the university for one small corner to catch an infrequent signal from the school's massive server—and composed an email outlining the situation.

Within half an hour Gabriel and I had gotten to the dojo; my coach, Aaron, had me splinted up in a removable orthopedic boot; and I was more comfortable than I had been in a week of dealing with hospitals. Aaron explained that he could do a more traditional splint, but that it was supposed to be a warm weekend and the boot would be nicer because I could take it off if I got too hot.

"Do me a favor," he said, once he'd guided my foot into the boot and secured it for me. "Try to stand on that."

My mind was alarmed, but I trusted Aaron implicitly. He was a damned good coach: he pushed us all to the edge of our endurance, but never asked us to do anything we couldn't do. I posted the majority of my weight on my left leg, carefully put down my right, and stood on the soft mats of the dojo floor.

"How's that?"

I responded to my coach's question by smiling and giving him a surprised nod.

He nodded in turn, knowingly. "You'll be back at practice in three weeks. The doctors will tell you six, but they say that for everything from a hangnail to open-heart surgery. You'll be fine."

His confidence boosted my spirits immeasurably. Just that little display of standing on the mats was tremendously reassuring. *I can do this. I'm getting better already.*

Gabriel, watching from beside the mats, gave me a thumbs-up gesture.

"Thank you!" I felt like throwing my arms around Aaron in gratitude.

"Hey, don't mention it."

One of the other guys from the club, who was also a firefighter, dropped by in the fire department ambulance to see if he could lend a hand, but I was already fixed up, happy, and on my way out the door that Gabriel held open for me.

Monday's visit to the other hospital did nothing to improve my mood toward mainstream medicine. My next email to the judo club was titled, "Sarah's Adventures in the Land of Scalpel-Happy Quacks," and told of how, in less than three minutes of actually seeing me, and without having palpated my broken foot at all, the doctor I had seen informed me that I needed surgery on both legs. I concluded that I was better off dealing with my own recovery.

The healers of ancient Greece had a saying: "First the word, then the plant, then the knife." In other words, surgery is a last resort, to be tried only when all other options have been exhausted. Doctors of the past recognized that cutting the human body is a serious procedure, and they treated the matter with grave consideration. The advances in knowledge and technology of the late nineteenth and early twentieth centuries have reduced the risks inherent in surgery; they have been an enormous boon to humanity and our species owes tremendous gratitude to the great men and women who developed them. However, it is a deep shame when modern surgeons forget that the fact that something *can* be done does not necessitate that it *should* be done.

I knew what was needed. Common sense and logic would have surmised it, even if my therapeutic-massage text had not outlined the physical therapy procedures and prior experience with foot injuries had not already taught me how to deal with recovery. Knowing how difficult it was going to be made me more determined, rather than discouraged, to take care of it myself.

The bones had been set, the one productive thing a doctor had done for me throughout the whole fiasco. It was arguably the lowest-tech element of anything that had been suggested, and it was the one thing for which I was grateful. Beyond that, healing was largely a matter of time and appropriate weight-bearing.

The human body has special cells that build up new bone tissue. Called osteoblasts, they are always present and working, because like all other living tissue, bones constantly replenish themselves. As I pored through my physiology texts, I felt more than a little vindicated at my rejection of pain-deadening drugs when I learned that pain actually triggers the brain to release a chemical (somatotropin) that stimulates these repair cells to go into overdrive. In other words, feeling pain makes the body create vastly more of the cells, which it uses to heal itself. I joked with Gabriel that this might be the reason the doctors were pushing drugs so hard: they'd make more money if the healing process were slowed down. My osteoblasts would shore up the basic damage; to make sure they'd have the raw materials they would need to do it, I shifted my diet and added extra supplements to significantly increase my intake of calcium, magnesium, and phosphorous.

About two weeks after I had broken my foot, Gabriel's mom asked if I was using comfrey on it. I lightly slapped my forehead. Comfrey! Of course! One of my previous jobs had been at a plant nursery, where amongst other duties I had taught classes on herbal folklore and history, and I felt like an idiot for not thinking of this myself. *Symphytum officinale*, or comfrey, is an herb that has been associated with healing fractures for so many centuries that one of its old common names is "knitbone." I sent Gabriel out to acquire some for me and consulted my herbal reference books to learn how the plant would have been used by a Victorian woman—or her even earlier forebears.

Gabriel returned with comfrey ointment from Whole Foods Market and dried comfrey root from a natural health care supply store. Following the instructions in my herbals, I soaked and boiled the root into a strong decoction, which I then used to soak my foot several times a day. Always, after soaking my foot, I would massage the swollen area, using the drainage techniques I had learned in massage class to force stagnant blood away from where it was pooling; then I would slather the sticky, jelly-like ointment thickly over my foot before carefully replacing it in its protective boot. Beyond these procedures, I knew it would be the job of my conscious body to restore strength to the framework that was being rebuilt. The best way to strengthen bone is to make it bear weight; the trick was not to stress it so much that I would refracture the delicate new tissue.

I waited four weeks for my bones to lay down their framework again. During this time, one of my very few entertainments was "window shopping" online for antique clothes. I spent many minutes watching for the Wi-Fi signal as a bird might watch for a silkworm. When it emerged, I would flutter to websites that sold antique clothing and imagine myself on a Victorian shopping trip, dreaming of what my wardrobe would have been like had I lived in that bygone era, or of what I might buy even now if my bank account were vastly larger than it was. Admittedly, seeing the prices of these lovely garments sometimes made me as morose as my broken-foot situation. Only once did I find an item that fit within my budget, and purchasing it was the one bright, shining experience from the whole time of my convalescence.

When I thought my foot must be ready for the challenge, little by little, I started putting weight on it. From judo practice, I had learned the difference between productive pain, the body's whinging while it pushes itself to the limits to make itself strong, and the pain that is nature's alarm system for injury. It was the difference between fighting through a submission and tapping out of one, the difference between overcoming my weakness and knowing my limits. Now, it was the distinction between encouraging the bone to heal and breaking it anew.

I created an elaborate physical therapy regime for myself based around a combination of techniques I'd learned in massage class, exercises from past injuries, advice from friends with medical training, and knowledge from textbooks (anatomy, physiology, and kinesiology books I owned from the classes I was studying, along with texts that Gabriel brought to me from the University of Washington's medical library). I spent every available minute following this regime, and Gabriel helped to the best of his capacity.

Throughout all this, I managed to keep up with my regular massage courses, getting rides to school from friends, or taking the bus since I obviously couldn't ride my bike with a broken foot. The day that I'd spent hobbling to the hospital then being ignored in the waiting room was the only occasion when I was absent from class. Massage school did get a bit interesting at times since being in the practitioner's position meant I would have to adapt moves so that I could do them from a seated position or standing on one leg, but I managed. The bright side of the circumstance was that it afforded all of us—my classmates as well as myself—opportunities to truly practice therapeutic techniques that mostly seem theoretical when practiced on healthy subjects. (Lymphatic drainage, for example, took on a whole new meaning for the class when "That feels nice" was replaced by "Check it out! Ten minutes ago Sarah's foot was nearly the size of a cantaloupe and now it's normal size again!") I'm sure that the massage therapy from my classes helped a lot more than the surgery the doctors had wanted to perform.

I knew I was on the road to recovery one morning when I asked Gabriel to help me with my corset and suddenly realized I wasn't leaning against anything. I was standing evenly, both feet planted. Later that day, I was walking. I had a pronounced limp for a while, but I fought it with intense concentration, and ultimately walked it away. Within a week, I could hop lightly on the tiptoes of the foot I had broken, putting all my weight in a jump against the very same foot that the doctors had told me would never work properly again without surgery.

I had broken my foot on the last night of May, and my debut sans crutches was at a Fourth of July party for the judo club. (Total time spent on crutches: four weeks. Admittedly I hadn't quite lived up to my coach's "back at practice in three weeks" prediction, but I wasn't too far off—and a far cry from the doctors' dire proclamations.) The judo coach was hosting a barbecue for Independence Day, and I was determined to show him and everyone else how well I was doing. It also seemed like a good opportunity to return the borrowed boot to its owner. I didn't need it anymore.

Most of the club members had seen me only ever during practice. Since that was the one activity for which I had continued to remove my corset, the majority of them had never seen me in anything other than an oversize gi (an Asian garment worn for martial arts) with sloppy pants and a bike jersey. I considered digging deep into my drawers and unearthing some of my few remaining loose clothes to hide my figure, but after a private debate, I decided not to bother. These were my friends, however I was, and if I was showing off the condition of one part of me, I might as well show off what shape the rest of me was in. I put on a light modern summer dress, concentrated very hard on minimizing my limp, and went proudly to the party.

There were many questions about my foot and congratulations for how well I was recovering, but no one said a word about my figure. I was glad of it. These were my rough-and-tumble buddies who had always taken me exactly as I was; if I happened to look a little differently than they had usually seen me, it didn't matter to them in the least. There was something immensely gratifying about that sort of camaraderie. I had already decided not to return to practice (breaking my foot had made me think long and hard about the wisdom of carrying out this activity for the sake of health and safety); but I was tremendously glad to see that my friends would remain my friends, in sports or out of them, and regardless of how I looked.

Once I could walk again, I did so as much as possible. I had missed my favorite exercise, and beyond that, it was great physical therapy. One day when I was out for a stroll, I stopped by a heretofore unvisited coffee shop, thinking I would sample their chocolate croissants.

The café was around the corner from a hospital, and as I waited I noticed that the man in front of me in line was a doctor. He was dressed in a doctor's lab coat, wearing a doctor's clip-on badge. He was also glaring at me.

I smiled cheerfully when I noticed him looking my way. He scowled, looked down, scowled even more darkly, looked down again. At first I thought he was glaring at my foot. I wondered if this was one of the doctors who had told me I'd never walk normally again without surgery on both legs (remember, I'd broken only my right foot—the left was just fine, and I hadn't hurt my legs at all—but they had been very eager to cut up the whole kit and caboodle of my lower regions) followed by a minimum six-month recovery. I could see how, having made such a statement, a man used to having patients submit to his authority would be angry to see me a few weeks later, uncut and prancing about easy as a lark.

He didn't look like my memory of those doctors, and we were near a different hospital altogether. Yet the way he was glaring downward made me wonder. It was a look of distinctly personal offense.

I checked his badge. Cardiology. That's not it, then. It took me a minute longer to realize that his dark looks downward were directed not at my foot, but at my waist. *He's glaring at my corset!*

The realization amused as much as annoyed me. I truly do wonder how people develop their prejudices sometimes. Why are some body modifications considered normal and others freakish? Perfectly straight teeth are just as unnatural as a small waist, yet no one (except me) objected when I was nine years old and braces were put on my teeth. That had been an alteration involving bones and was meant to be permanent. (A few years after the braces were removed, my teeth went back to being crooked anyway. It actually took them less time to revert than it had to get them straight in the first place.) Yet it was praised as good parenting on my mother's part, as it always is in modern America. Nearly everyone I know has worn orthodontics at some point, usually inflicted on them by their parents at a young age in an attempt to artificially straighten naturally crooked teeth. In the twenty-first century, this is considered the right and proper thing to do.

In the nineteenth century, no one had straight teeth, but most women had small waists. What right does a straight-toothed person have to criticize a straitlaced one? Both are artificial. Wearing any clothing at all is unnatural, but I do like to think it is progress from the days when our species was running around naked and barefoot, under blazing sun and over jagged rocks, alternately hiding from predators and stealing their scraps.

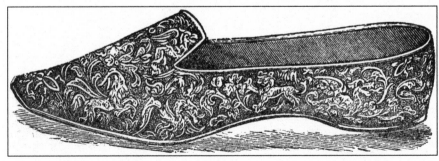

Gentleman's slipper.

Godey's Lady's Book (January 1890).

12

Customized Curves

Fashion plate for an 1890 walking dress.

Peterson's Magazine (April 1890).

Well healed, the next step was being well heeled again: a few weeks later, I was back in my kitten-heel boots. I've heard other corset enthusiasts say that wearing high heels takes pressure off the lower back, but back pain hasn't been an issue for me. Besides my one early and very brief experience when the knot from my laces had gotten poorly situated and pressed against my spine, I've never had any back trouble at all from my corset. On the contrary, I find it quite supportive and enjoy being the only member of my family who doesn't have a bad back. My back didn't need any help from my heels. However, my walk benefited from them enormously.

Edwardian actress Camille Clifford[29] caused an international sensation by her walk alone. By all accounts, she had average acting talents and her singing was unexceptional, but the simple sight of her walking across the stage with her eighteen-inch waist set the stage aflame when she played in *The Prince of Pilsen* in London. A contemporary newspaper stated that the world would be much poorer if Miss Clifford's mother had neglected to teach her to walk. Journalists weren't the only ones smitten: she soon after

[29] Arguably the most famous of the Gibson Girls, Miss Clifford had a beautiful swan's-curve figure and an eighteen-inch waist. She had started out a poor, immigrant laundress in New York, but later became world famous. When I started corseting, any time I felt low or frustrated I would gaze at pictures of Camille taken from the Long Island Staylace Association's website (http://www.staylace.com/gallery/gallery05/camille-clifford/index.html). Just seeing her black-and-white pictures would cheer me up; she was that beautiful.

eloped with a member of the British nobility.[30, 31]

Since I'd started wearing stays, I had given a great deal of thought to the motion of a corseted figure, and the contemplation only deepened with my foot injury. There has been much derision made of the perceived stiffness of a tight-laced woman. Modern women's studies texts include criticism of nineteenth-century fashion as "both physically constricting and voluminous . . . Such clothing made it difficult to move easily, reinforcing society's idealization of women as sedentary, ornamental creatures."[32] Ironically, comments like these appear alongside quotes from early suffragettes

Camille Clifford.

Public domain image (early twentieth century).

defending their clothes[33] and pictures of women now hailed as feminist heroes who seem quite clearly to be tight-laced.[34]

Mostly, the modern complaints against corsets tend to come from individuals who have never worn corsets, certainly never worn them properly, and have likely never even seen a corset rightly worn. At most, they may have put them on for an afternoon's experiment or seen them on actors or weekend reenactors. To judge corsetry by these standards is as "fair" as to judge ballet by the exertions of a bored retiree taking a single afternoon lesson, rather

[30] Robinson Locke Collection of Scrapbooks, NAFR + ser. 2, vol. 74, 49–92, Billy Rose Theater Collection, New York Public Library.

[31] NAFR + ser. 3, vol. 332, 31–68, Billy Rose Theater Collection, New York Public Library.

[32] McMillen, *Seneca Falls,* 128.

[33] Ibid., 130-31

[34] Ibid., 49, 55, 190: These pages show, respectively, Antoinette Brown Blackwell (who said the opening prayer at the 1888 National Council of Women of the United States in Washington, DC), Susan B. Anthony, and Victoria C. Woodhull (who in 1870 announced plans to run for the presidency of the United States). In all these photographic portraits, the women seem to be wearing corsets under their clothes.

than by the art of a Bolshoi dancer. This is why actresses so very seldom resemble the women they portray in period pieces: they are, at best, stumbling imitations.

Women of earlier times learned motion in stays from an age when the body learns easily, when acts of motion are not yet set by too much repetition. Victorian girls had training corsets in much the way modern girls have training bras: simpler than their mother's garments, different in form, but kindred in spirit. Corsets encourage an upright posture and stable core, adding to the grace of all the motions. However, they are really only the beginning.

Susan B. Anthony.

Public domain image (1856).

Each Victorian element I added to my wardrobe gave me new insight into the movements of a bygone era, and I came to realize that a Victorian ensemble, taken in its entirety, is an elaborate system of balances and counterbalances, each adding to grace of motion.

The corset, as I've said, was the first step. It held me up proudly, positioned to gaze down upon the world rather than scurry away from it. Next came the heels. Once I'd developed the knack for walking in them, those beautiful, arching kitten heels made the ground meet my steps more promptly than a flat foot, encouraging strong, purposeful strides. At the same time, they shifted my center of gravity forward. As my motions became more natural and I moved about, graceful and light on the balls of my feet, people started to ask me if I was a dancer. It reminded me more, though, of positions I'd practiced in judo.

Sears, Roebuck & Co. Catalogue, 1897 Skyhorse Publishing reprint (2007).

An 1897 Ball's Child Waist.

"I can't think of any sport," my coach had said, "that's practiced with your feet flat." He would instantly spring to a ready position, quick as a tiger. "You've got to be fast."

I would remember these lessons as I strode about, and I felt confident I could put up a good fight against whatever the world threw at me.

Wearing a hat brought my head up to hold it in place, and once I started winding my hair into a bun as an anchor for my hatpin, I found my cranium counterbalanced. During college, I had stared so habitually at the ground that I had been in danger of developing an obsession with collecting gutter change. Now, though, my head was high, and I viewed the world from a new perspective.

By the end of summer, I could slip both arms down inside the front of my twenty-four-inch corset and wave them around. Clearly, my waist was eager to become smaller. My hip bones, however, were at their limit. Below a twenty-four-incher, the next size down in off-the-rack corsets was twenty-two inches—and that one squeezed the flesh against my pelvis so hard that my legs started to go numb in short order. So, I wanted something smaller in the waist and bigger in the hips than anything I could buy ready-made.

It was time for a custom model.

Having been overwhelmingly intimidated by the prices I'd encountered in my first researches, I tried to find an alternative. On the Internet, I'd read of a business in Vancouver, Canada, that made custom corsets, and when I contacted the proprietor, I was quoted a very reasonable price and turnaround time—so reasonable, in fact, that she convinced me to order two corsets. She promised that this would make the costs even cheaper, since they would be cut and sewn at the same time.

I should have gotten her assurances in writing.

We made an appointment, and Gabriel and I arranged our schedules so that we could drive up to Vancouver. The store was in a part of Vancouver we had never before visited, despite many trips to the area, and it took us a while to find the shop. I experienced my first feelings of misgiving when I saw the dingy storefront window in the run-down neighborhood, but I tried to reassure myself.

Rent's pretty high in most of Vancouver—she must be trying to keep costs down. I bet corset-making's not that lucrative.

The inside of the store was clean. This reassured me. The handcuffs for sale, on the other hand, did not. The biggest surprise, and the first real moment of doubt, however, came when I saw that the store's owner, the self-styled corsetière, was not wearing a corset. There had been pictures on her website of her wearing a corset, but it seemed now they had just been for marketing. I thought back on all that wearing a corset twenty-four-seven had taught me—all that I had learned about breathing, movement, history, and poise from wearing corsets, how experience had made me understand them and was continuing to deepen that comprehension.

How can she make a good corset if she doesn't wear one herself? It's a bit like going to a dentist who has no teeth.

I tried not to dwell on this thought. We had come all the way to a different country for this; I felt I was in too deep to turn back. Besides, the price she had promised was very reasonable. So was the turnaround time she'd pledged. Although, again, I hadn't gotten anything in writing.

She took my measurements and I explained very clearly what I wanted, even leaving photocopies of historical corset pictures with elements circled and notes written detailing exactly how the finished product should look. We discussed size, and I specified that the finished corset should have a nineteen-inch waist, but should be roomy in the hips. At that first meeting, the store owner was very friendly. When I handed over a down payment of several weeks' worth of wages in cash, it felt impolite to ask for a receipt, but some small voice inside me said that receipts are always a good idea. I was later to feel that asking for one was the wisest decision I made that day.

(I think part of the spur for that internal advice to myself was the fact that, since her original quote, the owner had doubled her initially promised price. She seemed so nice, though, that I tried not to worry about it. I told myself that it was still cheaper than the estimate I'd been given by another business, since this price was in Canadian dollars, and the other had been in American dollars. Later, the quoted price was to be amended yet again—to American dollars, even though this was a Canadian store.)

Measurements taken, assurances given, and money down, we went back to Seattle with the promise that the store owner would call me when things were ready for a fitting "in a few weeks." That was the last I was to hear from her for quite some time.

A few weeks passed.

And then a few more weeks passed.

Gabriel started pestering me to call the store.

"Well," I said reluctantly, "I don't want to bug her . . . I'm sure she's working hard."

More time passed.

Summer started to draw to a close.

Eventually I heeded Gabriel's advice and tried to contact the store to schedule my fitting. First I tried emailing. When that met with no response, I bought a phone card so that I could make a long-distance call to Canada. Several international calls later, I learned that the store owner had gone on vacation. No one knew anything about my order.

Pages fell from the calendar, and squirrels started checking their hoards.

Finally, when the deadline by which I had been promised the first of my ordered corsets had long since passed, I received a call. She asked me to come in for a fitting, and I made another trip to Vancouver. Another huge chunk of cash was laid down, and I returned home for further waiting.

When all was said and done, the first corset ran over a month past its promised deadline and was twice the price originally quoted. The second ran three months past due, three times the quoted price, and was still unfinished when I made a third trip to Vancouver. It was structurally done, but was bare white, completely without ornamentation. When placing the order, I had asked that it be flossed (stitching added to support the bones; I had asked for blue flossing to give a little bit of color to the plain white expanse), and this was supposedly included in the initial quote—now already *three* times higher than it had started. At this last fitting, the owner wanted to double the price yet again (*six* times her original quote!) to add the flossing. There was a scene in the fitting room that ran very much like something out of a poorly written penny dreadful:

After she'd had me strip down to nothing but my panties for the fitting, she started screaming at me that she was an artist and I should be grateful to pay whatever she asked for whatever she was willing to make for me. "My corsets are made with love!" she shouted, brandishing a handful of very sharp pins. "And I'm just not feeling any love from you!"

If you think love is supposed to come into business transactions, you've got a really warped view of business, lady.

This was ridiculous. Maybe some of her customers reacted favorably to this sort of treatment, but I certainly didn't. To me, corsets are about Victoriana,

Me, before I started wearing a corset.

Winter visiting dress, circa 1890s.

Custom corset.

Portrait taken in the Suzzallo Library.

Gabriel at a presentation.

Gabriel and I put in an appearance at the State Capital Museum in Olympia.

I get stopped by a photographer en route to
the State Capital Museum.

The 2009 Port Townsend Victorian Festival.

An example of the amazing Victorian architecture of Port Townsend, Washington.

Independence Day 2009: My last day on crutches after I had broken my foot. I hid the crutches behind my back when Gabriel said he wanted to take a picture: if you look closely, you can see one of them peeping out below my skirt.

Half-in/half-out of an era: Victorian-style gray wool skirt paired with a modern sweater pinned in the back.

Reading at the Better Living Through Coffee café in Port Townsend, while everyone else engages with technology.

Back to the future: Contemplating the DeLorean.

Preparing for presentations.

Writing the text for this book.

Portrait of me modeling Édouard Manet's *Nana*,
painted by artist Frances Gace.

A presentation on the history of cycling at Port Townsend's 2013 Victorian Festival.

Photo courtesy of Barbara Chrisman.

We show off our bikes.

Photo courtesy of Don Willott.

Gabriel learns to ride a high-wheel bicycle.

not sadomasochism. My idea of proper wrist accessories are jeweled bracelets, not handcuffs.

She already had the lion's share of my money, so I paid enough to get a receipt for the unfinished corset and removed it and myself with all possible haste. (I later did the flossing myself. It took me a few hours and five dollars' worth of thread.) It boggled my mind that the store owner, so friendly and full of promises before she had my money, could have turned into such a harpy after she'd parted me from my cash. The whole experience—which had started out as so much fun when I'd been planning the corset, and into which I'd launched with such bright hopes—seemed sullied, and I spent a great deal of time whinging to Gabriel about it over the subsequent months.

Besides the time delays and exorbitant price inflations, there were, of course, issues with the corsets themselves. I had requested that the waists be nineteen inches, but the tags read twenty, and when I actually took a measuring tape to them, they proved to be twenty-two. Corset boning is manufactured with smooth, rounded edges, but some of the bones had been snipped short with no finishing. This left sharp, pointed metal edges that eventually punched through the corset lining and cut me in very tender places. To amend this, I had to buy a metal file from the hardware store, file the edges down, and darn up the holes.

In the end, the best lesson I learned from the whole experience was one I should have known from the beginning: always get everything in writing.

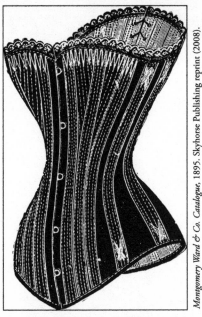

Montgomery Ward & Co. Catalogue, 1895. Skyhorse Publishing reprint (2008).

The 1895 corset, specifically designed for "tall, slim figures." Price: $2.19.

13

The Freedom of the Corset

Peterson's Magazine (July 1890).

Fashion plate, 1890.

Despite the issues involved, when I finally did get my custom corsets, they were a lovely upgrade from the off-the-rack models. In the first place, they were overbusts: the corset extended sufficiently far up my torso to do away with bras altogether. Instead of being pulled from above by straps, which dragged down my shoulders, my breasts were now supported from below by the structure of the corset. This sudden liberty from brassieres gave an immense feeling of freedom that shocked me. I had never realized how much pressure my bras had put on my shoulders until that pressure was removed. The women in my family were lamentably near the back of the line when nature handed out the gift of breasts, and I am not well endowed. It had never occurred to me that my modest breasts could put strain on my shoulders while my bras dragged me into a poor posture. With this burden suddenly gone, however, I realized how heavy it had been.

My shoulders were suddenly free—freer, even, than on prior occasions when I had left off a bra and gone completely unsupported. On those occasions, the weight of my breasts had still been pulling on my shoulders, albeit distributed a little more evenly than the point-specific pressure inflicted by a bra. With the overbust corset, though, the weight was completely shifted. The corset carried the whole weight of my breasts and was itself supported by not only the entire muscular structure of my torso (much stronger than the shoulders), but also my hip bones. The weight that had been an unrealized burden on my shoulders became completely negligible when distributed over such a large portion of my body. I was free to cultivate the proud, shoulders-back posture so striking in Victorian ladies—and so much better for the back.

Another freedom came with corseting, which likewise took me a while to appreciate. My whole adult life, I had fretted about my weight. I had constantly kept tabs on what I ate, attempting to calculate complicated equations of food intake versus exercise output in my head. No matter how old I grew, some part of me was still that fat girl from high school who sat at home during dances. At the same time, I had been very close to a number of people with eating disorders and was even more terrified of going down that path. Meals were a constant internal battlefield of warring insecurities: If I eat this, will I get fat? If I don't eat it, will I develop an eating disorder?

One day after I had been corseting for several months, I came home very hungry for lunch, my mind fighting itself in the old debate. What should I eat? How much should I eat? If I eat "x" will I get fat? If I get fat my clothes won't fit . . .

Then, suddenly I had an epiphany. Wearing the corset had made all these questions obsolete. It was no longer a matter of biology, but of simple physics: my stomach could not expand past the diameter of my corset. If I started the day with my corset at twenty-eight, or twenty-four, or twenty inches, as long as I did not loosen it, I would have the exact same measurement at the end of the day, no matter what I ate or what I did in the interim. I could eat until I was full at every meal; my stomach got full faster with the pressure of the corset on it, and it would not allow my stomach to grow beyond its boundaries—boundaries I set whenever I tied my laces. I could eat ice cream—or cubes of butter, for that matter—until I gave myself stomachaches, but my waist would not change.

I cannot adequately express how freeing this realization was. Years of insecurities and worries suddenly lost all force, like chains that prove to be made of paper. Knowing that I had complete control of the exact form I wished my body to take—not by some abstract equation of constantly changing variables, but by an actual physical means that I dictated absolutely—was freedom beyond measure. All the world's weight loss products, scams and schemes, diets, programs, the billions of dollars spent by people desperate to throw money away on ineffective treatments, all seemed suddenly very frivolous. To be free of all that, joyously free, and know beyond a doubt that I had absolute control of my own body: that was the freedom the corset gave, and that freedom alone would have been worth the wearing.

Peterson's Magazine (January 1890).

An 1890 fashion plate.

14

Objections

A Widow and Her Friends (1901). A Charles Dana Gibson drawing poking fun at the differing attitudes displayed toward a woman's behavior. The title of the piece is "Some think that she has remained in retirement too long, others are surprised that she is about so soon."

Due to my broken foot, we had been involved in relatively few social activities throughout the summer. After I'd regained the ability to wear high heels and the weather turned cool, we received another invitation from the group of historical costumers we had met in the springtime. They were holding a workshop on the history of corsets, and I was tremendously eager to attend. (Gabriel wasn't allowed to come, as it was specifically limited to women only.) I sent in my RSVP and hoped that one of my custom corsets would arrive in time to wear it. The first did—barely—reaching me by mail the day before the event. The morning of the workshop, Gabriel helped me into the new corset. He left it somewhat loose at my request, since I had a significant bike ride ahead of me to get to the workshop's location at a group member's private home. I tied the ribbons I had added to the waist of an old dress to cinch it in and hopped on my bike to ride the 11.88 miles to the event location.

Sun sparkled on the waters of Lake Washington as I skirted around its perimeter. Road conditions were perfect for riding, and I arrived a bit early. After locating what I believed to be the proper address, I knocked on the door but, receiving no response, sat down on the steps and waited.

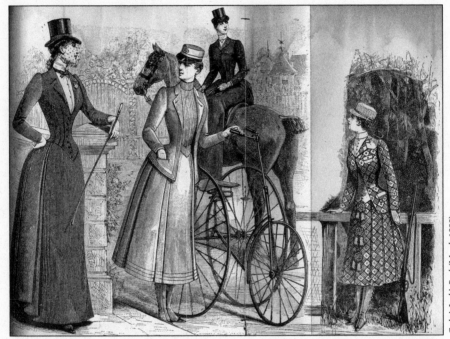

Godey's Lady's Book (March 1890).

Ladies' riding outfits, for horse and cycle, circa 1889. In the high-wheeler days of the 1880s, women preferred tricycles like the one seen in this fashion plate to the penny-farthing bicycles that men rode. When the safety bicycle (with its two same-size wheels and more modern look) boomed in popularity in the 1890s, its use was eagerly adopted by riders of both sexes.

In a short time, a car parked nearby and a woman with a long gray ponytail emerged, carrying a large cake box and several bags of groceries. This turned out to be my hostess, and I soon found myself swept inside and recruited for arrangement of tea things.

"Well, you really dressed up for the occasion!" she commented when I took off my coat.

I looked down at myself.

"No . . ." I was wearing a cheap polyester dress meant to look like wool. "Not really."

As a poor college student ten years previously, I had bought the dress at Target to wear when meeting Gabriel's parents.

"I . . . sort of . . . always dress like this."

Having thrown out about two-thirds of my wardrobe since I'd started corseting, I had very few choices remaining. This dress had survived the purges largely from sentimental value, and I had sewn ribbons in the back to allow myself to draw it in and show off my waist.

"You're kidding!"

"No, I—I sort of do," I stammered. I don't like to contradict people when I'm their guest, but I didn't want to lie, either.

The hostess gaped for a minute, then went back to giving directions on how to set up the tea. I tried to stay clear of her waist-length hair as it whipped about her in her scurries around the house, and, when a particularly vehement gesture sent her gray strands streaking through frosting, I made a mental note not to eat any of that specific cake.

Exiting the kitchen, I looked around for a place where I could display the books and underbust corsets I had brought to show people. I glanced at the coffee table in the living room, already covered with books and half-finished sewing projects, then examined the dining room table, which was soon to be laid out with all manner of sticky sweets and streaked frosting. In the end, I left my private materials in my waterproof pannier.

When the other workshop attendees arrived, I was glad to see that Polly Esther (she of the neon blue ball gown) was not amongst them. She had never uttered a civil word to me (or to anyone, as nearly as I could tell), and on the way home from the last event Ellen had specifically cautioned me against discussing corsets with her. Half an hour into the presentation, I was quite enjoying the calm atmosphere, the frosting-haired hostess's insights from her experiences sewing costume corsets, and the polite questions directed at me regarding my own experience wearing corsets on a daily basis. Then, Polly Esther let herself in the door.

The fact that she was late did not prevent her from taking a front-row seat; she simply unseated an earlier arrival and took her place. When she saw my corset, she screamed that it was too tight, and began storing up an armory of criticisms to fire when the presentation paused for refreshment. At that point, she cornered me in the kitchen.

"Well!" she exclaimed in a loud, accusatory tone, rolling her eyes. (Polly Esther always accentuates her criticism by rolling her eyes. In a larger woman, it might create resemblance to a horse; in her case, the mental picture generated is more that of a small, rabid rodent.) "I certainly hope that you talked to your doctor before embarking on such a *drastic* course of action!"

Would that be the doctor who wanted to perform surgery on my healthy left leg for a broken right foot?

"There's nothing drastic about it," I began, in a much calmer tone than the one used to confront me. "In the past—"

I would've finished my statement with, "all Western women used to wear corsets on a daily basis," but she cut me off.

"On *Grey's Anatomy*," her tone of conviction was stronger than that generally used to quote scripture, "they brought in a man who had been wearing a corset, and *he died!*"

I stared at her a moment. Was she seriously citing a television show as scientific authority?

"You do realize that that's fiction?" I asked slowly.

"It's based on fact!" She was fervent, her eyes gleaming.

I cautiously stepped away, careful not to turn my back on her until I had exited to the next room. For my seat, I deliberately chose a portion of the table that was already crowded so I could not be followed and further harassed. I do not enjoy arguing with zealots, no matter how strange their choice of idols might be.

It seems a common symptom of the human condition that in any given time period and society, the majority of individuals will accept some fallacies as gospel truths. The specific erroneous beliefs vary over time and between places, yet there always seem to be some of them. For example, the ideas that gypsies steal children and that Jews eat babies were historically popular amongst various communities, and many individuals who held these beliefs could not be persuaded otherwise. Having no evidence themselves to support their ideas never seems to bother such people, and even overwhelming evidence to the contrary often does not disillusion them. Some people are too far gone in their prejudice to benefit from education.

It is often difficult to pinpoint exactly where and when a certain misconception originates. Someone is disliked or something is misunderstood, a story is created and enlarged for dramatic impact . . . The beginnings of rumors and falsehoods are often so obscure as to be totally untraceable. Sometimes, however, one can pinpoint a nexus for the dissemination of false information—something that sends out an error like a starburst emits light. The most effective of these nexuses are created when an old error is repeated within a popular context; and in modern American culture, there are few contexts more popular than that of moving pictures.

The 1939 film adaptation of Margaret Mitchell's novel *Gone with the Wind* did not contain the first media portrayal of a woman grasping a bedpost while being laced into a corset (humorists have been drawing the same picture since at least the eighteenth century), but the immense popularity of the movie guaranteed the dissemination of the image and its implantation in the collective consciousness of American audiences.

Most modern audiences recognize that the African Americans in the movie—indeed, in the same scene as previously described—are portrayed as racist caricatures. To believe that slaves in the antebellum South actually behaved like those in the movie is absurd. Yet the same people who admit this are often all too eager to accept the equally stereotyped image of white Victorian woman as gospel truth.

Perhaps part of the reason audiences have become so obsessed with the bedpost scene is because the image is such a sexually charged one. The sexual innuendo inherent in a scene where a scantily-clad young woman takes tight grasp of a large pole, her breathing becoming increasingly labored as she makes inarticulate little vocalizations, makes good Hollywood drama. The lascivious nature of the image burns it deeply into the psyche of even innocent viewers with less-than-Freudian minds. The provocative scene was so effective that it was later copied in other movies, including the 1997 blockbuster *Titanic*.

However, it is not the memorability of an image that makes it true. (This should be obvious from the fact that a number of movie characters die unforgettable—and often bloody—deaths, yet the actors who portrayed them continue to walk the earth leading extremely vibrant lives.) Tying the laces of a corset, like tying any variety of thin cord into a slipknot, requires a bit of dexterity, but no exertion, and it is really best to leave the furnishings out of it. Groping an article of furniture and adopting the breathing patterns of someone in the early stages of foreplay is no more necessary in order to tie a corset than it is to engage in such activity to tie one's shoes.

The bedpost-corset scene is rather more obvious to the camera than when an electric cord is seen dangling from an "oil" lamp later in *Gone with the Wind*'s story line,[35] but these things are equal reminders that what viewers are seeing is a fantasy created for entertainment, not a documentary and certainly not reality. It is really a pity that so many people fail to keep this in mind. The image of Scarlett O'Hara groping her bedpost is one that arises with wearying frequency.

The most memorable of many occasions on which this image was brought up to me stands out by virtue of being so absurdly dramatic. I could never include it in any sort of fictitious tale precisely because it was too unbelievable. And yet, it happened.

I was chatting with an acquaintance at a community center one day when a paunchy, red-faced man who was invariably seen about the center (and always complaining about something) blustered over to us. That day's chosen topic for his tirade proved to be my figure, although I must confess that I was not flattered by the distinction.

"Those things," the man roared, pointing at my waist, "are horrible for you!" His triple chins wobbled a bit as he bellowed.

I stood my ground. "Have you ever worn one?" I asked calmly. I heard a smothered laugh from my companion as she covered her mouth and turned her face away.

The man's face shifted from the color of an underripe strawberry to that of a very ripe tomato. He spluttered a bit, paced angrily across the room and back, then launched a fresh attack. "I know all about those things!"

Oh really? Though the large man was gesticulating wildly at me, I remained exactly where I was.

"They're totally unhealthy!" the man continued. "They hurt like hell!"

"Actually," I countered, in a tone several decibel levels below his, "they're quite comfortable. I'm the only one in my family who does not have a bad back."

"Like I'm supposed to believe that!" he spit. "I heard of an interview with that actress who was in *Gone with the Wind* where she was auditioning for the role and all the girls in the audition for that scene—"

My companion and I were subjected to the tired old pantomime of exaggerated lace-tightening.

---

[35] This occurs about two-thirds of the way into the movie, when the character of Ashley is pretending to be drunk to hide the fact that he has been shot. Melanie (played by Olivia de Havilland) is holding the lamp in question (http://www.moviemistakes.com/picture3541).

"—had to be laced in, and they were all complaining, and all black and blue!"

I calmly folded my hands behind my back (a preventive to keep them from forming fists). This man was really getting on my nerves. Certain behaviors and levels of ignorance would inspire pity if not for their being so overwhelmingly exasperating. In such cases, a healthy degree of self-protective frustration rather kills the possibility of sympathy.

I could have pointed out that, just as sex sells film, the idea of suffering for art increases artist prestige, but I didn't want to engage that far with this red-faced, irritating man. I just wanted to end the conversation as quickly as possible so he would leave me alone.

Reaching back to memories of university lectures, I pulled out a rhetorical sledgehammer that I hoped would silence him.

"Well, if you want to believe an actress, whose entire job revolves around telling lies, as opposed to a real person who's right here in front of you, that's your choice."

The reason for acting being considered a dubious profession during various historical eras is one whose sentiment I do not necessarily share, but I was irritated enough to use this argument, since it is such a hard one to rebut.

"Lies?!" Mr. Tomato Head spluttered, his round face a deep crimson. "You think actors are liars?!"

"They've historically been seen that way," I responded cheerfully.

Strictly speaking, it is the truth: an actor is literally someone who is paid to lie. That was what made the argument so difficult to refute.

Mr. Tomato Head strode angrily away, my conversational companion retreated to a place where no one could see her laughing, and I used the opportunity to exit.

The next day, the woman with whom I had initially been chatting and who had witnessed the entire altercation, saw me walking home from the store and asked if I would like a ride.

"You know that guy you were talking with yesterday?" she asked as I settled into her passenger seat. "Well, you were talking," she corrected. "He was screaming."

I laughed, then shrugged with a sigh. "Yeah."

"He had a heart attack later."

"What?!" I stared at her, dumbfounded. "An actual heart attack?" My jaw dropped halfway to my chest. "You're kidding, right?"

"No, he really did."

I was inclined to think she was putting me on, until I again encountered the man himself several months later. He was considerably more subdued as he confirmed that he had, indeed, experienced a cardiac attack after the last time he had seen me, when, as my friend put it, I had been talking and he had been screaming.

"I guess I gotta stay calmer, huh?" he concluded.

"Might be a good idea," I agreed, nodding. I fought against a devilish impulse, then gave into it. "And maybe be more careful about telling other people their lifestyles are unhealthy?"

He had, after all, been quite nasty to me on numerous occasions.

He looked surprised, then he grinned almost sheepishly.

"Yeah," he said slowly. "Maybe."

Accident to a Young Man with a Weak Heart (1900). Illustration by Charles Dana Gibson.

15

Votes for Women

The Weaker Sex. (1903). Illustration by Charles Dana Gibson.

Occasionally, an event that seems entirely minor can have more ramifications than ever anticipated. Such was to be the case of a small notice Gabriel had forwarded to me from the Washington State History Museum's monthly email list. At the time, however, neither of us could have known where that mild little missive was to lead us.

The announcement had read as follows:

> High Tea Reception for the Publication of *Women's Votes, Women's Voices: The Campaign for Equal Rights in Washington*
> Oct. 17, 1 to 3 p.m.
> State Capital Museum
> 211 SW 21 AVE
> Olympia, WA 98501
> Suggested donation $2

A celebration in honor of the publication of the book *Women's Votes, Women's Voices: The Campaign for Equal Rights in Washington,* by Shanna Stevenson, Women's History Consortium coordinator, in conjunction with the suffrage centennial. Wear your 1910 period dress and enjoy a traditional high tea with the author and members of the advisory board of the Women's History Consortium. Enjoy performances, sing-alongs, and special remarks by Stevenson, Senator Karen Fraser, and Washington State Historical Society Director David Nicandri. Stay for a book signing and tea, all in the elegant Lord Mansion.

The aspect that caught my eye the most was the injunction to "wear your 1910 period dress," but the location was attractive as well. I had lived in Olympia for my first year of college, and although I had subsequently transferred and graduated from a different school, the town itself had a certain sentimental appeal for me. It had been there that I had met Gabriel. I had also made a number of other friends during that period with whom I had lost touch over the years, and any time an occasion arose to return, a part of me hoped that this might result in a serendipitous reunion. (I was, ultimately, to meet someone of significance that day, although it would not be an old friend, as I had expected, but somebody entirely new to me.) I marked my calendar and eagerly anticipated the date.

Gabriel was undecided as to whether he would join me or not. He didn't want to drive the DeLorean into bad weather (Olympia is located at the edge of the Hoh Rain Forest), and the trip is well over two hours each way by bus. My husband liked excuses to dress up with me, but he wasn't sure he was quite *that* desperate for one.

The weather on the morning of the event cemented his decision to stay home: it was absolutely pouring. Rain was coming down at a sideways angle in massive gray sheets, thick enough to obscure the buildings across a two-lane street. The storm had the force and violence of those more typically seen on the East Coast, but the staying power of Pacific Northwest weather that has no intention of coming to a hasty conclusion.

Through our window, which normally gave a view of the entire Seattle skyline and the Olympic Mountains beyond, the only thing visible was a sallow halo of light from a drowning streetlamp. Gabriel looked outside, then to me, then outside again. "Are you sure you want to go out in that?" He turned to me once more. "In your good clothes?"

I had been planning to wear my antique linen dress, silk petticoat, linen jacket, and Gibson Girl hat. It would be the perfect outfit for the period requested; as nearly as we could tell, the dress was from 1905, the jacket from 1910 exactly.

"Well . . ." I looked at the biblical deluge outside, half-expecting to see animals filing past, two by two. "I do have an umbrella . . ." I looked dubiously at the brightly colored, rose-covered item in question. It would be incredibly anachronistic, but I wasn't going out in that weather without some sort of shield.

"Is the bus stop covered?" Gabriel asked, definitely concerned.

"Yeah. And I'll be inside once I get there." Some part of me just felt I should go. I attributed it to that old conviction about Olympia—that I would connect with someone worth remembering there. "I'll be careful with everything."

Gabriel helped me on with the antique dress, making sure the tailor's weights hung properly, that the celluloid boning was straight in my high lace collar, and that the myriad of hooks and eyes were fastened, tracing my spine. I put on my beautiful blue velvet hat myself, fastening it with a long, silver hatpin. To prevent the pin from inadvertently injuring me or (even worse) tearing the dress, I covered its sharp tip with my only hatpin clutch, a hollow little nickel-plated pod the size of a small aspirin capsule, filled with cork. Wearing a hatpin without a clutch means having the very sharp tip of a nine-inch (or longer) steel rod waving about at the back of one's neck, eager to tear any clothing or stab any flesh with which it might come into contact. I owned one, and only one, of these indispensable little safety stoppers. (I had been looking for a source from which to buy more of them for years, but had not yet managed to find one at that point.)

Dressed and properly hatted, I took a firm grasp on my umbrella and ventured out into the storm. I held my skirts well above my calves to keep them out of the splash zone as I carefully stepped my way around eddies and rivulets in the street. Water growled down with ruthless brutality from the angry maw of the sky, and I was grateful for the tall buildings surrounding me, which at least broke some of the force of the wind. I stayed in their lees as much as I possibly could, cowering under my umbrella and pulling it low to protect my beautiful hat.

The bus came soon, and I gratefully sought its shelter. I took a seat next to a middle-aged woman, who regarded me for a long moment, then made an inquiry as to my destination. I explained about the centennial celebration of women's suffrage in Washington State and clear interest bloomed in her face.

She eagerly asked if I did a lot of work for women's rights, if I was a women's studies major.

I paused. At university, I had generally tried to avoid people majoring in women's studies, since the ones I had met seemed, by and large, to be disconcertingly rabid. But, how to express this diplomatically?

"No . . ." I began slowly. The stranger started to give me a reproachful look, so I continued, choosing my words with care. "I'm grateful for what the suffragettes did, and I'm happy to have the vote—"

This was a bit of a diplomatic stretch. Actually, since reaching the age of majority, I really hadn't seen much benefit yielded from my much-touted vote. In the first presidential election after I became old enough to vote, my preferred candidate had won the popular election, only to be toppled by a political numbers game a few hours later.

"But," I continued, treading into paths where I held more conviction, "I think that the really important work was done a long time ago, and a lot of what people have been trying to do more recently has been sort of counterproductive. I think that in a lot of the efforts that women have made to try to prove they're the same as men, a lot of the power that women used to have has gotten lost along the way."

She gave me a curious look, so I elaborated, using an analogy from a different culture.

"I used to live in Japan," I explained, "and one of the things that really struck me when I was living there was what an incredible amount of power women had over domestic life and everything that happened within the family. When I would visit people's houses, the husband would nearly always be hidden away in a very small room, sometimes just a closet, really, while the women had the run of the entire rest of the house. There's a lot of talk about Japan being a patriarchal society—and in business and government, the men do have a lot more power— but when a husband comes home, he gives his wife his entire paycheck, and she gives him an allowance, even though he was the one who earned the money!"

The woman to whom I was speaking giggled at this.

"So," I continued, "when you take the culture as a whole, what I saw wasn't so much that one gender overpowered the other in an overarching way, as much as just that the genders had very different spheres of control, and within those spheres, they each have an enormous amount of power."

I took a long breath, lining up my thoughts.

"Of course, our culture is very different, but I think that in the past there was a lot better understanding that women can be different than men and still be very powerful. Biologically, we are really different—there's no point in trying to deny it." I shrugged. "You know, I'll never be able to lift as much as my brother, no matter how hard I try."

I explained, "He's a six-foot-five police officer, I can't compete with that!"

My listener laughed.

"But," I smiled, "I can do things that he can't do. I think it's important to remember that we can be very different, and it's okay to be different, and there's nothing negative about that. It doesn't mean that either gender is inferior to the other. Just that we're different."

Stepped On. (1901). Illustration by Charles Dana Gibson.

Public domain image (early twentieth century).

In my own mind, I reflected that part of why I enjoy wearing a corset so much is that it is an accentuation of this difference. A woman is not an inferior man, so why should she dress like one? (Skirts are actually far superior to trousers for many needs of the female form, especially when paired with pantalets.) I am very proud to be a woman, and I had learned to enjoy flaunting that pride.

My seat-partner was intrigued, and said that I had given her a lot to think about. With the bus rapidly reaching her stop, though, she asked if she might change the subject to a far less weighty matter, to satisfy a curiosity before she departed. After my assurance that this would be perfectly fine, she asked, "Is it accurate for you to be wearing earrings? Did they really have pierced ears back then?"

I laughed. I had once asked my mother a nearly identical question when watching the medieval fantasy *The Princess Bride*. I had been about seven years old at the time, though.

"Oh yes!" I reached up, feeling an earring to remind myself which ones I was wearing. "Actually, these are quite a bit older than the dress. These are from about the 1860s or so, and the dress is more like 1905. People have been wearing earrings since, oh, about the time they figured out they could poke holes through their ears with sharp things!"

We both laughed, and I went on.

"There's a really famous painting that's actually called *Girl with a Pearl Earring,* and that was done a few hundred years before this dress."

She had still seemed dubious up until this point, but that bit of information clinched the earring question for her.

"Oh yeah!" she exclaimed. "I saw that movie!"

I usually cringe at citations of Hollywood portrayals as though they were actual facts, but I let this one slide, given that it supported my point, and also that it was based on a book, which was inspired by the painting in question.

The bus reached her stop, so she bid me a friendly adieu and we parted ways. Soon, the vehicle reached my own point of first disembarkation. (I would have three before finally reaching my destination and three more to come back home.)

The storm had, if anything, grown even more intense. Getting from the drop-off point to the transfer stop was the longest uncovered portion of the journey: it meant going down a steep hill on which I'd been known to stumble even in clear weather, and on the exposed, rain-blasted side of the street. I looked out at the deluge in horror from the shelter of the drop-off point, took a deep breath, and entered the storm.

In high heels down a slippery slope, holding my silk and linen skirts high, I raced down the hill, sprinting for the shelter of the other bus stop. My mad dash was halted by a red traffic signal. The rain was too obscuring and the cars too swift to cross against it, so I stood imprisoned on the wrong side of the street, helpless to protest against that electronic authority as I saw my bus approach the empty stop—and pass it.

The light finally changed and I darted into the grudging shelter of the three-sided bus stop. I positioned myself in the relative (if scanty) protection of the corner, using my umbrella to fence off as much of the open side as possible, and took stock of my condition. My linen dress was slightly damp, but luckily it was clean rainwater, not mud, and the linen had shielded my silk petticoat underneath it. Using a small hand mirror from my purse, I ascertained that the umbrella had protected my hat. I had, however, lost my hatpin clutch. Since I had roughly an hour to wait until the coming of the next bus, I briefly considered the possibility of retracing my steps to search for it. I looked past my umbrella to the torrential sheets of water gushing from the sky and thought better of the concept. The likelihood of tracking down an item that small was minute and not worth the risk to my hat and dress. I had a small bead in my purse that I had wrapped with thread and used as an emergency clutch on a previous occasion, so I ferreted it out and pressed it into this service once more.

(Throughout the rest of the day, people would mistake this for the top, rather than the end, of a pin. By the time I arrived home that night, I was to grow rather weary of people telling me that my "stickpin, or something, is falling out." For the record, it is not remotely possible for a hatpin to fall out; the ornamentation at the top prevents it. The only way it would even be conceivable for a hatpin to fall out of its wearer's hair would be for the lady in question to hang upside down and allow the weight of her hat to pull it off. Needless to say, this happens very seldom.)

Sheltering behind my umbrella, I spent the next hour highlighting vocabulary words in a book chosen by a pupil I was tutoring and making private, snarky comments in the margins. (The book in question was being made into a big-budget movie, but in my opinion had no literary, or even grammatical, merit whatsoever.)

At length, the bus arrived and I sighed with relief at being within its protection for the ensuing hour until the next transfer point. Missing the first bus meant that I had also missed my transfer, so I faced another hour under a different bus stop, although this one was thankfully more substantial. I furled my umbrella, set it aside, and carefully folded my skirts about myself to keep them from touching the ground as I perched on a little, flip-up seat designed to deter loiterers. Nearby, a young woman in her early twenties watched my movements. After a few moments' observation, she worked up the courage to inquire, "Does it make you . . . feel different? To be dressed like that?"

I smiled at her. "Well, I won't deny that it's a pleasant sensation to have four yards of silk twirling around my legs."

She laughed and a very pleasant conversation ensued. I told her about my pantalets, an element of the outfit not visible to the outer world, but probably my favorite article of Victorian underwear. Also called "split bloomers," pantalets are like light, blousy undershorts—but with a significant difference: they are split right down the middle, and open in the back. Victorian women did not wear panties. Pantalets meant that they had perfect freedom of choice while answering the call of nature: they could do so sitting down or standing up like a man. The young woman laughed anew when I explained my conviction that women's liberation had taken a dramatic step backward when we had given up this equality with the rougher sex. She had questions upon questions, and our amiable chat helped the time pass more quickly as the storm raged around us.

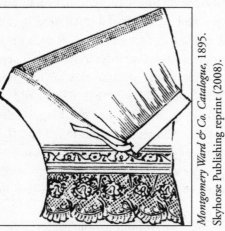

Pantalets: *Montgomery Ward,* 1895.

Montgomery Ward & Co. Catalogue, 1895.
Skyhorse Publishing reprint (2008).

When I finally reached Olympia, the rain had eased somewhat. I still could not shake that persistent idea that I would surely encounter someone I knew while I was down there, and I found myself searching each face in the small town as I walked under my umbrella toward the State Capital Museum. It was an absurd conviction, but I was unable to cast it aside, no matter how illogical I told myself I was being.

I even stuck my head into a coffee shop along my route and scrutinized its occupants. By now I knew I was being ridiculous. Resolving to cease this nonsensical behavior, I removed my head from the café's door, determined the most direct route to my destination, and strode out to complete my actual goal in visiting the city.

A block along, I heard steps running up behind me. I turned and saw a dainty young woman with a very large camera. Grinning broadly, she explained that she was a photographer. She had seen me from the coffee shop and wanted to take my picture.

I was flattered, albeit incredibly surprised. I could remember only two other occasions in my entire life when a stranger had wanted to take my picture: on the first, I was helping to haul a twenty-two-foot Christmas tree behind a tandem bicycle, and on the second, I was in a small-town fish market in Japan, holding a turnip the size of a BMX wheel. For someone to want my picture as I simply walked down the street was an entirely new experience for me.

Honored by the request, I saw no reason not to oblige. We were under the cover of a shop, so I started to fold away my anachronistic umbrella to get it out of the picture. "No, no!" the photographer insisted. "Keep it up! It looks good—it'll hide the street." Glancing behind me, I saw her point. The flowered umbrella might be anachronistic, but aesthetically it was more agreeable than the modern cars and cracked concrete at my back. I kept it up and smiled while she snapped off some shots. After she'd finished, I gave her my email address and she promised to send me digital copies.

A bit farther down the road, a distinguished-looking woman pulled her car over next to me and asked if I was going to the museum's presentation. Initially I was surprised at her insight, then it occurred to me that the outfit might be a bit of a giveaway. She invited me to get into her empty passenger seat, and we drove the rest of the way together.

When we got to the museum, I was significantly amused by the way this woman took me around to all the other attendees and showed me off, rather as if I were the feather of some exotic bird she had chanced upon while on her way to the museum. There was an especially great fuss made over the soutache trim on my linen jacket, which surprised me because I had almost left that garment at home, thinking it would not be of interest to people. (Also, the jacket was rather boxy, and I wanted to show off my waist.) I initially hung the jacket in the museum's coat closet, but was asked to retrieve and model the item so many times that I grew weary of the back-and-forth trip and resigned myself to a bit of concealment as I donned it for good. As a compromise, I positioned my hands behind myself so that they would tuck back the jacket's edges and show off my waist, just a bit.

Everyone was quite interested in my dress, and I was asked to tell its story repeatedly. I explained how my husband had bought it via eBay from a seller in Nebraska. It had been stored in the seller's attic for nearly a hundred years, and when my husband had presented it to me, it had been an extremely different color from its current shade of light brown. When Gabriel gave it to me, it was a very grungy rust color, and the dress was my first experiment in washing an item of antique clothing. It had been a nerve-racking experience, but an educational one.

Ever the researcher, Gabriel had turned up the information that the preferred cleanser in such cases is Ivory bar soap. I pared thin slivers into a basin of warm water, pressing them and working them with my hands until they dissolved. I strained this soapy water several times to get out the stubborn bits that refused to dissolve once the solution had reached saturation point, then let it cool to room temperature. I made sure our bathtub was pristine, filled it with cool water, and then added the soap solution.

I was extremely uneasy about immersing a century-old dress in water, but Gabriel and I had both agreed that the degree of pollutants darkening the item was detrimental to it. Not only did the dirt detract from the craftsmanship of the beautifully constructed garment, but the longer it remained, the more it would degrade the fibers of the dress. The real question was which would ultimately be more destructive: allowing the dirt (and the acids within it) to stay and certainly eat away slowly at the fabric, or washing it and risking a catastrophic deterioration? Had it been a silk garment, the risk would have been too great, but linen is sturdy. I had decided to try.

Having prepared the bath more carefully than I generally did for my own bathing, I had retrieved the dress and cradled it, looking down at the pearly water. I took a long breath and swallowed deeply. *Here goes.* I carefully laid the dress the length of the bathtub, as though I were laying it out on a bed.

As water soaked the old fibers, it released a century of scents. The first was the dirty smell of tobacco smoke: pollution that had gotten into the dress through decades in an attic. After this dissipated, underneath it I could smell wetted dust, the dirt of ages. As the slippery water slid amongst the dress's fibers, this smell too washed away, revealing the last, most mysterious scent. I knew the fragrance. It came like the unexpected appearance of a face from childhood: known, but rendered unfamiliar by strange context.

Rose hips? It was not the flower I smelled, which might have been dismissed as old perfume, but its fruit. The association puzzled me. *Did they dye it with them?* I knelt close to the water, inhaling deeply. *It's definitely a fruit. They might have used rose hips as a dye, if they had a lot of them, but it's such a weak dye . . .*

I had experimented with quite a lot of plant-based dyes over the years, and I knew that rose hips imbue a light, reddish-brown color, which is an agreeable hue, but doesn't hold up to much washing. Picking enough hips to dye such a large garment would be a major task and hard to credit if the effort would go to waste. They must have known that. This last scent blossomed and started to fade, and I suddenly had it. It was not the fruit of roses I smelled, but their botanical cousins, the temptations of Eve. Apples! They dyed it with apple must!

It made perfect sense. Apples have been an important mainstay of American life for centuries. When communities still pressed their own cider in autumn months, they would have had an abundance of the brownish, pulpy by-product left behind. Cooked down, it must have made a fine dye.

Happy to have solved the mystery, I had left the dress to soak in the soapy water. When I checked it several hours later, the wash water was black. I folded the dress away from the drain and pulled the plug. Liquid the color of samovar tea—with none of its appealing aroma—gushed from the fabric.

The dress was too heavy from its soaking to risk stressing the fibers by lifting it, so I carefully folded it away from the faucet, and held a plate under the spout to angle the water toward the side of the tub itself, keeping any direct water pressure away from the dress as the tub refilled slowly. An entire day of repeating this slow and careful rinse process still did not make the water run clear, but the dress was far cleaner than when I started: a lovely light brown color, like very creamy cocoa. This was the color that the event attendees saw when they viewed the dress on me, and they were fascinated by the tale of it.

I kept lifting my skirt just enough to flash the silk petticoat underneath. The dress made for an interesting account of preservation technique, but for me the petticoat had the more emotional story behind it. While I had been recovering from my broken foot the preceding summer, my single connection to the outer world during many apartment-ridden days was a sporadic wireless Internet connection, which my computer picked up at certain times of day, from the very corner of the room, when atmospheric conditions were just right. I used these fleeting opportunities to look up websites selling antique clothing, and to dream. One particular site grasped especially firm hold of my imagination and my heart. The clothes on it were beautiful, and perfect, and utterly, *utterly*, out of my price range. Minute upon stolen minute, I must have filled hours with sighs.

It's a special kind of self-torture to gaze upon much-coveted items that one knows are entirely unobtainable. I'm really not sure why I feel compelled to inflict it upon myself from time to time. Combined with the already depressed state I was in from my broken foot, I managed to stew myself into a truly morose sulk of self-pity. When I had seen the most exquisite item of all on the site—an amazing, English watered-silk petticoat in peach, striped through with bold black and soft silver, edged in a ruffle to whirl and eddy around its wearer's ankles—I decided that this auto-flagellation had gone on long enough and resolved not to even look at the price. *I should put it all away, give up selfish, impossible fantasies, and resign myself to reality*, I thought. Then a perverse curiosity got the better of me; I peeked at the price.

It was pristine, and peachy-perfect, the most amazing item on the entire site. And it was the only item on the entire site I could afford. My jaw dropped. My eyes glued themselves to the computer screen. I had worked myself into such a sulk over my bad luck, I could not believe this change in fortune. Before the spell could break or the wireless signal dissolve, I whipped out my debit card and placed the order. I held my breath until the transaction went through, then let out a sigh of absolute contentment.

"I'll wear it when I can walk again," I told myself. My luck was changing.

This museum event was one of my first opportunities to wear that beautiful petticoat, and I tipped my skirts as much as possible to show it off. I adored the rippling, flowing feeling of the watered silk, liquid-soft against my legs. Most of all, I loved the whispering, rustling sound and feel of the pleated ruffle at the bottom, eddying around the proud ankles poised atop kitten heels above my newly mobile feet.

The event itself was a lovely affair, with suffragist songs and sweet tea dainties. I took great care not to soil my dress as I nibbled small cakes and cookies, refilling my plate often but scurrying away from anyone whose plate overflowed. I sat well away from the table and chatted companionably with a handsome old woman. She had been a museum docent for decades, and I enjoyed hearing her wonderful stories of the mansion housing the collection and the family who had once lived there.

When the event drew to a close, I was offered (and accepted) a ride from the same woman who had seen me walking to the museum and given me a partial ride there. As we were leaving together, a curly-haired woman with the face of a middle-aged cherub came running after me.

"Did I hear you say you have more outfits like this?" she asked, referencing an earlier conversation.

"A whole collection of them!" I explained enthusiastically. "My husband and I have been hoping we might get a chance to do a historical fashion show at some point. We think it would be a lot of fun."

At this, she was even more enthused. We exchanged emails, and she promised to call me. This was to prove the fortuitous meeting I had somehow known would occur that day, although not in the way I had at all expected. At the time, I could not have anticipated where that simple meeting would lead.

Thanks to the friendly woman who had given me a lift from the museum, the first bus was achieved without difficulty. It was a comfortable ride, and I passed the time amiably chatting with the man seated next to me about fashion and the history thereof. The skies had cleared in Olympia when we left, but by the time the bus reached my transfer point in Tacoma, the rains had resumed. It was pouring in earnest by the time my next bus pulled up to the stop.

Actually, "to the stop" is a rather generous way to express the actual fact of the matter. A good driver will halt the bus within feet of the shelter, especially in inclement weather. This one overshot it by at least fifty yards.

Anxious about my dress and hat, and certainly not wanting to miss this— the *last* bus—home, I kept my umbrella up until the last possible moment and I sprinted for the bus. The other riders were nearly as eager to get out of the rain as I was and pressed against me with muddy clothes and dirty hands. The step up into the bus carriage was a particularly high one, and as I tried to make it, folding my umbrella to get it through the door and avoiding the wet, pressing bodies behind me, I heard the small *rip* of a few stitches parting. I looked down in horror.

Was it my dress?

No, worse: two little pleats hung loose from the ruffle of my silken petticoat. My peach petticoat, which I'd so proudly ordered from England, the one bright spot in my whole wretched summer! That little rip seemed an affront to history, a blank ingratitude on my part to the lovely garment I'd declared my reward for walking again. *Oh no!*

I was horrified to see this mar, this injury, to my beautiful, beloved petticoat, but if I'd known what brutality was immediately to be inflicted upon it, I would have run shrieking back into the storm. What happened next ranks very high in the lists of "Reasons Some People Should Be Weeded from the Gene Pool" and "What the Bloody, Fucking Hell Were They Thinking?!"

The bus driver—the *idiot* woman bus driver—grabbed the poor, torn little pleats and pulled. It happened too quickly for me to stop her; my scream for her to stop died halfway out my lips as two yards of ruffle accordioned out, her vicious yank slaughtering the delicate, old thread. The beautifully pleated ruffle, which had been dancing around my proudly heeled feet all day, hung like intestines ripped from a living thing.

Physical assault of a bus driver is a felony in the state of Washington. If they filed equivalent charges for noncontact actions, I surely would have gotten the death penalty for the poison I injected into my look and tone.

"*Don't*. Touch. My. Clothes!"

As it was, I just barely held myself in check from inviting felony charges.

She threw the sundered ruffle at me. "I's just tryin' to help ya out!" she bleated in a very low-class Southern accent, rolling her eyes at me.

I held my head up high and from my eyes spat venom at her. I did not ball my fists, and I most deliberately did not reach for the nine-inch rod of pointed steel holding my hat in place. Drawing attention to these choices, I do not mean to imply that the thought was far from my mind.

There is a scene in a piece of classic children's literature[36] where a young boy gathers up his cherished pet's intestines after it has been savaged by the "devil-cat of the mountains." In such a way, I delicately placed the distressed pink coils over my arm, and with as much dignity as I possessed, passed on to my seat.

I was subdued through the rest of the bus rides, trying to work out whether the damage was reparable. I knew that it would never be as it had been, but knew equally that I would try. It would join a great heap of mending projects, and it would be over a month before I could face this particular repair without the sewing tools shaking in my furious hands at the memory of how it had come to be injured, but I would return to it. I have an ingrained hatred of waste, and to let such a beautiful piece of history lie neglected would have been a terrible shame upon me.

Nearly all my antique items had some element needing repair; it is virtu-ally inevitable after they have spent more than a century on this Earth. Humans don't usually last that long—and if they do, they generally require more extensive mending and upkeep than a bit of darning. My cedar chest was full of tattered treasures from the past that I had been slowly, painstakingly repairing, stitch by labored stitch. For several years I had been working on repair of a Belle Epoque–era cape, which Gabriel had given me as a gift: It was ornamented with thousands of jet and steel-cut glass beads, some of them so tiny I could barely pick them up. The thread holding them onto the cape had rotted with age, and I'd passed season after season restitching each one individually. Many of the original beads had been lost over the years, and I scoured every bead shop to which I could possibly travel to try to find replacements. I was never able to match them exactly, so I had to make do with close approximations: I used the smallest iridescent glass Indian beads I could find to replace the original, minuscule glass beads that strained my eyesight and fingertips so much. The jet beads were even more challenging. Jet (known to geologists as lignite) is a dark, shiny substance related to coal. It was popular in Victorian jewelry and other ornamentation—so popular, in fact, that it was mined out. If it were an animal instead of a stone it would probably be on an endangered species list. The beads I found to replace those originals are onyx.

---

[36] Wilson Rawls, *Where the Red Fern Grows* (New York: Bantam Doubleday Dell Books, 1996).

Some garments had ripped seams, others wanted replacements for lost buttons and similar fastenings. Nearly all had holes—from use, from moths, from the gnawing teeth of time.

The petticoat, though, my beautiful petticoat, with which I had rewarded myself for learning to walk again after a frustrating convalescence, had been perfect when I'd bought it. It had sailed through untold tempests of time and come to me in pure condition. Then it had been ravaged by an ignorant brute for absolutely no reason whatsoever. The galling remembrance of this infuriated me every time I tried to repair the damage. My mending stitches looked coarse and clumsy next to their fragile antique sisters, and I felt intense guilt that my skills were unworthy of this beautiful relic, which I had failed to protect from a savage.

I wondered what a Victorian lady would have done if a coarse driver had deliberately torn her skirt. I like to think that she wouldn't have needed to take action herself, that any gentlemen seeing the attack would have dragged the savage forcibly before the nearest magistrate, while administering a suitable number of justified and well-placed blows. Even if chivalry missed seeing the assault, I picture a few affronted words of the encounter dropped in the ear of the nearest constable, sending the law to enact the swift justice of the billy club, then requiring the ruffian to pay for the damages. Perhaps I romanticize. In any event, it gave me something to fantasize about during the long hours I spent mending my beloved petticoat.

Montgomery Ward & Co. Catalogue, 1895. Skyhorse Publishing reprint (2008).

Reproduction of statue of Justice: *Montgomery Ward,* 1895.

16

Feminine Anatomy, and Matters of Hygiene

Godey's Lady's Book (September 1889).

Victorian fashion plate showing 1889 dresses. Note how much shorter the girl's skirt is than the skirt of the grown woman. Mothers didn't quite trust very young girls to keep long skirts clean, so skirts were extremely short on toddlers, then grew progressively longer as a girl matured.

Over the summer, my everyday clothes had largely been light cotton dresses, which had been easy enough to fit to my new figure, although they had never been designed with corsets in mind. Once the weather had turned decidedly chill, however, these light dresses were simply unfeasible. I had grown rather vain about my figure, but I couldn't see how it would do my beauty any good to catch pneumonia over it.

After so long in skirts, I found pants needlessly cumbersome, even downright uncomfortable. I disliked the feeling of my legs being divorced from each other and my limbs bound. Having grown accustomed to the freedom of Victorian-style undergarments, negotiating pants in a lavatory seemed by comparison like something Houdini might have conceived. (As I'd explained to my seatmate on the bus, using facilities in Victorian ladies' garments is simply a matter of spreading fabric; pantalets are split right down the middle.)

I couldn't get used to moving in pants again, either. I'd grown to love the way my skirts swished around me, and, like a cat's whiskers, communicated subtle information about the air currents and objects around myself. Extending my proprioception, it was like an extra sense I had developed without considering its presence—until I found it cut off.

Besides all this, most pants looked absolutely ridiculous with the corset. Since trousers are modeled on male anatomy, the waist is nearly always cut as a straight line up from the hip, in no way at all taking into account the curve of the female pelvis. Stays enhance those curves, and trying to put pants over them becomes a sort of visual *reductio ad absurdum*. Any pants large enough to be pulled over my hip bones would hang so loosely around my waist that I could have dropped an apple down the front. It was the fashion at that time (Seattle, circa 2009) for pants to be cut with waistlines more than a full handspan below the natural human waist, so unless I wore an excessively long and baggy top, I'd be left with several inches of my corset exposed. To get any sort of proper fit to this situation meant belting (or pinning) the blouse in addition to the pants.

Skirts, I decided, were far superior; but at this point, my waist was so small that even many modern skirts did not fit me; most of them had elastic waists that hung as low as the detested pants. They also tended to be very much not my style and unsuited for winter wear. Polyester, rayon, and flimsy cotton abounded in light, summer colors and droopy waistlines, but what I really wanted was a long, sturdy woolen skirt that would fit me properly. I sketched out pattern ideas and started hunting for fabric.

I was absolutely determined to avoid synthetic materials. I had seen enough costumes made of materials invented a century after their patterns had gone out of fashion to impress on me that something can be made to look real only if it *is* real. I was adamant that the quality of the materials should correspond to the labor required in sewing a garment by hand: I was not making a costume, but clothes.

The distinction between costume and clothing was—and is—very important to me. The word *costume* does derive from the French term, which simply denotes a suit of clothing; the educated classes of Victorians often had fairly extensive training in the French language, and when they used the term in this way, they did so with full understanding of its cultural and linguistic context. However, the idea of costume as normal clothing is no longer in keeping with the way the word has come to be used in twenty-first-century American culture. To anyone who would dispute this fact, I invite consideration of the following scenario: You wake up on a typical morning, yawn, and reluctantly roll out of bed. You start to pull on your everyday shirt and whatever else you happen to wear on a normal day. Someone else in the household, still half-asleep, asks what you are doing. Do you reply, "I'm putting on my clothes," or "I'm putting on my costume"? I think not many people would give the latter response.

The word *costume* has acquired strong associations with things that are false, such as children's Halloween fantasies and theatrical roles.[37] A costume is window-dressing for playacting; something worn in a specified context by someone pretending to be something they are not. For an individual with this heavy cultural load in his or her subconscious to refer to historical clothing as costumes is to partially deny the veracity of those who wore them, perhaps without even realizing it. The antiques packed away in my cedar chests, which I had studied, worn, and learned from, were *not* costumes. They were real clothing, worn by real people on a daily basis.

On the very first day of my first French class in college, my teacher made an insightful statement that stayed with me throughout my studies and beyond. "French people," she said, "don't say something in French because they mean it in English and don't know any better. French people say things in French because they mean them in French!"

---

[37] For this reason, even the term *cultural costume* strikes me as rather patronizing, for all that it might be technically correct in anthropological settings. Americans do not refer to a bride's white gown as a costume, so why should we use that term to describe the traditional dress of other cultures?

The clothing of the past was not worn because those creating it didn't know any better; it was worn for a myriad of very specific reasons, practical as well as cultural. I had already learned that corsets support the back and aid in good posture. Likewise, Gabriel had discovered that the small, and very deliberately placed, pocket at the front of a man's waistcoat keeps his watch (an extremely delicate and valuable piece of technology) in the place where it is least likely to be broken, easiest to access, and at the same time most difficult to steal owing to the visibility of its location. Even the tiniest detail had something to teach us about the daily life of history—things we could never learn from books because they were too commonplace or too intimate to be written down, and things that could certainly never be taught by costumes because playclothes often leave out the details altogether.

One of those very important details—more than a detail, really—was the material of the garment. There are legitimate, scientific reasons why natural fibers (as were available in the Victorian era) are superior to synthetics. For example, when moved into a cold, wet place from a warm, dry one, real wool actually creates its own heat by a fascinating physical exchange involving water vapor.[38] Humans have been playing around with synthetic fibers for only around one hundred years, but breeders have been perfecting wool for thousands; and the animals themselves from whom the wool is gathered have been evolving the fiber far longer than that, with nature, "red of tooth and claw," ensuring that the stakes were life and death for optimal material choice.

However, when shopping in twenty-first-century Seattle, real wool proved remarkably elusive. I hadn't quite appreciated how thoroughly plastic fibers permeate the vast majority of winter fabrics currently marketed until I attempted to find pure examples. Scrutiny of entire shops of fabric would generally unearth, at most, one or two bolts of woolen fabric that were not adulterated to one degree or another, and the odds of this being in a pleasing color and appropriate weight verged on nil. Gabriel finally convinced me to order from an online supplier, from which the offerings were far more numerous.

Once the fabric had arrived, I based my first skirt roughly along the same lines of a pattern I had worked out years before for my wedding-dress skirt. As I neared its completion, I asked Gabriel to help me make sure that I had pinned the hem straight around my ankles before I ironed and basted it.

---

[38] Phillip W. Gibson, "Effects of Wool Components in Pile Fabrics on Water Vapor Sorption, Heat Release and Humidity Buffering," *Journal of Engineered Fibers and Fabrics* 6, no. 1 (2011): 11.

From *About Paris* (1901). Illustration by Charles Dana Gibson.

"You know," I reflected, as I modeled the skirt, taking care not to tread on any pins. "The idea that clothes should fit their wearers must have totally gone out the window when women stopped sewing for themselves."

"Hmm?" he asked, circling me slowly to see if I had missed any uneven portions outside of my own field of vision. "How's that?"

"Well," I pontificated, "before, women used to sew their own clothes, so they'd make them fit themselves. Naturally, what's the point of spending days sewing something if it's not going to fit?"

"Mmm-hmm." Gabriel tugged at a panel of the skirt that had gotten hitched up, straightening it.

"But when people started buying stuff, off-the-rack stuff can't fit everybody."

"Well," he pointed out, "they used to sell a lot more sizes in ready-made clothes."

"Yeah," I continued. "They certainly fit better than today, when everyone's supposed to fall into three size categories—small, medium, and large."

"Not that a small is really small anymore," he smirked.

"Right," I laughed. "More like large, extra-large, and ginormous. Anyhow," I continued, brushing a hair off the skirt in progress, "no amount of sizing can take into account that every body is completely different. Some people have longer legs than others, some have wider hips . . . Even if you try to buy something like 'long-leg' jeans, they still don't really fit, because one person's legs might be one inch longer than someone with the same waist size, and someone else's legs might be three or four inches longer. Basically, with ready-made stuff, you can have it fit in one dimension, and all the others are going to be a compromise in some way. They sell clothes these days that are supposed to be 'one size fits all' but what they really mean is 'one size fits nobody'!"

Gabriel nodded and stepped back.

"Oh, you're completely right." He nodded at the skirt, having completed a full circuit of it. "It looks good to me."

When the skirt was finished, I was pleased with the result: a warm and practical skirt, with minimal complications. There was no elastic to wear out or zippers to break: the worst that could happen would be that I might lose a button, but even if I did, replacing one of these was far easier than attempting to repair a more modern fastening like a zipper. I had made the garment entirely for its practicality; I was unprepared for the number of compliments it was to receive.

"It's just a gray skirt!" I told Gabriel in bewilderment one day, having received my third compliment in the course of a relatively short walk. "Why do people think it's so extraordinary?"

He chuckled. "It's a nice skirt!"

"Yeah, but—"

A woman who had been walking the other way stopped us. "I really like your skirt!" she told me, giving it an admiring look. "That's beautiful!"

I smiled and thanked her, but after she'd passed, I shot Gabriel an uncomprehending look. I held my shoulders up, my hands out and palms up. *Why?*

My husband laughed at the gesture.

After the kind stranger had passed out of possible earshot, I resumed the line of conversation. "I mean, why?"

Gabriel seemed to find my whole confusion incredibly amusing. "Not many women wear skirts these days."

"But, if they like them so much, why don't they?"

He shrugged. "They think they can't."

"It's a skirt; it's not a Nobel Prize in physics!"

Gabriel was still laughing over this comment when another stranger crossed over from the opposite side of the street. "I like your skirt!"

My summer dresses had taught me how much freedom skirts can give; having an ankle-length skirt opened up new realms in understanding their usefulness. Coming down just to my ankles—not below, where it would have picked up dirt, but just to them—meant that it trapped a bubble of warm air around my legs, which moved with me wherever I went. Many animals have evolved fur that serves this exact function, trapping warm air underneath guard hairs to act as insulation. As a species, man lost this. It was woman who evolved it anew.

Accustoming myself to daily wearing of a long skirt added another level of grace to my movements, at the same time increasing my awareness of my surroundings. Plunking down unceremoniously onto a public bench would often have meant throwing that much-admired skirt onto city detritus, used gum, or worse. I learned to sweep it up around myself before sitting, a fluid motion that was soon as natural as wiping boots on a mat before entering a home. On uneven ground, I would lift the skirt clear, and after I'd made myself new petticoats (ones I could wear with less anxiety), this action flashed bright silk from under the somber gray wool. (People often think these underskirts are purely decorative; they have no idea of the luxurious sensation that comes of having six yards of fine silk swirling around soft skin.) As all these little subtle movements became second nature from daily living, a new depth was added to my antique clothes on the special occasions when I wore them.

After I'd sewn myself a simple white blouse to accompany the skirt, people started asking me why I was "dressed up." At first, it embarrassed me. There was something accusatory in the question, as though any garment that showed a modicum of care, and was not three sizes too big and off of a Third World assembly line, was shamelessly formal. After a time, though, I grew enough accustomed to the query to answer it in complete honesty. I would cock my head, giving my interrogator my own curious look.

"This is just what I wear."

One of the side effects of wearing nice clothes that were important to me was that I grew more fastidious in my habits. I could no longer simply wipe any grease and dirt from my hands onto my pants and throw them into a series of metal boxes to make electricity wash and dry them for me. (The complaints that came later—about the cost of replacing them when the depredations of the magical decontamination machines wore out the cloth—were also unnecessary now.) Rough mangling by a mechanical device might be good enough for something that fell off a mechanical assembly line, but not for a garment I had labored over for weeks to produce. As they had been made by hand, so they should be washed by hand, and I took great care to minimize the necessity of this chore. I took more caution with my movements, to minimize their picking up dirt, and this care itself added grace.

I was astonished by how long natural-fiber clothing could stay fresh and clean when given a modicum of attention. I had known that polyesters and all their high-end derivatives are petroleum products, but for some reason had never followed the clear logical steps to the realization that plastic clothes quickly become foul to the senses. I had taken for granted the idea that a shirt worn for several consecutive days of moderate exertion would reek to the rafters; it hadn't before occurred to me that this tendency was directly related to a high synthetic content. Natural fibers are far less conducive to odor. My main concern with my woolens was keeping them free of visible dirt.

I started carrying a small glass bottle (a size meant for perfume) of rosewater in my purse, along with an extra clean handkerchief, and used these to clean my hands when washing facilities were unavailable. It became second nature to keep my hands neat after I started wearing gloves; they served as a constant reminder to keep my hands clean, as well as protected them from contamination. Clean hands meant cleaner clothes, since I wasn't passing on soil from other sources.

One of the little girls whom I tutored in English as a Second Language at this time noticed me washing my hands in this way after eating a piece of fruit and took to calling my little bottle of rosewater "hand sanitizer." Given the context in which she saw me using it, this was understandable and I did not correct her. It would have been cruel to pick a pedantic quarrel with a term used by a small child already working through a language that was not her first tongue. There were, however, several significant distinctions. Hand sanitizer kills bacteria: it does not actually clean anything. All the dirt and sticky pollutants on the hands still remain after use. The germs stay behind as well, in blunt point of truth; the fact that they are dead does not make their destroyed corpses magically disappear.

When I had gone abroad one summer as a college student, my well-meaning grandmother had sent me off with a bottle of hand sanitizer. Eschewing the sinks in public lavatories, which I believed at the time to be hotbeds of infection, I had relied entirely on this chemical bottle from Grandma for the first few days, priding myself on my modern hygiene. It took very little time before I started noticing that my hands were covered with a layer of black grime the likes of which I hadn't seen since the days I had played in the dirt as a child. The hand sanitizer had been disinfecting, not cleaning.

Rosewater, by contrast, does what any water does: it breaks up dirt and sugars (such as might be left behind by fruit, etc.). These are then easily wiped away by the useful and high-tech cleaning device known as the handkerchief. As a pleasant side effect, rosewater leaves an agreeable scent behind, too.

I started to wonder how much water and electricity I'd wasted over the years by following my mother's habit of wiping soiled hands on my pants, then dumping the filthy trousers in the washing machine every day. I'm not sure whether it has been enough to drain a lake and power a small city, but I'm certain it's been quite a lot. Simply by taking greater care, I had reduced this consumption dramatically. When I followed out this train of thought to consider it in the macrocosm, it seemed ironic to think that while I live in a society that prides itself on environmental consciousness, in some ways our forebears had a much gentler touch upon the world.

Peterson's Magazine (November 1890).

Walking dresses.

17

"All the Pretty Girls"

Peterson's Magazine (March 1890).

Parisian fashions.

My debut outing in my completed ensemble (after I'd finished the blouse to accompany the skirt) was a shopping trip with Gabriel. There is a large Asian grocery in Seattle, and it was a simple but long-standing enjoyment of ours to make a trip there, sometimes spending hours perusing the fascinating foods and wares before making a small purchase.

Pocari Sweat. Calpis. Bright labels bearing that mishmash of languages that Anglophones in Japan call "Engrish" were one of the many charms of the store for us. As we pointed them out to each other, statements such as "It gathers and it is pleasant" and "The way of using is up to you!" brought smiles to our faces, although our gaily upturned lips were prompted by different motivations. While Gabriel was amused at the unorthodox grammar, my own merriment was born of nostalgia.

Not so very long before, I had spent an entire year teaching English in Komatsu, a small Japanese town in Ishikawa Prefecture on the western shore of Honshu. Divided from Nippon's major metropolises by a massive range of mountains that easily rivals the Alps (all my Japanese friends, even the ones who lived in Ishikawa themselves, considered it to be a remote outpost at the very edge of civilization), Komatsu's residents rarely saw foreigners, and at the private English academy where I taught, I was the only native speaker of the language. A tall, grayish-green-eyed blonde in a country of raven hair and eyes of velvet brown, I grew accustomed to being stared at unabashedly. One day, while visiting the nearby larger city of which Komatsu is a suburb, I went shopping with a friend who was half-Japanese, half-Caucasian, and 100 percent Canadian.

"You know . . ." I told her after a man carrying a small child had passed us, the baby extending a chubby arm ending in a pointing finger toward me the entire time they were within view, "I can never quite decide whether I should feel like a celebrity or a circus freak."

My Canadian friend's mouth turned up at one corner, and she shook her head. Tall and buxom, she received some of the same treatment, although it was moderated slightly by her having her father's dark hair and Asian eyes.

"A little of both," she shrugged resignedly. "A little of both."

On the day when Gabriel and I were visiting the Asian grocery store in Seattle, a bit of the old celebrity/circus freak feeling started coming back to me. In my new clothes and with my corseted figure, people were staring at me. Just as it happened in Japan, a small boy tugged at his mother's coat and pointed at me. A woman started to go down an aisle in the store where I happened to already be, stopped, and simply watched me until I'd passed.

Before I'd lived in Asia, this sort of scrutiny would have horrified me, made me cringe in apology for my own difference. Had I set out on this course at that less-traveled time of my life, continued experience of the same sort might have dissuaded me. Yet, the memories of dwelling in a place where I was so clearly, irrevocably foreign, gave a familiarity to such treatment. Because I had lived in a place where there was no option for me of blending in, regardless of how I was dressed, I did not fear the stares and the pointing as I once might have. It mattered little that the staring eyes, now in my own country, had a greater diversity of color, with blues, greens, and shades of gray joining the browns; or that more, or less, melanin was present in the spectrum of pointing fingers. I knew the behavior. I had lived through a long period when it was simply another normal part of life, and I had grown stronger for the experience.

On this particular day, I wasn't hungry, but Gabriel had skipped lunch earlier. I contented myself with a bottle of exotic dragon fruit juice while he settled down with a scatter-line meal in the store's eating area. Next to Gabriel, and thus just to the right of being directly across from me, sat a very old man. His pure-white hair was carefully combed, and his pale blue eyes had a dreamy alertness as he watched every motion of my form, a slight smile on his face.

I didn't mind his staring, but I thought he might be embarrassed if I drew attention to it. I pretended to take no notice as I chatted pleasurably with my husband. At last, the old man turned to the woman across from him. "She's somethin' outta a book!" he said happily, pointing at me.

I'd assumed the other woman to be his granddaughter, but the way in which she shrugged and barely looked up from her meal caused me to realize that she didn't know him. She was simply a fellow diner at the crowded table.

I didn't want to seem as though I'd been eavesdropping, but this seemed like an appropriate juncture to open a conversation with the lonely old man. I smiled at him.

"You're somethin' outta a book!" he repeated, addressing me this time.

I smiled more broadly and thanked him, blushing.

He told me how wonderful it was to see a woman dressed like me, and how long it had been since he'd seen it. "Is that a twenty-two-inch waist?" he asked.

I blinked, astonished. He had pinpointed my measurement exactly!

"Why, yes. Yes, it is." I smiled again, and he nodded.

"My first sweetheart looked like you," he explained, the dreamy look coming back into his eyes, shadowed slightly by a distant sadness. "She's gone now, of course . . ." He shook his head and that distant pall was banished. "I'm ninety-eight years old!" he told me proudly, sitting up with the proper posture of his age. He was surprisingly tall and cogent for one so advanced in years.

His smile came back and he told me of all the pretty girls he'd known, many years ago. The brightest glow came into his eyes when he spoke of the one who had married him—"The prettiest one of all!"—his wife. I was charmed by the sweet way he described those pretty girls, the obvious enjoyment he took from their memories.

When Gabriel had finished eating and helped me on with my jacket, the old man watched us both with the same happy nostalgia. I thanked him sincerely for talking with us and wished him the best of health as we took our leave of him.

Walking out of the store, Gabriel smiled at my happy expression. "That was nice."

I nodded. "Yeah, he was such a sweet old man."

My dear husband slipped a tender arm around my waist. "You clearly brought back some good old memories for him."

I smiled and laid my head against Gabriel's shoulder as we waited for a light to change.

All the pretty girls.

"I think so."

Hairstyles for dancing.

Godey's Lady's Book (September 1889).

18

Duck the Malls

Peterson's Magazine (April 1890).

An 1890 fashion plate, showing lady waiting on bench with umbrella.

Autumn poured into winter, and Seattle December flooded onto the calendar with all its customary damp. The holidays approached, and another occasion arose for me to visit Olympia. This time I had a logical reason to believe I truly would see an old friend there.

Mairhe had been my neighbor during my freshman year of college, and while we'd made several attempts to stay in touch over the intervening years, we hadn't actually seen each other in nearly a decade. I did know that she was still in Olympia, designing and making jewelry. When I saw that her work would be featured at an event called "Duck the Malls," promoting the work of local artists, I decided another long bus trip was in order.

I didn't dress up in any special way, but by now even my normal clothes were attracting attention. After I'd tracked down Mairhe and we gushed through the customary hugs and pleasantries that inevitably accompany a meeting of old friends, she stepped back, eyeing my coat.

"Did you fit your jacket?" she asked, taking in the alteration immediately with an artist's eye.

"Mmm-hmm." I smiled, unzipping the fleece to show my outfit. "And I made the blouse and skirt."

Her jaw dropped. "Are you corseted under there? You must be!"

I nodded, affirming her assessment.

"I am fascinated by corsets!" she told me, banishing any fear of disapproval I might have had and replacing it with pride at her enthusiasm. "Tell me all about it!"

"Well," I began, "it's sort of like a hug that lasts all day."

She laughed at that, one of her characteristic, effusive laughs that draws everyone around her into the merriment. "I knew you were going to say that. Go on—what else?"

I started to go into the standard questions and curiosities, but she was soon flooded with customers. Not wanting to interfere with her business, I promised to email her and slipped away, returning briefly to drop off a bag of cookies for her before I caught my bus back to Seattle.

The next day I wrote Mairhe the promised email, largely in the form of my most frequently asked questions. I concluded with an injunction to stay in touch, added that we should arrange a meeting soon, and filed the more academic portion of the missive for future use. Despite both our best intentions, it was to be another season again before I would see my old friend in person once more. When I finally did so, it proved to be an interesting encounter involving not only herself, but also the kind lady to whom serendipity had introduced me on my previous trip to Olympia.

At this point in the narrative, however, that meeting remains in the hidden and unpredictable future. I was currently more concerned with the present season, the one of short days and goodwill. Christmas was sweeping into the world with all its customary ebullience.

19

Waisted Flight

"The Game of Travel": *Montgomery Ward,*
1895.

Montgomery Ward & Co. Catalogue, 1895.
Skyhorse Publishing reprint (2008).

We had decided some time previously to spend the holiday with Gabriel's relatives in New Jersey. There was some last-minute scrambling to make schedules mesh as we planned our itinerary, but once we had our plane tickets, Gabriel breathed a sigh of relief. I, on the other hand, did not: flight schedules had me far less concerned than the idea of confronting airport security with three pounds of steel strapped around my ribs. Some modern corset-wearers leave their stays off for air travel, but aside from an obstinate disinclination to let a corporation's security policies dictate my choice of underwear, I had few clothes left that would have fit me without my corset. I needn't have worried quite as much as I did: there was one element of the corset upon which I hadn't counted, one which worked in my favor.

As a globe-trotting student years before, I had grown sufficiently accustomed to the invasive, rough procedures of airport security to absolutely detest them. Were trains a bit faster or ships more economical, I might have renounced air travel long ago, despite the fact that I enjoy flying. As a hassled student clad in denim and T-shirts, I had been legally groped and my luggage torn apart for nothing more threatening than coins and solid-stick deodorant.

With a metal body binding my torso, I feared nothing less than a cavity search. I had neglected to take into account the psychological impact of the corseted form and the perfectly tailored garments with which I had clothed that figure.

Among social species, alpha creatures never question their right to travel unmolested amongst their kind. Subordinate animals know themselves as such, and show their submission—their susceptibility to harassment—by every statement that their body language communicates. As a stoop-shouldered student, my whole posture had been that of a cowering animal. I had hoped that by showing the world how nonthreatening I was, my fellow *Homo sapiens* would ignore me as too weak to bother. In actual fact, the truth was quite the opposite. I should have learned it years before when I'd kept chickens: the lowest animal in a pecking order is the one most likely to suffer ill-treatment. The superior animals are never bothered: they are known to be too ready to retaliate.

Through centuries of culture, clothing ourselves has become an ingrained method of asserting dominance structure within the human pack. Social standing has become inseparably tied to money, family, and education, and we show all these things by our manner of dress. A wealthy, high-class woman with a university education can wear a ten-dollar T-shirt from Walmart, but she seldom will. Similarly, if a modern, uneducated, low-class person happens into fifty dollars in disposable income, they are more likely to spend it on an electronic gadget than on a garment.[39] We mark our social class by our clothes, alpha through omega. Well-tailored garments in quality fabrics declare their wearer to be someone with the means for legal defense when they find themselves offended.

However, there was also something more primitive to it. Deeper than the social cues of dress, this stretches back into the animal forebrain. We are biologically hardwired to recognize certain signs of genetic superiority, and a favorable hips-to-waist-to-breasts ratio in females ranks very highly in the sphere of genetic politics. Good hair is mostly a clue to good diet and nice hygiene, sound

---

[39] Out of curiosity, one day I went into a Walmart to mark exactly what the demographic of Americans who shop there are willing to spend on products. On October 9, 2010, in the Walmart in Auburn, Washington, the prices of various things were as follows: the cheapest articles of clothing were a multiway tie, between socks, panties, clearance-rack shirts, clearance-rack shorts, and clearance-rack dresses, all of which were priced at $3 each. The most expensive article of clothing was a $35 parka made of synthetic materials. By contrast, the least expensive autonomous electronic item available (a cellular phone priced at $39.98) cost more than the most expensive article of clothing. (There were phone cords for $3.46, computer mice for $9.97, and similar cheap gadget components, but nothing that could serve a function on its own for less than the highest range of what people were willing to spend on clothing.) The highest-priced electronic item was an LCD HDTV priced at $1,708. These prices would indicate that a typical Walmart shopper is willing to spend 4,880 percent as much on electronics as they are on clothing!

teeth and eyes aren't seen clearly except at close proximity; but a well-formed figure marks out an alpha animal from a vast distance.

At the airport, I was experiencing how these hardwired responses still dominate social interactions. When I passed through the metal detector the airport's security guards apologized profusely for the inconvenience of the beeping alarm, and treated me with courtesy bordering on deference as they very politely requested that I have a seat nearby. A portion of my mind wondered if the bullies I remembered from prior encounters had since been dismissed—but, no. Nearby the same officials who treated me with such respect were demolishing other passengers' luggage with gleeful deliberateness.

Gabriel had gone on ahead of me, his belt buckle being the only element of his respectable, although modern, clothing that had set off the metal detector. He took charge of our small pile of carry-on items and waited for me a few paces away, watching to see what would occur. I was not kept waiting long before a plump airport matron bustled over to me, a smile on her face. "Do you think it might have been any jewelry you might be wearing that set it off, dear?" she inquired most politely.

I shook my head.

"It was my corset."

The likelihood of several pounds of steel triggering a ferrous-metal detector before a few fractions of an ounce of gold and silver did so did not have a difficult time passing Occam's razor.

Her round face took on a sheepish look.

"I'm very sorry." She added her own apology to the vast quantity of unexpected contrition I had already received from her fellow guards. "But, since it beeped, the rules say I have to wand you."

She asked me to stand upon two painted footprints on the floor, and as she watched my graceful movements, she inquired very sincerely as to whether I was a dancer.

I laughed involuntarily at the question. *Me, a dancer? Me, who had been "the fat girl" and "the klutz"? She thinks that I am a ballerina?* I had no idea the corset had taught me that much poise.

When I answered that I wasn't, disappointment vied with surprise on her face. She took another look at my upright posture, my thrown-back shoulders, and tried again.

"Are you a singer?"

I shook my head, further amused, and she gave me an apologetic smile as she waved the wand over me.

Regulations required security guards to pat any area that causes their equipment to indicate metal. Naturally, this encompassed an area around my entire torso. The pleasant old matron accomplished this with broad swiping motions downward, as though dusting away any invisible contaminants that might have been left by the wand.

"What are you doing to yourself, girl?" She giggled with embarrassment as she felt the stays underneath my clothes. The pat-down completed, she handed me my shoes from the X-ray machine's conveyor belt and sent me on my way with another apology and a friendly wave. Behind her, a small child's soda pop was being confiscated as a security risk.

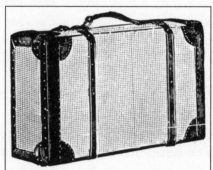

Montgomery Ward & Co. Catalogue, 1895.
Skyhorse Publishing reprint (2008).

20

Straight-Laced Security

Montgomery Ward & Co. Catalogue, 1895. Skyhorse Publishing reprint (2008).

"Across the Continent": *Montgomery Ward*, 1895.

Since New Jersey lies so close to New York and I had never been there, Gabriel and I had decided beforehand that we would spend a few days of our trip exploring the largest city in the United States. I had grown used to second glances and being stopped by complete strangers in my own town of Seattle, but I had expected that in a metropolis of over eight million people, a city that a number of celebrities have chosen to make their home specifically so that they could blend into the crowds, I would merit not a second glance. Gabriel disagreed—and he had been there before.

Our New Jersey relatives had warned us of the bitterly cold wind that roars in off the Hudson, so we bundled up in our warmest winter layers. When we faced that howling wind and I finally understood why it is called *bitter*, I was glad of my antique mink coat, even if it hid my waist. I was equally as glad of the very steampunk, polar-fleece petticoat hidden beneath my wool skirt insulating my long legs. (A real wool petticoat would come later, but such things must be budgeted. For now, the primitive underskirt Gabriel had made for me out of an old blanket kept me warm. Knowing it was my dear husband who had made it for me kept me warmer.)

Gabriel had been right about me standing out, even in New York. People kept stopping me to compliment my skirt and to ask if I was a model. People believing I was a model surprised me even more than the inquiry as to whether I was a dancer had done. *A model? Me?* Gabriel kept encouraging me to show my "blouse" (an excuse to show my waist) to people, and my vanity was petted enough by all these compliments to do so, despite the glacial buffets of Boreas.

We skipped the most clichéd of the tourist attractions and instead visited locales more appropriate to our quietly geeky personalities: the public library, guarded by its twin marble lions of Patience and Fortitude, was first; then a smaller library where I pored over yellowed news clippings about Camille Clifford, the gorgeous Gibson Girl whom I so admired. I was flattered beyond words when an elderly gentleman, who knew nothing at all of my research, approached me when I left my table momentarily and told me I looked like a Gibson Girl myself.

After the libraries came a much-anticipated visit to a very special collection: the museum attached to the Fashion Institute of Technology (FIT). At the FIT museum, the questions as to whether I was a model were repeated by yet more passersby, and as we inspected the nineteenth-century garments on display, more than one person told me that I should be in the exhibit, not just a spectator of it. One elderly man told me that I looked just like the girls who used to ice skate on the lake in Central Park years ago. "They dressed just like you!" he told me, smiling at old memories.

The rest of the New York trip passed in a whirl as fast as the Hudson wind, and we returned to New Jersey rosy-cheeked and fortified with French sweets. We had a lovely time with Gabriel's relatives, cozy in a warm exchange of holiday cheer, while outside piles of snow

Public domain image (early twentieth century).

Camille Clifford.

created a symbolically white Christmas, although they were not quite new-fallen and the holiday was a bit greener than we might have preferred. The only blemish on this Rockwellian idyll was a breaking news story the day before we were scheduled to depart: one that chilled the New Jersey relatives, panicked Gabriel's mom, left my husband unfazed, and made me very nervous.

There had been a bomb scare on a plane flying from the Newark airport—the exact airport from which we were to depart. Eight years on from the decade's most notorious September 11, its events were still strong in the cultural subconscious of the area surrounding New York. It was understandable that a family that was New Jersey born and bred would grow pessimistically melancholy upon hearing of another alleged attack near their home. My mother-in-law feared greatly for our safety on the trip home, but Gabriel and I had no worries on that account. We knew that whatever minute danger might exist from terrorists on a normal trip dwindled to a practically negative figure after a scare, owing to the ridiculously hyperactive fever that turns all security manic after such events. I had no concerns about suicidal lunatics. The security worried me.

Newark is a far less congenial airport than our home base of Sea-Tac. There were no strolling tourists taking in new surroundings with blissful expressions, only grim-faced passengers who seemed to regard air travel not as a marvel, but as a rough business that must be forged through as quickly as possible. Despite being the hub of the Garden State, it somehow managed to seem more gray and forbidding than anything rainy Seattle ever created.

There were fewer apologies about the security this time, as passengers' bags were being dismantled at complete random. (I'm sure that a certain portion of the population applauds the idea of such harassment being entirely random rather than targeted where it might have cause, but really, does it make sense to rip apart diaper bags?) I was ordered into a small glass cubicle, then from there taken to a windowless back room where I was ordered to remove my clothes.

I wonder how far they're going to take this, I thought. My outer skirt came off first, followed by my petticoat. I happened to be menstruating at the time, and had on modern panties to hold my sanitary pad in place. *Not exactly my finest hour, but at least I'm not in pantalets with my rear in the open air,* my internal monologue continued. Next, the two women guarding me wanted my blouse off, so I was down to corset, panties, and socks, with my skirts pooled around my ankles. I tried putting my skirts on a nearby table, but the security guard stopped me. *Great . . . After all that time spent making sure I don't get my skirt dirty, and now it's lying on a grimy Newark floor. Wonderful.*

The shorter of the two women guarding me stood in the corner with a slightly bored look, occasionally casting put-upon glances at her taller colleague. The latter, a brunette with an accent I couldn't identify, kept asking me to do various things, then stopping me as I tried to comply. It seemed clear that she really just wanted to see how the corset worked, but wasn't allowed to ask me to do something that would bare my breasts, which obviously would have happened if I'd removed the corset. *Good. If she doesn't want to see my breasts, she won't want a cavity search.* That's really all that worried me: the dreaded cavity search. She kept standing back, looking quizzically at my stays, then moving forward to touch something or ask a question before stepping back and examining my body again. Her coworker kept giving her impatient looks and telling her, "It's a corset!" This phrase was spoken in much the same tone one might use to state "It's an hourglass!" or "It's a statue!" to a simpleton too ignorant to recognize these items.

Finally the curious guard ran a piece of cotton along all the edges of my body, then let me get dressed again after the fluff had triggered a green light on a large machine. She seemed almost as fascinated by the process of my dressing as she had been by the corset itself. *Well, at least I've added a rather unorthodox history lesson to her day.* I didn't mind her staring at me; I'm not excessively modest, and we had budgeted plenty of extra time to get through security. I was just glad she hadn't wanted to do a cavity search.

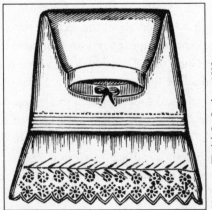

Muslin petticoat.

Montgomery Ward & Co. Catalogue, 1895.
Skyhorse Publishing reprint (2008).

21

Hatter's Logic, and Pinned Perils

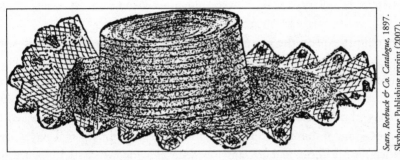

Sears, Roebuck & Co. Catalogue, 1897. Skyhorse Publishing reprint (2007).

An 1897 untrimmed hat, "Ladies' Neapolitan"-style. Price: 98 cents.

After I had made skirts, petticoats, and a blouse, the last item missing from my ensemble was a hat. I had several beautiful antique hats to go with my cherished antique clothing, but my experience in the November rainstorm had made me wary. As I had traveled down to Olympia, I had been full of anxiety about my lovely headpiece, and I shuddered to think of what might happen if I were caught wearing it in an unexpected downpour without an umbrella for protection. My antique hats were utterly lovely—and worryingly fragile. I didn't want to ruin them in Seattle's fickle weather. But I did want to wear a hat every day. My Victorian outfit seemed incomplete without one, not to mention I appreciated the solar protection they afforded. (Years after my grandmother's death, I could still hear her ghostly voice admonishing me at every turn of the elements: "You're hot? Put a hat on!" Then in winter, "You're cold? Put a hat on!" The logic of this had somewhat escaped me as a child, but the lesson had become ingrained deep in my psyche.) For years I had been seeking the perfect hat in shops, pursuing some platonic ideal of chapeau that proved perpetually elusive. I simply didn't care for the modern fashions in headgear, and they seemed only to get worse with each passing season. I wanted a hat, but antique models were too vulnerable for the purpose I had in mind, and I could not rely on modern millinery to provide one suited to my taste.

Gabriel expressed a severe degree of doubt when I announced my intention to make myself a hat for everyday wear. He had never once questioned my ability to sew any other article of clothing, no matter how complicated or exotic, but for some reason hats seemed somehow mysterious to him. He gave me a doubtful look as I studied my velvet Gibson Girl hat.

"How will you make the . . . the brim do . . . that?" He made shapes in the air with his hands.

I smirked sideways at him—very much a Gibson Girl expression. "I just will."

I couldn't explain the mechanics, but I could clearly see the way it would work as I inspected the antique buckram and felt the position of the wires within the cloth. I wondered why it was that he couldn't see it, too.

The creation of the hat caused considerably less frustration than making my blouse. I completed its structure in a matter of a few days, then asked my mom for some of the molted feathers from her cosseted parrots. I sewed these together onto a form of buckram to create a "wing," accented it with glass and crystal beads, then sewed this entire accessory onto the hat, backed up by ostrich feathers.

The first time I wore this hat outside on a walk, I was stopped by a lady who asked if I sold them. I was to find this question repeated again and again. It was occasionally varied by the flattering, "Where did you buy that hat?"

I was walking back from the grocery store one day when a shopkeeper rushed out of her store and stopped me on the sidewalk to ask if I would make hats for her to sell. It was not a proposal that required much deliberation.

Broad-brimmed hats are wonderful at keeping sun off the wearer's face, but they also have a tendency to catch breezes and become upset. The best way of securing one of them in place is with a hatpin, and I was fortunate to already possess some antique examples that had been gifts from Gabriel on previous birthdays and anniversaries. Made for the dual purposes of ornament and of anchoring a hat to a bun of coiled hair, my husband had never had to worry about fit or size when buying these extremely Victorian accessories, which made them an easy choice of present. They seemed to be one of the very few examples of an item from the Victorian era for which one size did fit all: each one of the antique hatpins in my possession was almost exactly nine inches in length.

Initially, I assumed that this was simply the most convenient distance from a hat brim to a lady's bun, reasoning that the head is one of the body parts with the fewest variations between individuals.

As a child, I had been quite fond of an old trope from cartoons and outdated movies, wherein an uppity Victorian woman pushed to extremity removes her hatpin and starts wreaking havoc upon the sensitive parts (usually the rumps) of those around her, to great comic effect. However, as a mature woman, I assumed this old chestnut to have been a complete fabrication created for the value of its humor and having no basis in fact. Correspondingly, when acquaintances commented that one of my hatpins looked like a weapon, I would roll my eyes at what I perceived as their imaginative ignorance. However, as I was researching the history of the hatpin one day, I discovered that not only had *I* been the one in ignorance about its potential lethality, but I also found that the uniformity of sizing I had noticed was, in fact, a legal requirement having nothing to do with head size.

In fact, hatpins really could be deadly—and demise by hatpin was not a pleasant way to go. Records of proceedings from London's Old Bailey court list a surprising number of violent incidents involving what I'd thought to be merely innocuous bits of prettiness. In a 1902 manslaughter trial, Medical Practitioner Richard Foster Owen testified to finding a three-and-a-half-inch length of broken hatpin lodged in an abscess in the victim's left lung during a postmortem examination. After being stabbed through the back with the hatpin later found by Owen, the victim had taken twenty-nine days to die of blood poisoning.[40] In another case, a woman confessed to manslaughter after her husband died a three-month lingering death resulting from a hatpin wound she had inflicted when he accused her of "immoral conduct."[41]

Even when not proving fatal, hatpin wounds could certainly be unpleasant. In November of 1909, when a man was accused of maliciously wounding his girlfriend with intent to do her grievous bodily harm, he claimed to have acted in self-defense, stating, "[S]ome four years ago the woman stabbed one of her old lovers with a hatpin and so seriously injured him that he is ruined for life."[42] The defendant did not specify in which part of the anatomy, exactly, the woman

[40] Old Bailey Proceedings Online (www.oldbaileyonline.org, version 7.0, 08 September 2012), trial of BENSON, Michael (61); PRESTON, Frederick (28); BRADLEY, Margaret (32); EDWARDS, Minnie (28); BENSON, James (35), (t19020505-413).

[41] Old Bailey Proceedings Online (www.oldbaileyonline.org, version 7.0, 12 September 2012), October 1908, trial of COOPER, Elsie Beatrice, (t19081020-31).

[42] Old Bailey Proceedings Online (www.oldbaileyonline.org, version 7.0, 08 September 2012), November 1909, trial of THOMAS, Arthur (31, traveler), (t19091116-34).

had stabbed her old lover and "ruined [him] for life." Considering it makes for interesting speculation.

With such tales in circulation in England, it is understandable that a certain amount of concern might have existed on both sides of the Atlantic. Various regulations of hatpin-wearing were discussed in America,[43] and modern websites devoted to collectors of the antique pins state that early twentieth-century laws restricted their length to nine inches, beyond which they were considered weapons.[44]

I found these historical tidbits fascinating, and I enjoyed sharing them with people, although perhaps the most interesting aspect of modern reactions was the ways in which their responses revealed the individuals' own preconceived ideas. A particularly good example of this is that of a woman who had opened conversation by marching up to me in the middle of a store one day and launching into an adamant lecture on how horrible she thought it was that I was wearing a corset and how she thought it was an awful reminder of terrible things inflicted upon women that were best forgotten. I offered all my usual rebuttals to the stereotypes in her sermon, then tried to defuse the situation by offering a bit of history that I thought (wrongly, as it turned out) might interest her.

Reasoning that someone who had just preached an unbidden ten-minute homily on women's rights might enjoy a suffragette story about women of the past who were decidedly not demure, I slid my exactly-nine-inch hatpin from its place anchoring my hair to my hat and recounted a story I read on the website of the American Hatpin Society. In the early twentieth century, an English judge faced with an entire group of suffragettes requested that the ladies on trial remove their hatpins, fearing they might be used violently. I explained that the suffragettes had proclaimed this an insulting request and went on to explain about the nine-inch-compromise that existed in various places.

The woman in the store glared at first at me, then at the nine-inch pointed steel rod in my hand. "Hmmph!" she concluded. "So that was just another way of oppressing women!" She tossed her head and stormed off.

---

[43] "Law for Long Hatpins: Chicago Council Considers One—Women Want Them for Protection," *New York Times,* March 1, 1910, http://query.nytimes.com/mem/archive-free/pdf?res=FB0712FB355416738DDD A80894DB405B808DF1D3.

"Short Hatpin Law Asked for by Women," *New York Times,* January 27, 1911, http://query.nytimes.com/ mem/archive-free/pdf?res=F50D12F63C5517738DDDAE0A94D9405B818DF1D3.

[44] "A Brief History of Hatpins," The American Hatpin Society, http://www.americanhatpinsociety.com/tour/ history.html.

"Modern, Vintage & Antique Hat Pins," Miniatures & Collectibles, http://www.miniatures-and-collect-ibles.com/hat-pins.html.

I was honestly glad to see her go, but I couldn't help but feel that her parting remark had been a slightly odd one. I gave the stiletto-like object in my hand a quizzical look before replacing it in my hat, being careful as always not to stab myself with it. Asking people on trial for disorderly conduct to give up potential weapons while in the courtroom constitutes oppression?

Historically, the English made a clear distinction between suffragists, well-behaved women (and men, as well) who worked within the law to obtain voting rights for women, and suffragettes, who favored more violent tactics. Early twentieth-century English suffragettes were prone to sensational acts that a modern court would consider terrorism, arson and vandalism by acid being two especial favorites.[45] When suffragette Emily Wilding Davison was brought up on charges of arson in January 1912, she already had six prior convictions (including assaulting the police) related to the suffrage movement. (It was noted at her trial that, outside the movement, she was a "highly respectable" woman.) Intended targets were mostly inanimate objects, such as ballot boxes and unoccupied property, but people could be, and were, injured if they got in the way. For example, in a 1909 case, suffragette Alice Chapin partially blinded a schoolteacher with acid when she smashed a tube of the destructive liquid over a parliamentary ballot box.[46] Ms. Chapin testified that her target had been the ballot box, not the man she blinded, but some attacks were more direct, and the most radical posed legitimate dangers to public figures and policemen carrying out their duties. In 1909, Winston Churchill was almost killed when a suffragette attacked him with a whip and tried to force him into the path of an oncoming train.[47] In 1913 London, suffragettes attacked police detectives with

---

[45] Old Bailey Proceedings Online (www.oldbaileyonline.org, version 7.0, 08 September 2012), January 1912, trial of DAVISON, Emily Wilding (36, tutor), (t19120109-20).

Old Bailey Proceedings Online (www.oldbaileyonline.org, version 7.0, 08 September 2012), March 1912, trial of PITFIELD, Eilen (45, nurse), (t19120319-14).

Old Bailey Proceedings Online (www.oldbaileyonline.org, version 7.0, 08 September 2012), May 1912, trial of PANKHURST, Emmeline (53); LAWRENCE, Frederick William Pethick (40, barrister), LAWRENCE, Emmeline Pethick, (t19120514-54).

Old Bailey Proceedings Online (www.oldbaileyonline.org, version 7.0, 08 September 2012), March 1913, trial of STEVENSON, Ella, otherwise Ethel Slade (53), (t19130304-67).

Old Bailey Proceedings Online (www.oldbaileyonline.org, version 7.0, 08 September 2012), April 1913, trial of HOCKIN, Olive (32), (t19130401-19).

Old Bailey Proceedings Online (www.oldbaileyonline.org, version 7.0, 08 September 2012), April 1913, trial of PANKHURST, Emmeline (53), (t19130401-67).

[46] Old Bailey Proceedings Online (www.oldbaileyonline.org, version 7.0, 08 September 2012), November 1909, trial of CHAPIN, Alice (45, no occupation), (t19091116-84).

[47] William Manchester, The Last Lion: Winston Spencer Churchill; Visions of Glory, 1874–1932 (Delta Trade Paperbacks, Dell Publishing, 1983), 403.

hatpins[48]—precisely the sort of assault the judge in the earlier trial had feared. Given previous cases of killings and men being "ruined for life" by such objects, my sympathies were rather with the judge.

As I ran the tip of my forefinger over the jet bead that topped my hatpin, I pondered the rather natural question raised by all this history: Why do modern people choose to view women of the past as demure victims of oppression?

People who are unhappy with the situation in their own lives may project that unhappiness elsewhere and exaggerate it in those imagined places. They thus comfort themselves through a feeling of dominance over those other places, forgetting that they themselves created their peculiar pictures of it. In the twenty-first century, it has become politically incorrect to proclaim that one's own nation is vastly superior in every way to all others. Those who denigrate contemporary cultures are denounced as xenophobes or racists; yet we have no word for those who treat the cultures of the past in this same manner.

"The past is a foreign country: they do things differently there."[49] Yet foreign countries have ambassadors and diplomats to speak for them. The past is far less able to defend itself; it cannot formulate rebuttals. Perhaps that is why it is such an easy victim. Thus, an opinion has become common that everything about the present is superior to anything that existed in the past. It is difficult for many people to grasp that lifestyles may have been different in the past, and yet still completely satisfactory to those living them. History has no emissaries.

I hold a university degree in international studies. When I was a child, I wanted to live in the Victorian era; when I had grown, I wanted to be a diplomat. In some ways, what I was becoming could be considered a combination of both: an ambassador for history.

Not that all diplomatic incidents are pleasant.

The more my appearance drifted away from the narrow constraints twenty-first-century America defines as normal, the more commonly I found myself verbally attacked by complete strangers for no other reason than that I happened to look different from how they felt I should.

Deciding to treat myself to a small splurge one day, I walked to a nearby café and bought a large drip coffee—considered by many (especially in Seattle) to be a daily necessity, to my penny-pinching nature this was an indulgence. I laced it liberally with half-and-half and settled down happily near a sunny

---

[48] "Escape of Mrs. Pankhurst: Rearrested after a Struggle; Detectives Attacked with Hat Pins," *The Age* (Melbourne, Australia), July 23, 1913.

[49] L. P. Hartley, *The Go-Between* (London: Hamish Hamilton, 1953). This is the first sentence of the prologue.

window to work on some writing I had brought with me. When I smelled patchouli oil and the corner of my eye saw a garish Indian print on the loose and unseasonable skirt of a white woman striding aggressively toward me, I withheld a sigh. Sadly true to my predictions, the hippie closed the gap between us and loudly berated me for oppressing the entirety of womankind.

I took a sip of my coffee.

Um, good morning to you as well? Why yes, it is fine weather we're having.

Sears, Roebuck & Co. Catalogue, 1897. Skyhorse Publishing reprint (2007).

Nineteenth-century illustration of coffee.

Inwardly, I sighed again, although I did not allow myself to show sign of it. And I had *so* been enjoying my coffee. I casually sipped the creamy-brown drink, being very deliberate about consuming it neither more quickly nor more slowly than I would have had there not been a human patchouli-bomb shouting abuse at me from across my table. She spouted an entire laundry list of stereotypes and misinformation, which I rebutted with memorized citations and quantitative data whenever she paused for breath. Her invariable response to these was first to call me a liar, then either repeat the very same stereotype or move on to an equally false one.

When I told Gabriel about the occurrence that evening, he paused for a moment, then laughed. "Who was oppressing who there? Really!"

I had noticed the irony myself. Sadly, the incident would become an oft-repeated one, in assorted places and with a different random stranger as antagonist, but with an otherwise unvarying itinerary. I eventually learned to expect it at least once every two or three weeks, although I sorely wish the expectation were realized less often than it is.

And yet despite the critics, I carried on; and the people who were receptive lent encouragement that helped me stay the course. It was rewarding to help individuals reexamine their opinions of Victorian culture, just as it had been satisfying to present an image of Americans that did not follow the stereotypes of my home country when I had lived abroad in Europe and Asia. Occasionally, opportunities now arise to invite study of both historical and geographical ideas of culture, and these are particularly edifying.

The Korean girls whom I tutored in English were especially fascinated by my hats. One day, after a lesson had run over its appointed time, the girl with whom I was working looked pointedly at the clock, then with a smile slid a sly look over toward my broad-brimmed, royal blue hat with its sparkling glass beads and bright parrot feathers. Since the lesson was over, I lifted the hat from the shelf to which I had removed it upon entering and asked if she wanted to try it on. She responded immediately with vigorous nodding and a broad grin.

The hat was, of course, far too big for the small girl's nine-year-old head, but like any child trying on grown-up clothes, that mattered to her not at all. She gazed at her reflection in a little hand mirror as proudly as the preening parrot from which the feathers atop the hat had originated.

"You know," she said as she handed the hat back to me, "before I met you, I had never seen a person who looked like you before."

I wasn't sure quite how to take that remark. "Do you think that's a good thing, or a bad thing?" I asked.

"A good thing," she smiled. "It's different. I like it."

Her mother might have overheard us from the hallway, or perhaps she had simply been recalling memories of a similar style. As I halted by the door to put my shoes back on (having removed them, of course, upon entering an Asian home), she fetched my jacket for me and, watching me, held it a moment.

"The first time I saw you, I thought, 'Such a small waist—is it, possible?'"

I had never actually talked about my corset with her before, and I was a little nervous. The family was one of those interesting cases of professional parents who had moved their entire family to a foreign country for a year so that their children could learn its language (in this case, English) in context. The father was a medical doctor, and the mother, the woman currently asking about my waist, was a psychiatrist. I wondered what an Asian psychiatrist would think of a choice that many of my own compatriots considered crazy.

I smiled nervously, considering it highly unlikely she had encountered a corset before, and wondering how on earth I was going to explain it across the language barrier. "It's because I wear a very traditional garment," I started slowly, "called a corset."

"I know," she nodded quickly. "We call it, 'ant-waist.'"

Relief broadened my smile and amusement brought a small giggle from me. "It has a similar name in English: 'wasp-waist'!"

We both laughed, and she agreed that a wasp was a bit like an ant, at least in terms of their waistlines. As I put on my jacket and returned home, I felt a great relief that, as opposed to the American strangers who accosted me on the street to tell me they thought I was crazy, this Korean psychiatrist, whose opinion I respected, merely considered my lifestyle to be a cultural curiosity.

Historical ambassador wins small victory.

Sears, Roebuck & Co. Catalogue, 1897. Skyhorse Publishing reprint (2007).

"The Latest Star Shaped Hats." Trimmed hat, 1897. Price: $3.25.

22

Veiled Glances

Fashionable veils, 1897.

In the old days, "fair" was synonymous with beautiful. There is a reason Snow White's stepmother asks her mirror in the old story, "Who's the fairest of them all?" A light complexion was the sign of a woman noble enough in birth not to have to work in the fields. Tanning for aesthetic purposes didn't start until the twentieth century, when most jobs had moved indoors into pallor-inducing circumstances and the prerogative of the upper class had shifted from the privilege of staying out of the sun to the leisure time of going out and lounging in it.

I have the approximate complexion of boiled cod, and any sun exposure beyond that of the rainiest of Seattle days tends to burn me like cream on a griddle. (I went to Spain once and got sun poisoning. The girl with whom I was traveling spent our entire time at the beach frolicking in the Mediterranean Sea, while I passed the time huddled under a parasol on the sand, slathering SPF 45 sunblock thick as frosting on a cake over every reachable body surface and repeating the application every five minutes. By the end of the day, Jackie was fine, but my legs were covered with heat rash so severe it looked as though I'd been trekking through poison ivy.) Anything to mitigate my annual summer boiled-lobster impression seemed like a good idea.

Victorian ladies guarded their skin with long, light clothing, gloves, hats, parasols, and veils. In particularly bright circumstances, an oriental fan could be spread into service as an extra shade. I had long clothing, and hats were no longer a problem. A lot of vintage gloves bought online had yielded three pairs of well-fitting, easily washed 1950s-era summer gloves, which neatly guarded the skin below the cuffs of my long-sleeved blouses. I owned a beautiful, antique parasol from the 1880s, which Gabriel had bought me as a gift. I even had some silk fans that I brought back from Japan. The only thing lacking was a veil, so I looked into my options.

I had never seen a surviving Victorian hat with a functional veil. It is rare to find any Victorian silk garment at all in good condition (which was part of what made my peach petticoat such a rare find). Victorian technology treated silks with heavy chemicals to give them a more luxurious "hand" (texture) when examined in shops, and over time these chemicals rotted the fibers. (Actually, eighteenth-century silk garments tend to survive in much better condition than their later counterparts because they were treated with less aggressive solutions.) Victorian veils were more or less exclusively silk, and the typical problems of chemical damage were compounded by their inherent gossamer fragility. Very few withstood the passage of time. Even if I had come across an antique veil available for purchase, I would not have bought it: the stress of wearing some-thing so delicate with intrinsic historical value would have rendered my nerves as fragile as the fabric.

The biggest hurdle to making my own veil was ascertaining suitable material. I had used tulle to stiffen the petticoat of my wedding dress, and I knew it would be far too stiff and scratchy for something that would be hang-ing close to my face. Silk veils were a staple in Victorian romances, but these tales' descriptions tend to focus more on the heroine's dewy eyes than on technical millinery terms for the type of silk involved. I knew that charmeuse would have been too thick, and the thought of brocade for these purposes just made me laugh. I had no experience with crêpe, but a bit of research made me realize that it was equally out of the question. Organza seemed more suited to a Scheherazade impression than a Victorian lady, and chiffon . . . I hesitated over chiffon. It was the thinnest material with which I had experience, but something still seemed not quite right about it. I waited, hoping something better would present itself.

It was Gabriel who, researching as always, read of silk tulle's difference from its synthetic counterpart. I had never even seen silk tulle, as it had been driven to virtual extinction by twentieth-century development of cheap nylon and rayon look-alikes. Whereas synthetic tulle was available at any fabric or craft store for the bargain price of $1.49 per yard, all of Gabriel's research had yielded a single supplier of silk tulle: mail order only, $75 per yard. I shuddered over the price, which was equal, at that point in my life, to about two and a half weeks' worth of grocery money, and hesitated.

By all accounts, silk tulle was much softer than the synthetic stuff I had used in my wedding trousseau, and it had been the standard fabric for Victorian veils. I watched the weather grow progressively brighter and

Godey's Lady's Book (January 1890).

Fashion plate showing a woman with a veil.

sunnier as April waned and the year waxed into May, and I finally decided to take the plunge. The fabric was expensive, but I did not believe it to be overpriced for what it was. Silk is a costly material, and naturally I understood that rarity value does add expense. If it helped keep me from yet another summer of solar-powered radiation burns, it would be well worth the price.

The smallest quantity in which the silk tulle could be purchased was by the quarter yard. (Naturally, small pieces had a higher cost per square inch, but I didn't need much.) I wrote to the supplier and placed an order for one quarter yard of green silk tulle to make a veil for my smaller hat and half a yard of navy blue to go over my larger one.

In a twist that emphasized exactly how small-scale the seller of this fabric was, my order was delayed for a week due to an unspecified "family crisis."

I couldn't help reflecting upon how the mighty had fallen: a material that had once been a major industry had shrunk to such a niche market that the problems of a single family could render it unavailable. Thinking back on the entire wall of nylon tulle I had seen the last time I visited a fabric store, I blamed the rise of synthetics.

When veiling material did come, I quickly decided it was worth the price, as well as the wait. The synthetic tulle I had used in my wedding petticoat was so sharp I had needed to underlay it with an extra skirt of satin because I feared the tulle's unkind edges would snag my stockings. That artificial tulle had borne the same resemblance to this material that a plastic pool toy does to the water lilies floating upon Monet's ponds at Giverny.

If Arachne had met with Iris, the rainbow goddess, after Athena turned the presumptuous weaver into a spider, the resultant web might have been something like this material. Soft as a kitten's breath, it lay on my hands with the weight of a butterfly come to rest, like a mist that swirled around me without intrusion. I lifted it up and watched its fey dance upon the air, laughing with delight.

I was beyond nervous as I cut the veils to shape, but they were simple to tack onto my hats. It felt a bit like the sensation of walking through a spider's web: light, unhindering, but present. The first time I wore one of them, it took very little time for me to comprehend the meaning of a "veiled glance." My eyes wanted to half-close against it, and my lashes fluttered on demurely lowered lids. It took some acclimation, but I came to enjoy the soft feeling against my cheeks, like a flutter of butterfly kisses.

Not long after the addition of veils to my hats, I visited a public street fair. Since crowds get so dense at these sorts of public gatherings, I'm afforded a bit more of an opportunity to hear comments meant to be private asides. One of my favorites was a little girl who, tugging at her mother's hand and pointing at me, called out, "Mommy! Look at her face! Mommy, look at her hair!" The adorable little thing had never seen a veil before.

I folded back the silk tulle from my hat and smiled at the little girl. "Hello." I gently waved a gloved hand at her. She hid behind her mother's legs, then peeked out shyly. "I like your butterfly," I told her, referring to a brightly colored picture painted on her cheek. She hid behind her mother's pants once more, but I saw a smile on her face before it disappeared.

Further on, a youth of about nineteen or so did a full arm-swing point at my waist, his hand starting at the level of his sideways baseball cap, then diving down parallel to his baggy pants. "Yo, man! That's some old-school shit there!" I couldn't help laughing.

Since I started wearing a veil, Muslim women smile at me a lot more. Actually, the increase in approving grins by women in head scarves started when I began wearing ankle-length skirts and long sleeves; the addition of veils simply took it up a notch. I can never quite decide whether this is appropriate or ironic.

Nearly everything I've ever read about Middle Easterners coming to America for the first time makes a point of discussing the culture shock they feel at seeing how much skin is visible on Western women in public. Modesty of female dress in Muslim countries is a popular topic of discussion in both politics and media. (When I lived in France as a visiting university student, there was heated debate over whether certain traditional Muslim garments should be banned in public.)

My Victorian-style clothes protect nearly all my skin; nonetheless, I really would not call them modest. They cover, but they do not conceal. My cotton blouse covers my arms to the wrists, but it is so tight over the torso that it requires hooks and eyes between the buttons to prevent the latter from popping off due to the strain. I've owned spandex shirts that didn't fit me as snugly. My wool skirt falls in long folds from my hips, but it traces and accentuates those hips in a way of which trousers can only fantasize, and it's held corset-tight against my waistline, showing off my body in several senses of the term.

Various religions have specifications regarding ways to cover the body in public, but I was fairly surprised when certain people started assuming my clothing must have a religious basis. Some will query through an entire index of theological possibilities, each more inappropriate than the last. Are you a Jehovah's Witness? No. Are you a Mennonite? No. Are you Amish? The Amish call themselves the "Plain People"; what exactly about what I'm wearing strikes you as *plain*?

If there truly is a world religion somewhere in the globe whose canons require the wearing of corsets, I would be genuinely curious to hear the details of it. Mostly, such inquiries just reflect the questioner's deep-seated ignorance about diverse beliefs. The pathos inspired by such cultural denseness is generally moderated by a bit of amusement, which is fortunate for my temper and sanity, although it would be impolitic to show it.

One of my Mormon friends was flabbergasted when I told him of how, a few hours earlier, a drunken frat boy had seen me crossing a parking lot and started screaming, "Look, it's a Mormon! A Mormon! Mormon!" Over and over again while pointing at me.

Hearing the story, my Mormon friend stared at me. "Why?"

I shrugged, chuckling. "Some people think I dress the way I do because of a religion."

"But why—" My cat jumped into my friend's blue-jeaned lap and started pawing at his T-shirt. "—that one?"

I rolled my eyes, shaking my head at the same time. "Why any of them?"

Pretty Kitty, whose own favorite form of evangelism (especially in warm weather) was the gospel of "Spreading the Fur," moved on to indoctrinate Gabriel. My atheist husband gave her a few quick pats and then set her back onto the floor.

"Why is it so hard for people to grasp that people can have deep-rooted convictions that have nothing to do with religion?" he asked.

I laughed. "I wouldn't exactly call wearing a corset a 'deeply rooted conviction'!"

"You believe people should have the right to wear what they want," Gabriel replied. "And you have a strong belief in the importance of history, don't you?"

"Well yeah, but that's different from religion."

"I don't think it is."

I like to tease Gabriel that history is his religion. Certainly he spends as much time poring over arcane texts as many theological scholars, and more than most casual religious devotees. He likes to point out that a person can have deep-seated faith in something without involving supernatural beings; and he prefers to base his ideas about truth on documented evidence and historical examples rather than on scriptures and deities.

I have my own ideas about divinities that differ from those of my husband; however, I do agree with him that history is important and worthy of respect, that it is something that deserves to be taken seriously. This shared respect is the reason why we both inwardly shudder at falsehoods. It is why we refuse to play along with stereotypes we know to be inaccurate, even if we sometimes maintain silence through them for the sake of diplomacy. It is also why, when the opportunity arises, we enjoy imparting truth and educating people.

Fashion plate.

Godey's Lady's Book (November 1889).

23

Crisis for Beauty

Godey's Lady's Book (February 1890).

An 1890 fashion plate showing women sharing sweets.

Whenever we heard of a new exhibit about the history of clothing, hope would spring eternal that the interpretations would be based around primary-source data, rather than simply regurgitating secondary-source stereotypes. Admittedly, when we learned of one titled "Suffer for Beauty," our hopes did not spring very high, but we reasoned that we should at least give it a chance.

The exhibit did provide some entertainment, if only because it appealed to our sense of the ironic. There is something intensely amusing about labels that describe women in photographs as oppressed or tortured when the women themselves beam out from the sepia tones with bright expressions of joyful vigor.

When we came to an electrical device in the corner, my eyes grew very wide. I glanced over at Gabriel, then riveted my eyes back on the display as I asked in a low undertone, "Is that what I think it is?"

My husband was grinning from ear to ear. "Yep! Definitely." He chuckled. "We knew they were a Victorian invention."

"Well . . . yeah . . ." We had actually watched a documentary (checked out from the University of Washington's library) about such devices only a few days previously. This model was even quite similar to one that had been shown in the educational film.

"But . . ." I looked at the sign near the door proclaiming the exhibit's "Suffer for Beauty" title, the modern interpretive labels with their sensationalist claims of how torturous historic beauty regimes had been. "It doesn't exactly fit in with their thesis, does it?"

It was a vibrator.

I glanced over to where a lump-shaped baby boomer was regarding a measuring tape that had been shaped into a circle at the eighteen-inch mark. "Can you imagine?" she was asking, shaking her head. "How awful!"

"I suppose someone who's never worn a corset might be willing to believe what they're told about them, but . . ." I let my thought hang in the air for a second, my voice was barely above a whisper. I gestured toward the device, which had been invented for the explicit purpose of relieving female tension. "A vibrator?"

I wasn't even whispering now, just mouthing the words, but it was easy enough for my husband to read my lips under the circumstances. "How could anyone think that equated with suffering?!" I asked him.

A lesbian couple came up behind us and looked curiously at the exhibit. The older of the two cocked her head at the vibrator, gave her partner a milder version of my own incredulous expression, then looked back at the device. "Now, what do you suppose. . . ?"

Gabriel, ever the helpful historian, chirped up. "It's a vibrator!" he told them in his most academically cheerful tone.

The women laughed, then nodded at each other. "Well, I thought so," said the older one, "but then I thought, 'Nah, couldn't be!'"

"No, it is," Gabriel confirmed.

Whatever my expectations had been when I'd left home that morning, I certainly had not anticipated discussing vibrators with a couple of lesbians in the middle of a museum. Truly, one never knows where educational paths might lead.

The vibrator is a marvelous representative case of an item whose dates invite reanalysis of the perceived prudishness of the Victorians. The electromechanical vibrator was invented in 1883 and was specifically adopted by physicians to bring about what they termed a "crisis" to alleviate female tension. Personal electronic vibrators for home use followed as home electricity became more common, and the personal electronic vibrator actually pre-dated the electric iron by ten years, the vacuum cleaner by nine years, and the electric frying pan by more than eleven years.[50] (This timeline makes a rather interesting challenge to the idea that the Victorians considered housework a higher priority than sex!) As "catalogue culture" swept the nation and items became available for purchase through the postal system, companies such as Sears, Roebuck & Company started selling vibrators via the convenience of mail order. It wasn't until fairly late in the twentieth century that certain states (Texas, Virginia, Colorado, Georgia, Kansas, Louisiana, and Mississippi) legally banned the sale of vibrators. One might pose the question: Which time period was more prudish—the one that invented the vibrator or the one that banned it?

The query is, perhaps, an unfair one; I do not believe that any given generation or culture is truly either more or less prudish than any other. (If that were honestly the case, certain societies would cease altogether.) Humans are mammals, with all the biological imperatives that implies, and those drives do not change from one generation to the next. A more reasonable question then becomes: Why does modern society think the Victorians were repressed?

Certainly, the monarch who gave the society her name was no prude. Queen Victoria was a great admirer of male beauty, and historian A. N. Wilson goes so far as to call her "highly sexed."[51] So, why does the 1999 *Oxford*

---

[50] Emiko Omori and Wendy Slick, "Passion & Power: The Technology of Orgasm" (documentary), 2008.
[51] Wilson, A.N. *The Victorians*, New York: W.W. Norton & Company, 2003. p. 57

American Thesaurus of Current English list "Victorian" amongst the synonyms for "prudish"?

Perhaps part of the answer lies in a common condition: few people enjoy pondering the sexual congresses of their own grandparents. Logic dictates it must have happened at least once, but most people really do not like to think about it. Attaching the couple involved with the label of prudish makes it easier to push the image out of one's mind. However, this is really too simple of an explanation to be credible on its own, so what other contributing factors are involved?

Misunderstanding of culture might be part of it. Modern American culture associates sex with skin: the more epidermis is shown, the sexier an image is generally considered. (Pornographic films are even colloquially known as "skin flicks.") Yet to the Victorians, luxurious clothing and sumptuous materials were considered sexy. Some of the most alluring sounds in the nineteenth-century world were the rustle of silk and the creak of whalebone; and cheap romance stories of the nineteenth century often give accounts of characters' clothing in detail verbose enough to rival twenty-first-century romance novels' descriptions of breasts and buttocks. A twenty-first-century American, seeing a figure clad chin to toe in velvet, might see a prude, while a Victorian seeing a woman wearing only a few torn threads might see a pauper.

It might be appropriate to briefly address a shift that has taken place in people's preference in erogenous zones. Some people wouldn't even think to list the waist among these sexual zones any more, but in the nineteenth century, it was one of the most erotic spots on the female form. Breasts had a stronger association with motherhood, but the waist—the waist was exciting. In one of the most popular novels of the nineteenth century, a woman describes how she would have seduced a man in her youth, starting with her waist: "If I was a young woman still, I might say, 'Come, put your arm round my waist, and kiss me, if you like.' . . . and you would have accepted my invitation—you would, sir!"[52]

There is also the issue of a private life versus a public one to consider. The Victorians placed a significantly higher value on privacy than do modern Americans; in all likelihood because—modern concerns notwithstanding—it was a rare commodity for them. For a Victorian of either sex to occupy an entire dwelling place by his or her self was unusual, and quarters could often

---

[52] Wilkie Collins, *The Woman in White*, rev. ed. (1860; repr., New York: The Heritage Press, 1964), 450.

be quite cramped. (Lascivious modern interpreters have been known to make a great deal of fuss over references to Abraham Lincoln sleeping with other men while traveling, but the reality of the matter is that sharing bed space in such circumstances was fairly common. Rich and upper-middle-class married couples could have private bedrooms as a sign of afflu-ence, but in the poorest classes, entire large families were known to share a single bed.) Gabriel and I had spent a significant amount of time discussing the ways in which helping each other dress must have affected people's relationships; the privacy issues in a culture where

From *A Widow and Her Friends* (1901). Illustration by Charles Dana Gibson.

the highest-paid servants had intimate knowledge of their employers' semi-nude forms must have been very interesting indeed.

The matter of hidden intimacies versus public display was in the back of my mind one day when a triflingly minor mischance brought it back to my attention. I was switching places with another student in my massage class, and as she removed her own linens from her bag, I noticed the clinging crackle of recently laundered items. She flicked one of the sheets open and something the electric dryer had evidently Velcroed to it via static fell loose: a small bit of polyester satin and pink lace. She gave a nervous little giggle, then glanced to her left and right before grabbing her underpants off the floor where they had fallen. It occurred to me that in the nineteenth century, clothing of all sorts would have been visible to the public on any sunny laundry day. Indoor drying racks existed (I own an antique example myself) and were certainly useful for rainy days and during freezing weather, but conducting the entirety of wash-ing and drying a large family's laundry indoors is a cramped process, to say the least.

The only way to maintain privacy in such settings was by setting up men-tal screens where no physical ones existed, to engage in self-discipline and actively not do certain things. Staring at the neighbors' damp underwear was unacceptable. (Yes, of course it happened; but society agreed that it should not.) Groping an employer's buttocks while fastening buttons just a few millimeters away from them? To use a Victorian phrase, "My dear, it was simply not done!" Overfamiliarity with a stranger or an acquaintance while sharing sleeping arrangements at an inn was likewise "simply not done!" These constant choices to act with decorum were ways people protected themselves and each other; they were mores that guarded privacy in a world where it could have been easily invaded.

Despite many modern fears about invasion of privacy, we actually have far more of this commodity than our recent ancestors did. Private quarters are significantly more common, and certainly private beds are taken for granted for all but lovers. Imagine the scandal that would ensue if a modern candidate for public office were to share sleeping arrangements with a political partner! Even siblings complain if they are expected to share a bed beyond a fairly young age. (Current Washington State law not only legally requires that a foster child have a private bed, but furthermore goes into great detail about the parameters of that bed and of the room where the child sleeps.[53] Any private bed, regardless of parameters, would have been a tremendous luxury to a foster child in the Victorian era, never mind the room.)

Technology such as that of the Internet makes it very easy to share information, and people forget that such sharing is voluntary. Transactions regularly occur where the individuals involved are represented by little more than the numbers of their accounts, and websites like eBay make it commonplace to exchange large sums of money between people known to each other only by pseudonyms. Yet in a sort of interesting cultural foil to this, people very openly choose to post private opinions and pictures of themselves on public forums. Even opinions that can cause damage to careers or relationships if they are seen by unintended audiences, and photographs that can be compromising, are often willingly put out for general viewing. Perhaps the twenty-first-century phenomenon of Americans flinging private affairs out into public view can be traced to the fact that it has become easier for us to achieve privacy.

---

[53] Washington Admin. Code § 388-148-0260, Washington Admin. Code § 388-148-0265, Washington Admin. Code § 388-148-0270.

Like the Victorians, I have never felt any shame in showing my clean laundry, but neither am I in any rush to air the dirty variety. Correspondingly, I choose not to stare at the metaphorical dirty laundry of others. People sometimes believe I am hard of hearing, or somewhat stupid, because more and more frequently I show no acknowledgment of the rudest remarks. It is not that I do not perceive them; it is simply that I discipline myself to draw my veil against them.

Godey's Lady's Book (February 1890).

Sharing information, Victorian-style: This fashion plate depicts one woman handing another her calling card. These were small, usually decorated, cards printed with a person's name and possibly one or two other details such as which day of the week they accepted visitors at their home.

Calling card (late nineteenth century).

24

A Year On

Chrisman Collection (circa 1891–95).

Photograph of unidentified woman.

Over the winter, I kept in sporadic touch with the pleasant-faced woman whom I had met at the women's suffrage event in Olympia. Mary Lee (we always spoke her name as one unit, as though her given and surnames were a joined piece) was immensely curious about our antique clothing collection, and in February we arranged an opportunity for her to view it. This simple afternoon of showing off was to blossom into quite a series of adventures.

We showed her all the treasures we had accumulated over years of saving and searching. (Most of them had been presents to each other on special occasions, such as anniversaries, birthdays, and Christmases.) She exclaimed over all of them, but was particularly taken by my mourning outfits. This rather surprised me, as I actually thought them to be my less impressive pieces. I had one in cotton and one in silk, and although they were nicely ruffled and tucked, they had always struck me as less pleasant than some of my other items, as they had been designed for bereavement. They showed off my figure to advantage, and I had done a passable job of making my repairs to them discreet, but still . . . They were entirely black, and not the sort of thing a young wife wears without some tragedy in her family. Mary Lee, however, loved them.

As soon as I'd taken the first one out of my cedar chest, she had stopped talking mid-sentence, and simply stared. She held the pose for an awed pause, and I wondered what she found so striking about the item. Finally, she spoke.

"There is a picture," she explained, "of Susan B. Anthony wearing that exact dress!" I passed it to her with a smile, and she took it with the air of a devout accepting the Shroud of Turin. "The exact one!" She almost whispered, glory filling her features.

It wasn't literally Susan B. Anthony's dress, of course, but a great deal of mourning clothing was strikingly similar. (The nineteenth-century convention of special clothing during bereavement had actually started the custom of mass-produced, ready-to-wear clothing. It would have been unseemly to start sewing mourning clothes before a death, but after a relative's demise, social convention required their instant appearance.) I was later to learn that Susan B. Anthony lost her favorite sister shortly before visiting the Washington Territory, so it was natural that she would have been photographed in black during her visit here. As part of this ensemble, she had worn a little black bonnet, and when Mary Lee saw my similar hat, she went into comparable raptures.

Gabriel and I had, by this point, seen a number of presentations alleging to be historical fashion displays. They had all fallen short of our high hopes, and many had promoted outright falsehoods. We wanted to give our own presentations promoting history, not erroneous stereotypes. We explained this desire to Mary Lee, and she agreed to help us. Thus, our adventures began.

Our first project was an appearance accompanying an exhibit opening at the state historical museum. Mary Lee helped us arrange the matter with the museum officials and specifically requested I wear what she called my "Susan B. Anthony outfit." Gabriel spent a great deal of time choosing his own ensemble and finally settled on a suit contemporary with my dress. I knew that there would be questions about my corset, and so I revisited the letter I had written to Mairhe several months before and tweaked it into a general question-and-answer broadsheet to hand out to the curious.

I invited Mairhe to the event, as well as all my other friends. Gabriel and I grew increasingly giddy contemplating the event, and we awaited it with most eager anticipation. All our conversations seemed to come back to it; we were effervescent with excitement.

Determined to make a good showing of ourselves, we both started researching suffragists and women leaders of the nineteenth century. Gabriel, the MLIS librarian-in-training, provided fodder for these researches in the form of towering piles of texts from the University of Washington's extensive library system. Early in my examinations of these venerable tomes, I turned a page and burst out laughing.

"Hmm?" Gabriel asked from the next room, where he was writing a paper. "What is it?"

I was laughing almost too hard to explain a coherent answer for my mirth. "Just come in here," I invited between guffaws. "Take a look at this."

"What is it?" Gabriel came over behind my seat at our table, looking around our tiny kitchen for something more worthy of such hilarity than the grim-faced photo in the dusty book before me. But that was exactly what had me laughing so hard. "What?"

"Just take a look at this!" I tilted the book toward him, starting to draw my chuckles under control.

"Yeah . . ." He recognized the picture, but he hadn't caught on quite yet. "It's Susan B. Anthony."

"Yeah!" I agreed, my laughter renewing itself. "And what do you notice?" I pointed.

"She's wearing a corset!" Gabriel smiled, starting to be affected by my merry amusement. "Of course she would be."

Of course she would be.

It was true. In the nineteenth century and early twentieth centuries, nearly all Western women wore corsets. The knowledge did not diminish my amusement in the slightest.

Susan B. Anthony (right).

Public domain image (1897).

Harriet Tubman.

Public domain image (nineteenth century).

"What do you think the really rabid, 'corsets oppress women!'–style feminists would think if they bothered to notice that? They worship Susan B. Anthony! She's like, the Supreme Deity to them! How could they possibly square her wearing a corset with all the nasty stereotypes they push about them?"

Gabriel gave the question a slight, sideways shrug. "I think they just don't understand what they're seeing."

"But it's so obvious if you know what a corseted figure looks like!" I blurted.

"Well, yeah." Gabriel tilted the picture, examining it. "But most people don't. They just think, 'Oh, people looked different back then.'"

"The women looked different because they were wearing corsets!"

"Oh, I know. It's not like humans spontaneously evolved into drastically different creatures when corsets went out of style. But people don't understand that." He shrugged, handing me back the book. "You should copy it."

Still amused, I went back to my reading. Later, when I came across a photo of Harriet Tubman wearing a corset, I cracked up even harder than I had over the Susan B. Anthony picture. I remembered Ellen's desultory comment, which I had heard ignorantly reiterated so many times: "Fine for the women who had everything done for them!" Imagining that comment made about the woman in the picture before me, I laughed so hard I nearly fell out of my chair.

By an interesting coincidence, the museum event was scheduled for the day after my birthday. This made it exactly one year and one day after my first experience with corsets. A year on, I privately took stock of my waisted year, which had been anything but a waste.

I had gone from a thirty-two-inch waist to a twenty-two-inch measurement around the outside of my corset. My shoulders never ached anymore, as they had on occasion from poor posture and the detriments of bras. My metabolism had increased: whereas I had long had difficulty motivating myself to physical exertion, now I disliked inactivity. My digestive system was functioning on a much more comfortable level, since I was taking more care with my meals and making them more balanced. I myself was more balanced, having learned the graceful steps of walking atop curved french heels. I had a wardrobe of pretty clothes and caring for them had taught me to be fastidious in all my habits, more particular care of my skin and hair among them. I had gone from grumbling to the world that I didn't care about my looks while hypocritically hiding from mirrors to learning that there is no shame in being able to turn that glass into a sycophant. My head was high, and I enjoyed the admiration I saw directed at me. My thirtieth birthday, a cornerstone birthday, and a year on from my first corset, I understood that the gift I hadn't wanted had transformed me into everything I had desired of myself.

Concerned over traffic, we left for Olympia quite early on the morning after my birthday and arrived hours before the museum opened. There was a small note on the main entrance instructing individuals with museum business outside the public hours of operation to approach through the back door. Following this advice, we soon found ourselves ushered inside, through what had been the old service entrance when the museum had been an upper-crust home.

The museum volunteer who had allowed us entrance glanced me over, from hair to heels. "Well! That is quite the outfit!"

I looked down at the very plain clothing I had made myself: white broadcloth blouse, gray wool skirt. *She ain't seen nothin' yet*, I thought privately. My amateur replicas could make no claims of skill when set against the antique garments Gabriel was carrying in a well-sealed garment bag. *Wait until she sees—*

"You must be dying in that!" the volunteer continued, breaking in on my thoughts.

"No." I smiled as I shook my head. I had developed a good metaphor recently, and I was actually quite proud of it. "A corset's just like a really good pair of shoes, really. A good pair of supportive shoes is the best thing in the world for your feet; but if you'd gone barefoot all your life and someone suddenly gave you a sturdy pair of hiking shoes, they'd seem like torture and you'd wonder why anyone would ever wear them. Once you're used to them, though, they're the most comfortable thing in the world and you wouldn't want to give them up."

She gave me the sort of cautious look usually reserved for bedlamites on day passes and quickly slipped down a side passage. I looked around to find where my husband had gone. The museum had originally been a private mansion, and it took a bit of wandering to locate him.

Once I had tracked down Gabriel, our next task was rather more difficult than finding our way through the complicated corridors: we had to get dressed. My own outfit was fairly straightforward, and in essence not dissimilar from what had, by this time, become my daily clothes. The main difference was simply that I had to be a bit more careful with the delicate old fabrics than with the sturdy newer clothing. Gabriel was the one who had a truly difficult task in front of him.

I was largely dressed and fussing with my shoes when a knock came lightly on the dressing room door.

"Can I just grab something really quick?" a soft voice asked.

"Oh, sure!" I called out, tightening a bootlace. I didn't mind if another woman saw me with one stockinged foot.

"Wait!" The plea was voiced with an almost desperate intensity, and I looked over to see Gabriel in his shirtsleeves—and not much else. Victorian men didn't wear what would be called underpants by modern standards.[54]

---

[54] Boxer shorts came out in 1925, and jockey briefs were not introduced until the 1930s. Long underpants had existed, but simply tucking the long tails of the shirt into the trousers was an option as well (and the one that Gabriel had chosen on this particular occasion).

"Oh, wait, wait!" I called out, but the door was already opening. Gabriel ducked behind the table and I rushed in front of him, spreading my skirts as a screen. He gave me a slightly hurt look after the young woman had left the room, smirking. After all, I was the one who'd invited her in.

After Gabriel had managed to don trousers, collar, collar buttons, cuff links, waistcoat, tie, tiepin, watch (complete with chain and locket fob), glasses, shoes, bowler, and finally, gloves, we were at last ready to present ourselves to the public. I had already run out to the bathroom and back several times throughout his dressing, although I'd tried to be discreet about it. We made quite a respectable pair as we strode out into the drawing room of the old mansion, still slightly empty and with a hushed atmosphere.

As soon as the public started arriving, we found ourselves drawing a curious crowd, the way that perfume draws honeybees. Gabriel was a bit more at home amongst the buzz of queries, and I found myself largely hanging back, doing my shy best to look picturesque. My main concern was not to draw too much ire from the author who was signing a book on suffragettes, as she clearly did not seem happy about the large crowd flooding toward us and dwarfing the trickle of attention she was receiving at her book table.

This was our first experience with an event at which our presence had been formally invited, and that formality inspired an initial switch of attitudes, which I had not expected. Gabriel, usually the quieter half of us, dove into academic expostulation with the happy air of a seal hitting saltwater. I, on the other hand, was struck by timidity. I stood ready to answer any questions with cheerful profundity, but felt I was out of my depth when no questions came. It was merely our presence that had been requested, no presentation and no laid-out obligations. The lack of structure planted a strange discomfiture of idleness in me, which a straightforward task would not have done. Gabriel chatted away merrily with a trio of fascinated women who followed his every statement and tracked his every move, while the larger crowd surrounding them shifted in and out like the breath of a living creature; I lingered on the outskirts, wondering what to say and shyly blushing at the compliments of grandfathers who said I reminded them of heroines in stories.

I found myself rescued by the arrival of a dear friend. I had invited her to the event along with nearly my entire circle of acquaintances, but since she lived several hours away, I had not expected her to attend. It came as a delightful surprise when she walked through the door with her new husband.

Robin is one of those wonderful women with a personality like granite bedrock: she has a quiet dignity that holds calm and steady while all the more mercurial sediments are erupting into metamorphosis. Seeing her enter, I rushed over and embraced her comforting frame like a tide-swept swimmer clinging to dry rock.

"I'm so glad you could come!" I told her earnestly, probably with something in my tone of an earthquake refugee grasping at sturdy footing.

She must have sensed my bewilderment because she chuckled reassuringly. "Of course!" she said, taking in the situation with a grin. "No problem!"

An 1890 walking dress.

Godey's Lady's Book (April 1890).

With Robin and her husband to show around, I had the firm comfort of a concrete task. Leading them around the exhibit soon drew a crowd, and I was relieved when the questions finally came. Perhaps none of the other attendees had wanted to be first to address me as I stood apart in stark black (Mary Lee had specifically requested I wear my mourning outfit—or as she described it, my "Susan B. Anthony outfit"), or perhaps it was simply the subtle magnetism of my friend's steady personality, but I soon found myself apologizing to Robin as she quietly withdrew with a grin, and I was left confidently addressing a crowded audience of questioners.

After a time, speeches were made about the exhibit, and we all withdrew to tea in the dining room. Having skipped lunch, I gobbled down tiny, sugar-dusted cakes between questions. One particularly sweet old man told me I reminded him of the women in his favorite Western stories, the mysterious woman who stepped off a train into town and always, always fell for the hero of the story.

Near the end of the event, another old friend appeared, this one slightly more expected. Mairhe came in just as most of the event attendees were leaving, and she watched with a jovial amusement as the event wrapped up.

"Sorry I didn't come earlier," she apologized, explaining that she'd had to drop off her son. She retreated with me back to the dressing room as I changed from my delicate antique dress into my everyday clothes for the return trip home. As I undressed, she asked me a number of intelligent questions about corsets, still expressing her earlier curiosity. Mairhe had recently become pregnant with her second child, and we discussed the anatomical science behind the changes in a woman's body from pregnancy versus the changes from corsetry. (The changes imposed by a laced form are actually far less dramatic than those caused by gestation.) I had removed my mourning dress and was stripped to my stays when the first museum docent from earlier walked in on us. She examined me with a critical look from hair to heels.

"You don't really wear that all the time!" she stated emphatically, indicating the corset.

"Well, actually, I do," I informed her, slightly irritated.

"Why would you do such awful things to your body?" Her tone was that of one addressing a lunatic found injecting depleted uranium with a nail gun.

Mairhe charged to my defense. "Actually, we were just talking about how it makes less of a difference than being pregnant does." I felt a wave of pride as she stuck up for me, remembering why I had so valued her friendship back in college.

"Well . . ." The antagonist took a few steps toward the door, and groped for a response. "It's not like women are pregnant all the time!"

Mairhe gave that argument a smirking laugh. "Some women are."

The other woman's eyes darted back and forth, she retreated farther toward the door, then attacked the subject from a different angle. "Well!" she huffed, folding her arms in front of herself. "You can't deny that it's an exaggerated shape!"

I shrugged. "That's the point."

"But it's not normal!"

She had retreated so much by this point that she was—barely—through the door, so I took control of the handle. "That's why I like living in a free country." I shut the door on her.

Mairhe rolled her eyes at the firmly shut door. "Do you get that sort of thing a lot?"

I sighed. "Sometimes. Mostly from idiots, so I try not to let it bother me."

She shook her head. "It's the same thing when you're pregnant. It's like your body no longer belongs to you or something."

A discreet hand cradled her belly defensively. She wasn't showing yet, but she did have one child already, so she spoke from unwelcome experience.

"Perfect strangers want to touch you and ask if you're taking your vitamins—like it's any of their business. *Are you taking your vitamins?*" The last was a muttered aside, as though directed toward remembered busybodies. "They even try to take food away from you that they don't think you should be eating—I'll damn well eat a tuna-fish sandwich if I want to eat a tuna-fish sandwich!"

I remembered the advice surrounding seafood from my childhood. "They used to say that children had to eat fish to make their brains develop properly." I had read fairly recent studies that still supported this idea; they even insisted on the benefits of piscine protein during pregnancy, concerns about mercury notwithstanding.

Mairhe nodded, agreeing. "And God forbid you should try to order a glass of wine with a meal. They'd probably call the cops or something."

I remembered my French host-mother from my foreign studies, lecturing me and the other *étrangères* girls about the importance of alcohol to women in maintaining cardiac health. I pulled on my modern petticoat.

"Everyone has so many different ideas of what constitutes a healthy lifestyle, it's pretty ridiculous to try to inflict your own opinions about it on a stranger." I paused, holding my blouse. "And even if it were unhealthy—which I don't think corseting is—what business is it of theirs, anyway?"

"Yeah, exactly: none. It's not affecting them, so what right do they have to complain about it?" She leaned back, folding her arms.

"The funny thing," I continued, pulling on my blouse and threading its shell buttons through their holes, "is that the people I get the most adamant objections from about the corset are the women—and it's *always* women—who are the same ones who'd be the first to say 'Hands off my body' about other issues."

Mairhe shook her head, taking a deep breath. "It's crazy. I wonder if you've heard about a campaigner for body issues . . ."

Our conversation grew increasingly academic as we cited and discussed various sources. Gabriel returned and Mairhe helped us repack the car. She gave me a big hug before departure and promised to see us at our next event.

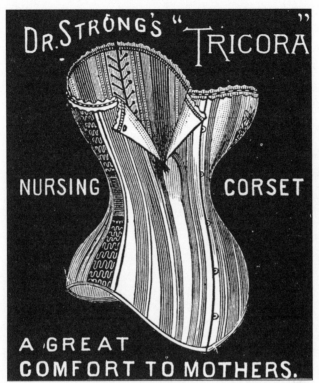

Montgomery Ward & Co. Catalogue, 1895. Skyhorse Publishing reprint (2008).

"Tricora" nursing corset. Price: 90 cents each.

25

A Victorian Lady's Dressing Sequence

Sears, Roebuck & Co. Catalogue, 1897. Skyhorse Publishing reprint (2007).

An 1897 *Sears, Roebuck & Co. Catalogue*
illustration of underwear.

Mary Lee had arranged three events for us, each of them slightly different. The
next was scheduled for several weeks after the first, and we used the interceding

time to organize and rehearse our presentation. This was to be a formal presentation of a Victorian lady's dressing sequence in all its layers, from the inner-
most intimate garments to the outer winter finery. I would be starting in a corset and pantalets (with modern panties underneath the latter to retain decency
in front of an audience), and Gabriel would act as my "lady's maid" while we
explained each item subsequently layered over these. By the end, I would be
dressed in a full winter visiting outfit, complete with cape and muff: a Victorian
lady prepared to go calling.

I was very much looking forward to the presentation, but it would be a
falsehood to say there was not a certain amount of anxiety laced into the idea
of appearing publicly in my underwear. I felt a little silly for this nervousness.
After all, the corset alone covered nearly as much flesh as a one-piece swimsuit,
and the pantalets I'd be wearing came down nearly to my knees. I'd be showing
significantly less *peau* than most women on modern beaches—as long as there
were no clothing malfunctions. This was my biggest concern: besides her rather
psychotic price increases and timing delays, my last corsetière had created figures with far too little room in the bust, cut so low in the cups that my bosom
could—and did—fall out on occasion. I had no desire to reenact Janet Jackson's
infamous Super Bowl blunder in front of a live audience. However, the corset
is such an integral and intriguing item of a Victorian woman's wardrobe that
I would have been remiss in presenting the sequence if I hadn't shown stays to
the audience.

I practiced motion in front of a mirror, experimenting with the exact
optimal position for holding my shoulders back in proper Victorian posture
without pulling my bosom loose of the mal-fitting corset top. For extra
security, I ordered yardage of "swansdown" (actually turkey down formed
into a fluffy boa, although the Victorians would have had actual swan feathers as a high-end trim, with cheaper turkey feathers offered as an inex-
pensive alternative marketed under the same name). I carefully sewed this
along the bustline of the corset I would be wearing for the presentation,
which added several inches of concealment to the top of the garment. I gave
Gabriel strict instructions to get the corset cover over me as quickly as possible, and we practiced the sequence in our apartment, going over the entire
presentation, but practicing this initial rapid-cover even more than the rest
of the dressing.

Once I was reasonably confident that I could manage this initial stage
of the presentation without inadvertently imitating Gypsy Rose Lee, my

anxieties calmed down by a significant extent. I scripted out the points we wanted to be sure to cover in our presentation, and we continued refining our speeches. Besides practicing the presentation inside and out, I poured myself into publicizing it. I invited nearly everyone I knew, however ancillary the acquaintance. First, all my friends were invited, as well as my family. I contacted casual acquaintances stretching back to high school, and friended people on Facebook whom I hadn't seen in more than a decade, specifically to extend invitations. I asked people to invite their friends, even going to the length of writing to an old buddy in a different time zone to request that anyone he knew still in the area be invited. I printed out flyers about the day and, keeping a supply in my purse, handed them out to everyone who complimented my outfits.

Our first event had been attending an exhibit opening; this second appearance would be a presentation to accompany a benefit event for local artists. Since we would be traveling more than 120 miles in a single day for the sake of this event, it seemed only sensible to take full advantage of the situation, so I decided to ask the officials in charge how far they were willing to extend the definition of "local."

I had, by this point, been writing books for several years, and binding them by hand for a portion of that time. The finished products were beautiful works of art, hand-sewn and bound in covers ranging from cloth, to leather, to silk. One showed off real seed pearls sewn onto silk charmeuse representing tidal foam, while on another (in whose plot bicycles played a major role) I'd hand-embroidered tire tracks and bordered the title with crystal. The event officials were delighted when they heard of my books and said that I would be welcome to set up a table from which to sell my books when we were not actively presenting our dressing sequence. The upcoming day grew increasingly anticipated with every added excitement.

One of our neighbors, Yukiko, expressed an interest in seeing us present; she was a sweet, kind soul (and we wanted more people anyway), so we pressed her to come. When she fretted that she had no transportation to Olympia, we offered her a ride. At the time, it seemed as though we were doing her a favor, but by the end of the day, we would develop a tremendous appreciation for the copious help she cheerfully provided. On the morning of the event, we piled ourselves and our carefully packed clothing into a borrowed car, then drove down to the state capital in high spirits.

Yukiko helped us carry our various garment bags, boxes, and accoutrements into the museum, along with my stock of books and accompanying supplies. It took several trips, and even before anything was properly set up, I was grateful for her help. By the time the day was over, I was to find that gratitude expanded by orders of magnitude.

While I set up the bookselling table, Gabriel sought out the office where we would be getting dressed for the presentation. (Rather, I should describe it as the office where he would be getting dressed. I would actually be getting undressed there, stripping down to my corset before descending the building's grand staircase for the presentation.)

I sold a respectable number of books once the artist's event opened. Yukiko offered subtle but very helpful assistance by steering people in my direction. She took over the table for me several times when I had to check on details about the dressing sequence, or when she had spotted particular delicacies appearing on the refreshments table and encouraged me to partake in them. I was quite lucky to have her minding my nutritional needs in this way; we had skipped lunch on the long ride down to Olympia, and it would have presented entirely the wrong image if I had passed out from hypoglycemia mid-presentation. I had spent more than a year trying to disabuse people of such stereotyped notions as corsets causing fainting spells; the last thing I wanted was to give them a false support of this image simply because I had missed a meal.

Mary Lee arrived and verified last-minute details. Having an actual, concrete task in front of me, I was much calmer than at the last event. Nevertheless, as the clock hands turned to the time of the presentation, I shouldn't deny that there were a few butterflies in my stomach, competing for space with my nibbled tea cakes and strawberries.

It was my custom at this time to wear my nineteen-inch corset (vanity sizing—the actual size was twenty-one inches) with approximately an inch and a half of open area at the back between the two

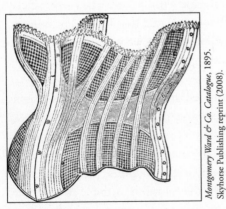

Montgomery Ward & Co. Catalogue, 1895. Skyhorse Publishing reprint (2008).

An 1895 ladies' summer corset, made of openwork material for coolness. Price: 40 cents.

halves of the lacing panel. Immediately before the presentation, I asked Gabriel to cinch it down that last increment of space, closing it completely.

He grinned, followed my instructions, then asked with an inquiring look, "Is that going to be okay?"

I took a breath, assessing the condition of my body. I smiled and nodded at Gabriel. "Ready."

He went down first, into the museum's main reception area, and explained the nature of the presentation. I waited upstairs amongst the exhibits, feeling very exposed in nothing but corset, panties, and pantalets, and ducking behind a display when a young man passed by.

At last I heard my cue from Gabriel: "And so, without further ado . . ."

I descended the grand staircase, stepping lightly on the carpet in my bare feet. "The corset was the foundation of a Victorian lady's wardrobe," I explained, treading carefully. "It gave the appropriate shape to her figure and provided support for her other garments."

Gabriel met me at the base of the stairs, corset cover in hand, exactly as rehearsed. I reveled in discreet relief that there had been no mishaps.

"This is a corset cover," he explained, tying it behind my back as I angled away from the audience. "Its function was to protect the dress from the metal clasps of the corset and to soften the corset's lines . . ."

We continued in this manner through an entire winter outfit: corset cover, garters, stockings, inner petticoat, crinoline, outer petticoat, boots, bodice, skirt, watch, rings, earrings, hat, cape, and muff. Mostly we used actual antiques from our collection; when showing the few exceptions to this (such as the garters), we explained the reason for the substitution. (Nineteenth-century garters, for example, had elastic made of natural rubber, which would have long since lost its elasticity.) In the case of the boots, Gabriel showed off our nineteenth-century antiques (which didn't fit me), while I laced up my modern replicas (which did).

Mairhe arrived partway through the presentation and took up a position at the back of the audience; her little boy beside her behaved remarkably well for a child so young. Mary Lee beamed from a seat front and center, and some of Gabriel's classmates perched in a corner. Yukiko took pictures throughout the lecture, in addition to watching over the table of book sales while Gabriel and I were indisposed. Speckled as it was with such a favorable bias, it would have been difficult to picture a more amiable audience. When I finally stood in full regalia, enrobed in furs, wool, and silks, we received a round chorus of applause.

Fashion plate.

Peterson's Magazine (March 1890).

26

Fifty Years of Fashion:
A Model Performance

Sears, Roebuck & Co. Catalogue, 1897. Skyhorse Publishing reprint (2007).

Catalog illustration.

The third event that Mary Lee arranged for us was the most ambitious. We were to be the entertainment at a "pink tea" Mother's Day fund-raiser, and we'd be presenting fifty years of fashion, from the 1860s through the 1910s. We would start with Gabriel modeling his earliest outfit, an itinerant Irish preacher's suit from the 1870s. We would each model three outfits in total (my own including an 1870s mourning outfit, an 1890s tea gown, and a linen dress we had dated to 1905), and end the timeline with Gabriel in a seersucker suit with a straw boater hat.

Since the event would take place during Mother's Day weekend, I offered to buy my mom a ticket to come see us. Wanting to be nice (since it was a gift, after all), I gave her a choice of activities for which I would pay: I would buy her a ticket to the high tea so that she could watch her daughter and son-in-law presenting or I could take her to the zoo. She opted for the zoo. We tried not to be offended that she preferred watching the funny monkeys to seeing us.

Maternal indifference notwithstanding, the event was sold out some time in advance and we spent weeks putting our presentation together. Sangmi, one of the little girls whom I tutored, learned of it (probably from her grapevine of friends, among whom there was a boy Gabriel gave lessons to history), and asked me if my mother would be going.

"Well . . ." I explained about my offer and my mom's response. Sangmi squinted, then cocked her head at me.

"If I were a grown-up," she informed me, clearly examining a situation she found odd in the extreme, "I'd rather see my kids than see monkeys!"

I sighed, shrugged, and directed her attention back to her grammar.

The idea behind the presentation was a fairly straightforward one—ambitious, but straightforward. We would model a series of outfits from the late nineteenth and early twentieth centuries, using the clothing as visual aids while we talked about the ways in which fashions had changed. We knew it would be difficult with only two of us as models, but we judged that we were up to the challenge. We forgot that fate often enjoys turning a moderate challenge into a much bigger one.

Since this presentation was much more complicated than our last and would involve a number of changes of clothing, the group for whose benefit we were performing arranged for a helper for each of us to aid us in getting dressed. Mine was a sweet young college girl, who *oohed* and *ahhed* over each article of clothing.

The organization for whom we were raising funds allocated us the spare lavatory as a dressing room. Though this was somewhat suboptimal, we decided we could make do with it. There was no way we could have anticipated what an absurd problem was to arise halfway through the presentation, because it would be so far outside the realm of reason.

The presentation of the first few outfits went beautifully. Gabriel showed off his suit from the 1870s, which had once belonged to an itinerant Irish preacher. The audience loved all the detailed work on it, most especially the gold shamrocks on its silken lining, and the "lovers' pockets." This type of pocket was *de rigueur* on Victorian men's frock coats and cutaway coats. Designed for tucking away gloves in a place where their bulk will not interfere with a man's silhouette and the fit of his coat, these pockets were located at the back, in the tails of the garment. Their hidden location made them convenient for hiding things, such as clandestine letters, hence their nickname.

My mourning outfit was similarly well received, with hushed exclamations of shock rippling through the attendees expressing amazement at the way it showed off my figure.

Even before we had timed everything out in our numerous practice sessions, we had known that our biggest challenge would be Gabriel's changes of outfit. There were so many layers and complex fastenings involved (not to mention the ties) that there was really no way around it. My dresses were much simpler, and it was my job to keep us on schedule. As Gabriel walked into the presentation hall in his 1880s business suit, I glanced discreetly at the clock. We were running a bit behind our ideal timing, but I knew I could make it up on the next change: my upcoming outfit was a simple tea gown, a one-piece flannel wrapper. It would take no time at all to don—barring extraneous circumstances.

This was the place in our carefully prepared presentation when something so absurd transpired we could not possibly have anticipated it. I had just gotten out of my mourning outfit and was in my underwear when an angry knock sounded on the lavatory door. "I have to use this bathroom!" called a belligerent woman's voice.

My helper and I looked at each other, at my half-naked form, and at the fragile antique clothing carefully arranged over every available surface in the makeshift dressing room. *Is she kidding?*

I poked my head out the door. A dumpy old woman glared at me, with much the same expression I imagined she had turned on the Grim Reaper several decades previously, before saying that she was too old to have truck with him and slamming the door in his face.

"Let me in!" she insisted crossly. Then she looked at all the clothing carefully arranged in sequence for our presentation. "You have to move all this stuff!" she snapped. "Hurry up!"

"There's another bathroom across the hall." I pointed to the door labeled WOMEN, not three feet behind and three to the right of her. She had walked past it.

She looked at my indicating hand and scowled at me. "I can't use that one! You have to move all this stuff! Hurry up!"

I gave my young helper an incredulous look. *Is this dame for real?* I glanced down the hall to check that there was no one to see me running around in bare feet and underwear, then darted across the hall, glancing into the ladies' room.

It was more than three times larger than our makeshift dressing room and it was totally empty.

"There's no one in here," I told Grandma Biddy, holding the door open for her. "There are three stalls you could use! We'll help you in!" The last statement was offered in desperation. The clock was ticking, and this was taking far, far too long.

"I can't use that one!" the crone repeated, pushing past the meek young helper. "Move all this stuff! Move it! Move it!"

Oh, for land's sake! My own grandmother's version of profanity came back to me. If I'd had the presence of mind to step back and view a very illogical situation from a logical viewpoint, I simply should have refused: told the woman this room was unavailable and gone onstage. However, she gave every indication of an intent to urinate all over my precious antiques if they were not moved at her command. And even stronger than this implied threat was the force of training drilled into me from childhood: that old people must be obeyed, no matter how ludicrous their instructions.

Ticktock, ticktock!

I was keenly aware of the havoc this interruption was creating with my timing as the helper and I hurried to shift a path to the spare toilet while the crone hissed at us. When I finally threw on my tea gown in the hall and darted back out to the presentation area, I was so flustered that my carefully prepared words flew away like notes blown off a podium by a gale. The audience looked at me expectantly and I groped through my mind, trying to gather the mental cards of my dropped speech.

"This is a tea gown," I told them, desperately trying to remember all the information I'd practiced and had perfectly queued up in my mind before the lavatory incident. "It's made of cotton flannel, and a woman would have worn it for entertaining at home . . ."

When I ran dry of information, I trailed off into ancillary branches from my main trail of thought.

"And as long as we're talking about entertaining . . ."

I picked up my calling card case from the display we'd arranged at the front of the room. Going through those customs bought me a few more minutes. Gabriel still hadn't appeared.

"And you'll notice the silhouette of this dress, so this seems like a good time to bring up the corset . . ."

This was really stretching, but at least it was a topic about which I could keep up speech for a while. Still no Gabriel.

When my husband finally arrived, I inhaled a discreet breath of relief. He would later explain that while I'd been grasping at straws up on stage first to recall and then to immensely prolong my speech, he'd been waiting on the old crone's interminable biological business before he could gain access to his next change of clothes, now horribly jumbled after the hasty rearranging.

After the massacre that had been made of our timing, I half-expected to be booed by the end of the presentation. Contrary to my expectations, we were applauded brightly. Later, Mary Lee would politely point out that we had run over our allotted time, but the audience had loved it.

Women swarmed up around us following the question-and-answer session. A pretty, young brunette told me, "I didn't know a modern woman could look like you!" The sentiment was taken up and repeated by several in the crowd.

Why couldn't a modern woman look like me?

"Well," I explained, "it takes a lot more than a hundred years to really evolve different body shapes. We can do everything they did."

There was something sadly wistful in it: to see these twenty-first-century "emancipated" women yearning after a freedom over their bodies, which their great-grandmothers had possessed, but which modern society had convinced them they could never have. It felt like a liberating rebellion to explain that they could.

They asked a number of questions about corsets and my experiences with them. Many suggested that I should write a book about it all. My mind turned upon this, and I hesitated. I had written adult novels and a children's picture book, dabbled in poetry, and won minor awards for my short stories, but . . . a memoir? About me? I'm boring!

I looked around at the bright-faced women smiling at me. I blushed.

"Oh . . . I don't know about that. Who would read it?"

A chorus of laughter met my befuddled expression as eyes turned pointedly to my linen-lace dress, my twenty-two-inch waist. They glanced amongst themselves and the answer chimed out the same from all sides: "I would!"

Godey's Lady's Book (October 1889).

An 1889 fashion plate.

27

Loose Laces to Tie Up the Tale

Sears, Roebuck & Co. Catalogue illustration.

When I was a child, there was a special popularity for "found object" scenarios in children's stories. The specific details were subject to variety, but the general plot was always the same: an ordinary (or more often, less than ordinary) person finds some magical object and by using it can transform into a superhero. In the early days, the corset felt a bit like that. Not only did the lines of steel and protective cloth feel physically like putting on armor, but it transformed my body, posture, and stance just as much as any superhero costume. Clark Kent just took off his glasses to become Superman; I had something that metamorphosed my entire body. Within those magical silken curves, I faced the world with a different attitude. The world in its turn saw this and changed its own stance regarding me.

Like those beloved childhood superheroes, in the early days I often felt I was leading a double life. Before it became a constant I never removed, I wondered what people who had never seen me in my corset would do if they suddenly encountered this other aspect of myself. (What would Diana Prince's friends think if they met her at the grocery store in her Wonder Woman tights?) Yet, when I did see it, I found that their reactions did neither more nor less than reflect the inner nature of their characters, confirm values already established. The suspicious and the antagonistic remained as they always had: suspicious and antagonistic of this piece, as they were of all things. My friends remained my friends, appreciating me for all the things they had always appreciated in me. The constants in this human experiment had remained consistent: it was me who was the variable.

When I opened my twenty-ninth birthday present and saw what the wrapping contained, it never occurred to me that this object of silk and steel would open up opportunities. The idea of a life where photographers stopped me on the street to ask me to model for them was even farther removed from my reality than Seattle is from Ishikawa. (As I mentioned earlier, in Japan, a stranger had—once—stopped to take my picture, but at the time I was the only blonde in a city of about fifty thousand people, and I was holding a fifteen-pound turnip.) But it does happen.

I was strolling alone through a springtime street fair a little more than a year after all this had started when a hand gently tapped me on the shoulder from behind. "Excuse me—"

I turned around. A dark-haired man approximately my own age smiled at me.

"I was wondering . . ." He looked down, then back up, and smiled quickly. I thought he was going to ask about the corset, so his next words surprised me. "I do fashion photography, and I wondered if you'd let me take your picture?"

I smiled, shocked but flattered. "Of course!"

He grinned, then looked left and right. There were thick crowds all around—less-than-ideal photography situations. "Are you on your way somewhere?"

"I'm just sort of walking," I explained.

"I'll walk with you!"

We went up and down the street a bit, then he recalled a nearby building with a scenic courtyard, just off the avenue. Moving away from the main street, I had misgivings. I noticed that he didn't seem to be carrying a camera and I started to worry. *Don't go inside with him!* a voice said in the back of my mind. *You don't know this guy!*

I felt palpable relief when he indicated a large rhododendron. "In front of here's good. That way we can get some flowers in the shot." He frowned slightly at them. "Too bad they're not lower down." He shrugged, unslung his backpack, and pulled out a large, expensive-looking camera. When I saw the heavy, professional lens, I felt distinctly silly for my earlier paranoia. "Have you done modeling before?"

"No, uh-uh." I smiled, relaxed now.

He looked surprised and snapped off a few pictures. "Turn a little more this way . . . Good!" *Snap, snap!* "Wow, you've got a great smile, too!"

I've been told before that people like my smile, but it's the compliment I have the most trouble believing. My teeth are a bit crooked, despite years of orthodontics, and I'm self-conscious about them. It made me grin in earnest to have my smile complimented by a professional photographer.

"Good! Now, look over your shoulder . . . Turn a bit—great!" *Snap, snap!* "Can you put your arms out a bit?"

I struck a pseudo-ballet pose and he frowned. I switched tactics, planting my hands on my hips. This met with approval.

"Perfect!" *Snap, snap!* "You can relax—I don't want to hurt your neck." (I was still looking over my shoulder.)

"No, I'm fine!" I assured him. Compared to the contortions I used to get into in the judo club, this position was about as stressful as having a butterfly land on my hair.

"Really? Okay, then let's do a few more!" He shifted angles. I rolled my shoulders back into maximum Victorian posture.

"Wow, you've got great arms, too!" *Snap, snap!*

I couldn't quite mimic the astonishingly narrow shoulders of someone like Alice Roosevelt Sr., who'd been practicing since childhood, but after a year of rhomboid work, my shoulders were capable of significantly more retraction than my average contemporary. I was really quite enjoying this.

A few days later, I met with another photographer. He had run up to me the week before as I passed through the university bookstore, a candid grin on his face.

"Miss! Miss!"

I stopped when I realized I was the one being called, and a young man with artsy glasses and curly brown hair caught up to me.

"Hi! I was just wondering, are you dressed up for something?"

I shook my head. "Nope. I look like this every day."

"Wow!" His grin got broader. "That's fantastic!" He put his hand on his chest. "I'm a photography major, and I was wondering if you'd let me take your picture sometime?"

I smiled. "Sure!"

I reached for my purse, and he reached for his bag.

"Let me write down my contact info for you—"

"Okay, I'll give you one of my cards." I pulled out my mother-of-pearl calling card case.

"Ooh, that's even better!" He closed his bag and flashed an apologetically sheepish grin. "I don't have any cards. I'm Max, by the way."

"Sarah." I shook his hand.

Contact thus established, we went on our separate ways, and later in the day I received an email from him that must have been sent within minutes of the meeting. A bit of back-and-forth electronic communication decided that the best location for the shoot would be the University of Washington's Suzzallo Library.

I adore Suzzallo; it was my favorite retreat when I was a UW student. Built at the turn of the twentieth century as a "cathedral of learning," it rests like a crowning gem atop a hill from which two separate mountain ranges are visible: the majestic Cascades and the rocky Olympics. Soaring Gothic architecture frames jewellike stained glass, guarded not by the saints imprisoned in stone upon religious cathedrals, but by effigies of history's great thinkers, from Socrates to Darwin. This architectural choice is actually a wonderful illustration of the changing values of the time: the United States was shifting from a religious culture to an increasingly secular one, where philosophers and scientists were revered over prophets.

It was raining on the day of the shoot, and I deliberately planned my arrival at the library to be punctual instead of early so that I wouldn't have to stand in the wet. I felt a pang of guilt when I saw Max waiting in the drizzle.

"I hope you haven't been waiting long," I said, folding up my umbrella.

"No," he replied. "Actually I just got here. Thanks for doing this today!"

"No problem!"

We started at the Grand Staircase inside the entrance. I sat on the beautiful marble steps, my skirt tilted up in some of the shots to flash the bright silk petticoats underneath, spread upon depressions worn into the stone by millions of footsteps.

After the staircase, we moved up to the graduate Reading Room, a chamber so photogenic that movie scenes have been shot inside.[55] We tried our best to be quiet as I posed in front of dark wooden paneling, carved with wildflowers and native fruits. I had brought the art-case editions of my own books, and for some shots I sat reading them, lit by morning light through stained glass windows.

The graduate Reading Room has all the beauty and grandeur of the interior of a cathedral—and the quietude of one. We shot as many pictures as we dared before Max whispered to me, "I think we're really going to start annoying people if we stay here much longer."

---

[55] Most notably, the 2002 blockbuster *The Ring*.

I nodded silent agreement, and we moved on to a side staircase that reminded me of walls I'd seen in European castles, thence to the map room.

Finally, we concluded on the bridge between two libraries (the second-story overpass that connects Suzzallo to the Allen Library). My handmade books were featured in more shots before Max did a close-up on my watch.

Afterward, he offered to buy me coffee as a thankful gesture for the modeling. This being Seattle, there was a café actually in the library, on the ground floor in a room that was formerly part of the computer lab. Max had to go shoot some stills of aged wood while the carpentry shop was open, so he left after he'd bought me my coffee. I settled down alone to drink my white chocolate mocha in quiet meditation. As I was finishing the last sips, a heavyset young man sat down across from me.

I was about to leave when the newcomer stopped me.

"Excuse me," he began, somewhat apologetically. "I was wondering, are you dressed up for anything in particular?"

It was a typical question, and I gave it my typical answer, shaking my head. "Uh-uh. I look like this every day."

He smiled. "That's cool! What got you started?"

"Well . . ." I briefly wondered where to begin. "I was the little girl who, when my mom took me to a Victorian museum, begged her to leave me there."

I clasped my hands and made little-girl puppy-dog eyes. "Please!" I mimicked my younger self. This was an anecdote I'd told before, and it was always good for a laugh.

"Then, one day," I went on, "I just sort of decided that I didn't care what everyone else was wearing, or what other people thought. I was just going to wear what I wanted to wear."

"That's wonderful!" The man across from me smiled approvingly.

I tilted my empty coffee cup, watching ecru drops twirl in the bottom.

"I also like introducing a bit of temporal diversity into life. I mean, people talk a lot about diversity, but . . ."

I hesitated. I knew what I wanted to say, but it took some effort to express the sentiment that had settled so deeply within me. I thought of the mass-produced banners and bumper stickers proclaiming Diversity, proudly displayed by women who described themselves as liberal, yet criticized my clothing.

"I think a lot of the time people get stuck on one set idea and forget about actual diversity." I shrugged. "I know that sounds strange."

(Gabriel liked to describe the popular, politically correct variety of this as "brand-name diversity": the philosophy that, aside from the acceptable variations in race, religion, or sexual orientation, everyone should otherwise live their life as an exact, assembly-line copy of every other person's life in their community—and by God, they'd better! For a contrasting term, he deemed what I was doing "off-brand diversity.")

The man in the coffee shop shook his head. "No, not at all. I totally agree!"

"The other thing," I confessed, taking a lighter tone. "Modern clothes look terrible on me."

"Really?" He laughed.

I joined in the chuckling. "Yeah, I just don't fit the modern ideal," I explained, closing one eye and drawing a straight line in the air with thumb and forefinger. "I'm not built like a twelve-year-old boy!" I rested my hands on the table, and glanced down at my curves. "But, that wasn't always the ideal. So, I decided there wasn't any reason I couldn't wear clothes based on ones from a time when the ideal was closer to how I actually look."

"Well," he responded, nodding. "All fashion's cyclical anyways, so why not?"

One of the most amusing ideas I encounter—and one of those I understand the least—is the utter certainty of some people that I must be living the life I do because I am paid for it. This is quite a peculiar thought to me: that a human being of independent mind, endowed by their creator with freedom of thought, should choose a lifestyle with slight differences from that of the rest of their herd only because they are being paid to do so. The first time it confronted me, I was taken aback.

"So, I can tell they provide your clothes," began a grocery store checker as she filled my bag. "But how much do they pay you?"

"They?" I stared at her a moment. "Who are 'they'?"

She stopped with a can of tinned peas in midair, her head slowly cocking to one side. I am sure my own puzzled expression cannot have been too different.

"I make my own clothes," I explained.

A brief but uncomfortable pause ensued.

"So . . ." she slowly lowered the peas into the bag. "No one pays you to do this?"

I shook my head. "To be me? No, sorry. It would be nice, though." I smiled at the thought.

As I have continued to receive variants of this question on other occasions, I've started amusing myself by speculating about "They." If "They" are in the habit of paying people simply to be themselves, I would truly like to meet "Them." I picture this mysterious "They" as some shadowy secret organization, with headquarters like a hybrid of a Masonic lodge and something out of a Marvel comic book. From some exotic eyrie-like location on a remote, snow-swept mountain top, "They" would make decisions on patronage for worthy benefactors, to support diversity of lifestyle. I enjoy imagining what "They" might fund. Dating services for gays and lesbians? Fertility advice for interracial couples? Speculation on the topic can provide endless entertainment.

Most of the commentary I receive tends to be warmly positive.

I was standing in line to buy candy at Bartell's one day when a tall man with a deep voice and an accent straight out of Chicago stopped and gave me an admiring look from hat to toes. "Miss," he said with a huge smile. "That's classic. Tell Great-Grandmama, it's working!"

The next afternoon, a woman passing opposite myself at a crossroads called out, "Your outfit is lovely! You look so serene and peaceful!"

It's rather pleasant to be able to invoke such comments from nothing more than a trip out for groceries.

Coming out of the supermarket on a different day, a little girl tugged at her dad's hand and, staring at me, told him quite loudly, "Look at that pretty lady! She's pretty!"

As I was walking home, an elderly man saw me through the window of the restaurant where he was eating lunch and actually left his half-eaten lunch on the table to run outside and call to me.

"Ma'am! Ma'am!"

I stopped, surprised and a little amused.

"I just want to say, you look beautiful!" he told me. "I was sitting having lunch, and I just had to run out here and tell you you're gorgeous! When I was a young man, this—" He made a sweeping gesture, encompassing me from hat to shoes. "—was the style. You've made my day! Thank you! And take care of yourself! That smile looks like it's worth about two or three trillion dollars, at least!"

Some of the approbation is nonverbal; I love it when men tip their hats to me. There's something wonderfully chivalrous about it, whether it's a full-on, off-with-the-hat bow, or the simple tapping of a baseball cap. Nor is it only old men who do it, although that would be easy enough to expect. It also comes from men far too young to remember the era of doffed top hats: thirty-odds, college boys, and some who seem barely out of high school; I'll never know whether their mothers taught them or perhaps their fathers, but someone out there brought them up properly. It's not something I see every day, but perhaps once every few weeks or so, and it tickles my heart every time, just as it gives me a warmly flattered glow when men open doors or give up their bus seats for me.[56]

Other commentators are not quite so complimentary. Sometimes, people are simply clueless. On the bus one day, a sloppily dressed white man glanced at me and plastered on a cheesy grin.

"Cinco de Mayo!"

I raised an eyebrow at this. "Pardon?"

"It's a Mexican holiday. I thought . . ." His voice trailed off.

I pointedly looked myself over: ankle-length wool skirt, three petticoats, cashmere-lined leather gloves . . . I'd have died of heat prostration anywhere in Mexico that wasn't at least a mile above sea level.

"Does this look Mexican?"[57]

Blanco looked embarrassed and muttered something incomprehensible before taking a seat elsewhere.

One of the sillier confrontations to which I'm subjected from time to time is when some clueless ignoramus starts berating me for makeup that does not exist. Very rarely it's a man but more usually it's a woman who launches into a patronizing lecture about how horribly anachronistic it is for me to be wearing makeup, which is actually present only in the scolder's mind. The situation always grows

---

[56] Incidentally, I think it's a dreadful shame that certain misguided people criticize such sweet and endearing gestures as sexist. The gestures are gendered ones, but ones that in no way imply male domination. Quite the contrary, in fact: It should be remembered that in traditional chivalry, hats are removed in the presence of one's superiors. A queen tips her crown to no one.

[57] I'd like to state, for the record, that I have absolutely nothing against actual Mexican clothing. I have a great deal against idiocy.

invariably more ridiculous when I point out their error and instead of apologizing they'll insist, "But you look like you are!" And then either resume their lecture or start spouting out a litany of archaic synonyms for prostitute, demonstrating that they have not the slightest clue as to the difference between wit and rude stupidity. I generally just walk away at that point and let my silence have the last word.

Some people recognize the corset for what it is; some don't. Waists have fallen so far off the radar of modern people that a significant number can't identify a corset when they see one. "What a pretty dress!" they'll say, attributing the entirety of the hourglass figure to a flimsy piece of cotton to which no one gave a second glance before I started corseting.

Some attribute my small waist to an optical illusion. "Is your waist really that small?" they'll ask.

To this question, I'm always tempted to reply, "No. Actually, I'm wearing a special device designed by a physicist I know at the University of Washington. It warps the physical space around me to make my waist appear smaller than it actually is."

It would be fun to see if anyone would actually be gullible enough to believe me, but unfortunately such tactics are not very educational.

Cross-cultural encounters are generally pretty fun. As I've mentioned, I have a degree in international studies (I also have one in French), so it shouldn't surprise anyone that I enjoy witnessing the differences in social reactions. Any human response is an individual matter, but I have encountered sufficient consistencies within groups to notice general trends. Asian women giggle behind their hands; the Japanese call me "cool beautiful" (*sugoi kirei*) in their own language. Mexicans demand to know where I'm from, then refuse to believe that I'm American. Tourists want to take my picture.

Often, encounters are just plain sweet. I was walking home from the library one day when a smile-faced babushka pointed at me emphatically and said something in Russian. She hurried over to me, pulling a little wire shopping trolley with one hand and pointing at my waist with the other.

"Hello," I greeted her, smiling.

She circled my waist with her hands. "You eat? Something? No!"

If an American had walked up and started groping me in such a manner, I would have been sorely tempted to practice some of my old judo moves on them; however, I was willing to cut a foreigner some slack in the interest of cultural sensitivity.[58] Perhaps issues of private space are different in Russia.

I nodded my head, laughing at her question. "I eat!"

"No!" She squeezed the corset, shaking her head. "Is no food in there!" I giggled. "How old, you are?"

I put my hand on my chest. "Thirty."

She shook her head and motioned to another woman who had just come out of the grocery store. The first pointed at my waist again, and there was a rapid-fire exchange of Russian at amusing volume. The first woman started to leave, and I decided to try one of my meager six words of Russian.

"Do svidaniya!" I waved to her. *Good-bye*.

"Do svidaniya." She was still shaking her head. After half a beat, she paused again. "Like doll!" she called out in English.

An 1890 fashion plate.

Peterson's Magazine (January 1890).

---

[58] When I lived in Japan, elderly women had wanted tactile experience of everything from my blond hair to my overly padded derriere. "You don't have to wear padding when you wear kimono!" they'd say, poking my bottom. I had drawn a line only when they'd wanted to touch my eyes, and even then I had made an effort to be polite about it. Since I was a guest in their country, I accepted that a certain amount of being treated like an exotic animal was inevitable.

For the record, however, I have no such patience with fellow Americans. Anyone with any modicum of decency in their character should recognize that a human being has a natural right to a certain amount of private space, and the amount of this space is specified by culture. An American should know how much space to give another American. I dress the way I do for my own benefit, not as an invitation for my erogenous zones to be groped by random strangers. (Yes, it happens.)

I could have hugged her for that last comment, so endearingly was it spoken. Instead, I giggled from behind a gloved hand, and waved to them both as they retreated a short distance.

After the well-received public presentation of "Fifty Years of Fashion," I faced a greater challenge: Mother's Day at the zoo with my mom. I had more or less resigned myself to Mom's sniping comments and incomprehension. We had so little in common since I'd grown up; maybe she just couldn't think of anything to say. The outing would be a bit more than halfway finished when I would get a small glimpse into the idea that there might be something deeper—and more tender—at work that I had not considered.

From the start of our zoological visit, I was getting the sort of comments that, by now, were standard to me. Little girls in the ticket line stared at me, open-mouthed, and told me I was beautiful. Their mothers said I looked lovely. A photographer taking pictures of hummingbirds stopped his avian shots to ask if he could snap some photos of me for a local blog. Given how many objections she'd made previously, I was surprised to see how proud my mom seemed through all of this.

Around afternoon and near the tiger cage, Mom got quiet.

"You know," she said, "the only problem with you looking like that is that people see your waist, and then they see this." She pointed at her own belly.

I sighed, not knowing how to respond. Mom had always been insecure about her physical appearance, and in all my years of trying to reassure her, I couldn't remember anything I'd ever said having had any effect. We walked on in silence for a while.

At the penguin exhibit, we joined a crowd of people in marveling over a wild heron that had paused amongst the captive birds. Serene and beautiful, it balanced on the highest point in view. It looked all the more elegant for being out of place.

As we stood there, a woman sitting on a large rock yelled a fairly typical question at me. "Is that an eighteen-inch waist?!"

Questions about the exact size of my waist are always problematic for me. "Waist" is another word for corset, and I was wearing a nineteen-inch corset. It would be perfectly truthful to say I had a nineteen-inch waist. I could have passed a lie detector with it. But the outside measurement when I took a tape to my midsection was twenty-two inches, and that's what counted when I sewed my clothes. For responses to random inquisitive strangers, I generally chose my answer based on the whim of the moment.

"Twenty-two inches," I told the woman on the boulder, who looked disappointed.

"The only problem with her looking like that . . ." Mom broke in, and I inwardly cringed because I knew what was coming. Mom loves to repeat herself. ". . . is that people see that, and then they see this!" She shook her stomach.

The stranger laughed cruelly. "Well, Mom, you need to go on a *diet!*"

My fingers clenched around the handles of my tote bag and I pivoted away, guiding Mom to come with me.

"Girdles don't work for us!" the stranger yelled after us.

I'm not wearing a girdle—and mind your own bloody business about what people "need" to do!

"You want me to slap her for you?" I offered once we were out of earshot, shaking my bag. "I've got a nice, heavy water bottle in here." Nearly a liter sloshed in the stainless steel bottle as I swung the bag.

I was kidding, of course. Clueless idiots aren't worth assault charges. But the desire was real. Had there been no danger of legal ramifications, I would have gladly beaten the obnoxious stranger to a pulp.

"No," Mom sighed. "I used to let stuff like that bother me, but now . . ." She looked into the distance ahead, and sighed again, a sadly resigned expression on her face. "Life's too short."

She looked down at her feet, unsure of her footing on the steep slope we were ascending. I put my arm around her back, taking some of her weight upon myself and letting the corset support us both.

"Well," I told her, dropping my voice. "I'll still slap her if you want me to!"

She laughed as I supported her up the hill.

John Chrisman and family: Gabriel's ancestors. John was blind, but his wife, Mary, still very obviously had a corseted figure.

Chrisman Collection (1889).

Epilogue

"What is woman's sphere? . . . Much may depend upon the times, says one; and another replies that the woman herself and not the times is responsible for the place she fills—responsible for her sphere."
—*Godey's Lady's Book*, July 1894

Fashion plate.

Godey's Lady's Book (September 1889).

I hadn't wanted the corset when it was given to me. I had no way of knowing what lessons it would teach, how many fulfillments of long-held desires I would find bound in its silken curves. Making this external object internal, taking all its lessons of graceful poise and assurance into myself, could happen only with time. This was not knowledge that could ever have been gained casually, any more than a dilettante could dance a role of Tchaikovsky's. The corset and my clothes have never been a costume to me, and I could not have grown under their tutelage if I had treated them as such. Costumes are for those who wish to playact, who put on a role they plan to remove shortly. A caterpillar cannot learn to fly by pasting on paper wings. True transformation can occur only if metamorphosis is fully embraced.

Having originally intended this to be a chronicle of my first corseted year, I find now that I have overshot that mark by several months. However, I hope it is not hubris in me to consider the tales of these extra moon-turns to be an enrichment, rather than a bloating, of my story.

Conclusion of an autobiography is necessarily a troublesome business. It cannot end in the protagonist's death, and the alternative in this case—the cessation of the experiment described—is one of which I have no intention of seeing drawn. That experiment has become my life, and it is ongoing.

At the time I write this, it has been more than four and a half years since that fateful birthday. Gabriel and I now live in Port Townsend, in the same neighborhood where I grew misty-eyed because I thought we could never dwell in a place so perfect and Gabriel told me that "never" was too strong a word for a world in which anything is possible. The very first time I stepped into my home, I knew it was truly that: home. The old Victorian house was more than 120 years in age and completely devoid of furnishings the first time I saw it, having been the property of an absentee landlord for a decade and empty of

tenants for more than a year. Yet I felt wholeheartedly welcomed there, as if the sunshine filling the high-ceilinged rooms were the smiling joy of a kind heart that had long been lonely. We are slowly restoring it to the beauty it once knew, and thus our adventures continue.

It is seldom that a birthday present leads to a complete shift in one's view of their placement in time and society, but in a way, it is perhaps appropriate that a token presented in celebration of birth's anniversary should lead to rebirth, that an honor to that first wakening should lead to a reawakening. With opened eyes I close this tale. May it lead to fresh sight in those who read it.

Godey's Lady's Book (October 1889).

Victorian fashion plate.

Further Reading

The following are resources on which I drew in learning about corsets and to which I returned when writing this book. Sources that I found particularly valuable and would like to recommend to others are marked with an asterisk (*). I would especially like to recommend Valerie Steele's *The Corset: A Cultural History*. It was invaluable to me in my early days of research, when I first started wearing a corset. I read it and reread it until I had virtually the whole thing memorized, and in point of fact, I actually did memorize some of the poetic citations verbatim. Ms. Steele has a remarkable gift for transforming the obscure into the obvious, and being able to call up many of her points from memory was to later prove invaluable to me when talking to people about corsets. I am sure that reading her extensive research had an influence upon my own lines of inquiry.

Articles:

Campbell, Nicole, Martin Richardson, and Phillip Antippa. "Biomechanical Testing of Two Devices for Internal Fixation of Fractured Ribs." *The Journal of TRAUMA Injury, Infection, and Critical Care* 68, no. 5 (2010): 1234–38.

Cormier, J. M.; Stitzel, J. D.; Duma, S. M.; Matsuoka, F. "Regional variation in the structural response and geometrical properties of human ribs." Proceedings of the Association for the Advancement of Automotive Medicine. 49 (2005): pp. 153–170.

Cormier, Joseph Michael. "Microstructural and Mechanical Properties of Human Ribs." MS thesis, Virginia Polytechnic Institute and State University, 2003.

Dickinson, Robert L. "The Corset: Questions of Pressure and Displacement." *The New York Medical Journal* (November 5, 1887).

Granik, Gerald and Ira Stein. "Human Ribs: Static Testing as a Promising Medical Application." *Journal of Biomechanics* 6 (1973): 237–40.

*Hustvedt, Siri. "Pulling Power." *New Statesman*, February 6, 2006, 40–42.

Kemper, Andrew R., Craig McNally, Eric A. Kennedy, Sarah J. Manoogian, Amber L. Rath, Tracy P. Ng, Joel D. Stitzel, Eric P. Smith, Stefan M. Duma, and Fumio Matsuoka. "Material Properties of Human Rib Cortical Bone from Dynamic Tension Coupon Testing." *Stapp Car Crash Journal* 49 (November 2005): 199–230.

Kemper, Andrew R., Craig McNally, Clayton A. Pullins, Laura J. Freeman, Stefan M. Duma, and Stephen W. Rouhana. "The Biomechanics of Human Ribs: Material and Structural Properties from Dynamic Tension and Bending Tests." *Stapp Car Crash Journal* 51 (October 2007): 235–73.

Kleinman, Paul K., and Alan E. Schlesinger. "Mechanical Factors Associated with Posterior Rib Fractures: Laboratory and Case Studies." *Pediatric Radiology* 27 (1997): 87–91.

National Cancer Institute. "Pregnancy and Breast Cancer Risk— Misunderstandings about Breast Cancer Risk Factors." http://www.cancer.gov/cancertopics/factsheet/Risk/pregnancy.

Pengel, Heloise M., Chris G. Maher, and Kathryn M. Refshauge. "Systematic Review of Conservative Interventions for Subacute Low Back Pain." *Clinical Rehabilitation,* 2002, 8.

Schultz, Albert B., Daniel R. Benson, and Carl Hirsch. "Force-Deformation Properties of Human Ribs." *Journal of Biomechanics* 7 (1974): 303–09.

Stein, I. D. "Rib Structure and Bending Strength: An Autopsy Study." *Calcified Tissue Research* 20 (1976): 61–73.

Stitzel, Joel D., Joseph M. Cormier, Joseph T. Barretta, Eric A. Kennedy, Eric P. Smith, Amber L. Rath, and Stefan M. Duma. "Defining Regional Variation in the Material Properties of Human Rib Cortical Bone and Its Effect on Fracture Prediction." *Stapp Car Crash Journal* 47 (October 2003): 243–65.

Theobold, Mary Miley. *History Myths Debunked: The Whole Truth and Nothing But the Truth.* "Myth #28: Women had ribs surgically removed to make their waists smaller." http://historymyths.wordpress.com

Books:

When possible, ISBNs are provided to help readers track down specific books.

Blum, Stella, ed. *Victorian Fashions & Costumes from Harper's Bazar: 1867–1898.* New York: Dover Publications, 1974. ISBN 0486229904

Crawford, M. D. C., and Elizabeth A. Guernsey. *The History of Corsets in Pictures.* New York: Fairchild Publications, 1951.

Cunnington, C. Willett and Phillis Cunnington. *The History of Underclothes.* London: Michael Joseph, 1951.

Flint, Austin. *A Text-Book of Human Physiology.* 4th ed. New York: D. Appleton & Company, 1893.

Graydon, Shari. *In Your Face: The Culture of Beauty and You.* Vancouver: Annick Press, 2004. ISBN 1550378570

Kahn, Selma Annette. *Merchandising Manual for the Corset Department.* Under the direction of John W. Wingate. New York: Journal of Retailing, 1939.

Kidwell, Claudia Brush and Valerie Steele, eds. *Men and Women: Dressing the Part.* Washington, D.C.: Smithsonian Institution Press, 1989. ISBN 0874745500

Lord, William Berry. *Freaks of Fashion: The Corset & the Crinoline.* Edited by R. L. Shep. Mendocino, CA: R. L. Shep, 1993. (Originally published in 1868 as two separate books: *Freaks of Fashion* and *The Corset and the Crinoline.*)

McMillen, Sally G. *Seneca Falls and the Origins of the Women's Rights Movement.* New York: Oxford University Press, 2008.

Mitchell, Sally. *Victorian Britain: An Encyclopedia.* New York and London: Garland Publishing, 1988. ISBN 0824015134

*Page, Christopher. *Foundations of Fashion: The Symington Collection; Corsetry from 1856 to the Present Day.* Leicestershire Museums Publication no. 25. Leicestershire, UK: De Voyle Litho, 1981. ISBN 0850220890

Shep, R. L., ed. *Corsets: A Visual History.* Mendocino, CA: R. L. Shep, 1993. ISBN 0914046209

Simmons, John Galbraith. *Doctors & Discoveries: Lives That Created Today's Medicine; From Hippocrates to the Present.* Boston: Houghton Mifflin Harcourt, 2002. ISBN 0618152768

*Steele, Valerie. *The Corset: A Cultural History.* Singapore: Yale University Press, 2000. ISBN 0300090714

Steele, Valerie. *Paris Fashion: A Cultural History*. New York: Oxford University Press, 1988. ISBN 0195044657

Waugh, Norah. *Corsets and Crinolines*. New York: Routledge Theatre Arts Books, 1954.

Waugh, Norah. *The Cut of Women's Clothes: 1600–1930*. New York: Routledge Theatre Arts Books, 1968. ISBN 0878300260

Williams, Peter L., Roger Warwick, Mary Dyson, and Lawrence H. Bannister, eds. *Gray's Anatomy*. 37th ed. UK: Longman Group, 1989.

Sound Recordings:

Dreyer, Dave, Lou Handman, and Herman Ruby. "When I Was the Dandy and You Were the Belle." *Performed by Walter Van Brunt*. Edison Blue Amberol, 1924.

Websites:

Long Island Staylace Association ("LISA") http://www.staylace.com

Corset Heaven (Corset Forum and Chat) http://www.corsetheaven.com/forum

Lucy's Corsetry http://lucycorsetry.com

Movie Mistakes *(Gone with the Wind)* http://www.moviemistakes.com/picture3541

Romantasy Exquisite Corsetry http://www.romantasy.com

Timeless Trends Corset Designs http://www.timeless-trends.com

Two Nerdy History Girls http://twonerdyhistorygirls.blogspot.com/

Acknowledgments

All the events described in this book are true, and as accurately portrayed as my memory can make them. Some of the names have been changed out of respect for the privacy of the individuals depicted.

To everyone who participated in the research for this book and to those who helped bring it to print, I would like to extend my sincere gratitude. Special thanks go to my wonderful editor, Nicole Frail, for all her amazing hard work and devotion; to my agent, Deborah Ritchken, for taking a chance on an unknown; to Tom Evans, for his encyclopedic knowledge of bones, anatomy, and all things biological as well as his eager cheerfulness to spread scientific data to the laypeople of the world; to Sue Lean, for her perpetual encouragement and efforts on my behalf; to Hillary and the Wornettes at *WORN Fashion Journal* in Toronto and Lucy Williams of Lucy's Corsetry for reviewing the book in glowing terms when I was still making every copy myself by hand; to Allison Arthur for the splendid newspaper features; to Angela Kirkpatrick for her beautiful artwork; to Max Kraushaar and Emily Decker for the lovely photographs; and to all my dear friends for their wonderful help and encouragement. And naturally, my most heartfelt thanks go to my beloved husband, Gabriel, for giving me the corset in the first place—and for everything else.

Peterson's Magazine (July 1890).

Illustration from Victorian lady's magazine.